The Neuroscience of Freedom ar

Professor Joaquín M. Fuster is an eminent cognitive neuroscientist whose research over the last five decades has made fundamental contributions to our understanding of the neural structures underlying cognition and behavior. This book provides his view on the eternal question of whether we have free will. Based on his seminal work on the functions of the prefrontal cortex in decision-making, planning, creativity, working memory, and language, Professor Fuster argues that the liberty or freedom to choose between alternatives is a function of the cerebral cortex, under prefrontal control, in its reciprocal interaction with the environment. Freedom is therefore inseparable from that circular relationship. *The Neuroscience of Freedom and Creativity* is a fascinating inquiry into the cerebral foundation of our ability to choose between alternative actions and to freely lead creative plans to their goal.

JOAQUÍN M. FUSTER, M.D., Ph.D., is Distinguished Professor of Cognitive Neuroscience in the Brain Research Institute and Semel Institute for Neuroscience and Human Behavior at the University of California, Los Angeles. In the 1950s Professor Fuster pioneered the neurophysiology of cognition. He is the first to have discovered and described "memory cells" in the primate brain. He is the author of numerous peer-reviewed articles and three books: *Memory in the Cerebral Cortex* (1995), *Cortex and Mind* (2003), and *The Prefrontal Cortex* (1980, 4th edition 2008).

The Neuroscience of Freedom and Creativity

Our Predictive Brain

JOAQUÍN M. FUSTER

CAMBRIDGE
UNIVERSITY PRESS

University Printing House, Cambridge CB2 8BS, United Kingdom

Published in the United States of America by Cambridge University Press, New York

Cambridge University Press is part of the University of Cambridge.

It furthers the University's mission by disseminating knowledge in the pursuit of education, learning and research at the highest international levels of excellence.

www.cambridge.org
Information on this title: www.cambridge.org/9781107608627

© Joaquín M. Fuster 2013

First published 2013

Printing in the United Kingdom by TJ International Ltd. Padstow, Cornwall

A catalogue record for this publication is available from the British Library

Library of Congress Cataloguing in Publication data
Fuster, Joaquín M.
The neuroscience of freedom and creativity : our predictive brain / Joaquín M. Fuster, Semel Institute for Neuroscience and Human Behavior, and Brain Research Institute, School of Medicine, University of California at Los Angeles.
    pages   cm
Includes bibliographical references and index.
ISBN 978-1-107-02775-6 – ISBN 978-1-107-60862-7 (pbk.)
1. Cognitive neuroscience.   2. Free will and determinism.   3. Creative ability.   4. Brain – Philosophy.   I. Title.
QP360.5.F88   2013
612.8′233–dc23

2013007947

ISBN 978-1-107-02775-6 Hardback
ISBN 978-1-107-60862-7 Paperback

To my younger brother Valentín,
fellow humanist, physician and scientist.

And to the memory of Václav Havel.

Contents

Figures

Preface

October 2000, University of Paris, La Salpêtrière Hospital, Charcot Amphitheater. I was invited to give a short acceptance speech on a subject of my choosing after being awarded the Jean-Louis Signoret Prize. Determined to deliver it in French, I gave it an ambitious title: "Liberté et l'Exécutif du Cerveau." In less than half an hour I tried to explain that the prefrontal cortex is the cerebral enabler of the human agenda. Further, that the achievement of biological and social goals is the outcome of the competition between demands of internal and external milieus continuously barraging that cortex. Further, that those demands include unconscious ethical imperatives in addition to instinctual urges. Of course, I dutifully cited Claude Bernard and Benjamin Constant. Human liberty, I concluded, is a phenomenon of the brain's ability to choose, rationally or not, between alternatives of action.

Only after my talk did I realize I had overreached. I had spoken about a sacred French theme in less than perfect French to an intellectual French audience in an august French forum. Now, a dozen years past, this book is an attempt to say all those things better, in English.

What motivates this brain scientist to write about such a lofty theme as human liberty? And what qualifications does he have to do it? He surely must know that the terrain is fraught with pitfalls. Emphatically yes, he knows the dangers. No one has to convince him that those dangers are very real, especially the disdain, or, worse, the implacable wrath, with which modern neuroscience treats the unsuspecting defender of free will.

Indeed, on neuroscientific grounds, the radical defense of free will is a lost cause, and it is not my intention to attempt it. What is defensible – my position here – is that the freedom or liberty to choose between alternatives is a function of the nervous system, especially the cerebral cortex, in its interaction with the environment. Further, that the freedom or liberty to choose between alternatives – including inaction – is relative, constrained by limits in both the organism and its environment. And further, that the subjective experience of freedom is a function of the intensity of the cortical activity that precedes and attends free choice.

A defense of freedom from the determinism of the brain's microcosm of genes and molecules is practically impossible if we ignore that such a microcosm obeys the laws of the nervous system and its environment, and is no less subject to them than the ink is to the written word. Nonetheless, most everybody has a reason to deny liberty a place in that system. No structure within it seems to harbor the immense breadth of human purpose and the biological roots of human institutions. However, even if choice had a specific place in the brain, there would still remain the question of how the brain creates the new from the old. Karl Popper will eloquently win the argument against determinism in human action, but then concede that his victory is insufficient to understand the essence of freedom, responsibility, or creativity. He will wistfully ask himself, now how can we explain Mozart?

Without much success, some philosophers and sociobiologists attempt to anchor liberty beyond the nervous system. Evolutionary psychologists anchor the "illusion of freedom" in the phylogenetic history of mankind, but are seemingly unaware that something truly new has happened in that history to liberate man from his past, to open him to his future, and to make him capable of freely inventing that future. That something is the evolutionary explosion of the cortex of the frontal lobes, especially its prefrontal region.

Aside from the urge to redeem myself after an imprudent speech in French on liberty, what compels me to undertake this intellectual adventure is having devoted nearly half a century to research into that part of the brain. This does not mean that I see any brain structure, not even the cortex of the frontal lobes, as somehow escaping natural causality or as being endowed with the power to choose and decide for us. Quite the contrary, I view the dynamics of the frontal lobes as ultimately determined by the genome and the environment. Furthermore, the attribution of ultimate executive power to the prefrontal cortex is, as I will explain, a major obstacle to the study of its role in liberty. Yet, because of its prospective functions, that cortex extends the executive freedom of the individual human to shape his future radically beyond the limits of any prior individual animal in the course of evolution.

I must mark for the reader a clear separation between the simplistic notion of the prefrontal cortex as a mythical "CEO in the brain," which it is not, and its central role in the conception and organization of goal-directed actions. This role is composed of several nervous subfunctions, including working memory, preparatory set for action, and inhibitory control. This book is not an apologia for a new theory of the prefrontal cortex to supersede all others. It is, rather, a synthetic view of the processes by which those subordinate functions of the prefrontal cortex, under its overriding function of temporally organizing action, serve our freedom and our ability to create the new, the good, the useful, and the beautiful.

The ultimate foundation of human liberty consists of two cognitive functions that radically differentiate us humans from all other organisms. One is language and the other our ability to predict the future – and to shape our actions accordingly. Language is vastly more than an extension of animal communication. It is a means of imparting information, emotion, experience, and logical thought to ourselves and to others. Because language is also a means of predicting future events (Latin *praedicere*, to foretell) and of constructing plans of action, language and prediction are largely inseparable. The two functions are intimately related to each other, though neither is reducible to the other. One purpose of this book is to explore the nature of that relationship. In any case, both functions stem from the dynamics of a complex adaptive system, determined by a finite past but open to an unlimited future. Both language and prediction are solidly based on the workings of the prefrontal cortex. For this reason alone the prefrontal cortex emerges from evolution as the cradle of liberty.

The vast majority of our daily activities carry success rates of nearly 100 percent. Most of those daily activities, however, are automatic, overlearned, unconscious, and reinforced by repeated previous success. By contrast, our most momentous decisions, that is, those that shape our future (such as career, marriage, emigration, financial investment, new research, or child-bearing), are rarely based on prediction with the highest probability of success, or, conversely, with the lowest risk of failure. It is those momentous decisions that are clearly within the purview of the prefrontal cortex, as the enabler if not the executive of the brain.

Consequently, also in the purview of the prefrontal cortex is all manner of creative or innovative activity in all fields of human endeavor, from the artistic to the social, to the professional, to the scientific, to the philanthropic, to the sporting. In the human agenda success and failure are defined by the attainment of goals not only in biological terms, including health, pleasure, and the absence of pain, but also in terms of values treasured by us humans: love, recognition, trust, credit, esthetic pleasure, praise, social acceptance, and others. Whether and to what extent those values are the result of the sublimation of biological urges is not essential to my present argument. What is essential is that our freedom to pursue them rests on the health and vigor of our prefrontal cortex.

The critical dimension of that temporal-organizing function of the prefrontal cortex, the one that bears on freedom and creativity most directly, is the future. Curiously, almost everybody concerned with frontal functions ignores it, except clinicians and the students of working memory. The first because the planning difficulty of the patient who has suffered injury to the frontal lobe is so glaring, and the second because working memory, for which the frontal lobe is so important, is memory retained to be used in the near future. Everybody else seems afraid to be accused of teleology, that is, of believing that the future can cause the present, which is the nemesis of the physical scientist.

There is another group of scientists, however, who are beginning to see the connection between the future and the prefrontal cortex: the neuroeconomists. The field of neuroeconomics deals with the role of brain structures in the prediction and probability of *expected* risk and value deriving from free choice – financial reward among others. The prefrontal cortex is one of those structures, heavily implicated in the physiology of choice and liberty. On the one hand, it is profusely endowed with neural detectors of pleasure and reward. On the other, it is endowed with the neural organizers of reward-seeking behaviors (behavioral economics), including the spoken language.

In recent years neuroeconomics has flourished, for the most part as a result of the application of certain conceptual approaches such as game theory, and a better knowledge of the role of the prefrontal cortex in reward and displeasure. Probability has entered animal neuropsychology much as it previously had entered the study of human behavior. Behavioral tests have been devised to measure how animals, especially primates, estimate the probabilities of reward or risk. Thus, neuroeconomics can make reasonably accurate predictions of simple animal decisions, and even correlate those predictions with neural activity. It does not quite come to grips, however, with complex human behavior. And neuroeconomics would fail to do so even if the mechanisms of the human brain were as perfectly understood as they can ever be. Here also, as in market economics, the interplay of variables cannot be predicted with precision. The reason is that interplay takes place in the cerebral cortex, a system of neural networks that is constantly submitted to influences from many sources, all of them different: influences and bias from past memory in the cortex itself, or from the instinctual, visceral, and emotional centers of the limbic brain and the brainstem.

Yet, it is precisely in the crucible of probabilities and uncertainties in the human brain that freedom comes to life. The ability to choose between alternatives literally derives from the variance and degrees of freedom of innumerable variables behind prospective human action. As in evolution, both determinism and straight causality dissolve in probability and, as they do, both yield to a teleological factor: *purpose or goal*.

Much as in liberal economics, the metaphor of the "invisible hand" of Adam Smith (the self-regulating behavior of the marketplace which leads to social good) emerges in the human brain in the form of imponderable neural influences leading the individual to better adaptation to his environment. Just as innumerable motives move the participants in the marketplace to determine values and prices, innumerable neural influences, some unconscious or merely intuitive, move the individual to make personal decisions. Among those influences are not only the "animal spirits" of biological drive but also the principles of natural law etched in collective evolutionary memory. There are also the principles of esthetics, altruism, and creativity, which are etched in our individual memory by tradition, family, and education – in sum by culture. It is the aggregate of collective and individual memory that allows our prefrontal cortex to invent the future and to make it possible in the present. Here we are going to deal with the functional anatomy of that "invisible neural hand," the memory of the organism in the broadest sense, which makes rational language, prediction, and freedom possible.

This book is primarily the product of my many years of cognitive neuroscience research at the University of California. In close second place, the book is the product of long clinical experience with the mentally ill. The phenomenology of mental illness is one of the best educators on the woeful consequences of the loss of personal freedom. This book is also the product of my earlier European education in the arts and humanities, especially music and languages, those marvelous creative tools that the human brain has bestowed on us. Finally, of course, this book is also the product of endless discussions with my academic colleagues and students at all levels of their development. I am persuaded that some young minds are better at discussing freedom and creativity than many a seasoned scholar with preconceived notions. Perhaps this is true also for other things so very natural and so very human.

To be sure, at times I have thought that the theme of this book is too big for me – perhaps for anybody. There is, indeed, still much we do not know about the brain at the threshold of what is to happen and our freedom to make it happen, or to prevent it from happening. More than once, I have detected a smile on the face of some of my fellow scientists on learning what I have been trying to do. It is a smile faintly revealing a mix of disbelief, compassion, and good wishes. But then, I never lost the sense of the importance of my task, and many are those who have taken it seriously and have lent me a helping hand with good advice and encouragement. To them, my sincere thanks: Warren Brown, Patricia Churchland, Gerry Edelman, Ignacio Fuster, Patricia Greenfield, Peter Hagoort, Daniel Kahneman, John Schumann, Larry Squire, Peter Whybrow, and others. I owe special thanks to Sally Arteseros for her expert editing of difficult portions of the text, and Carmen Cox for her help in the gathering of references and final preparation of the manuscript.

1

Introduction

I am myself and my circumstance.

José Ortega y Gasset

For as long as it can remember, the human race has been asking itself whether it is the master of its own destiny or, instead, whether human destiny is dictated by stars, deities, or genes. Today, few question anymore that the brain has a great deal to do with destiny. Modern neuroscience, however, is in the main deterministic and reductionistic, averse to the idea that there is a place in our brain for free will or any other sort of "counter-causal" entity.

Yet, thanks to recent advances in cognitive neuroscience, which is the neuroscience of knowledge, that panorama is about to change or is changing already. When it comes to the cognition of human action, both radical determinism and radical reductionism are no longer the beacons to guide our discourse.[1] That does not mean that free will can already claim a sovereign place in the brain in the form of a distinct entity or set of neural mechanisms. What it does mean is that our scientific understanding of the human brain is opening up to accommodate liberty; that is, to

---

[1] I do not want to be misunderstood. My defense of systems neuroscience makes it appear that I consider basic neuroscience irrelevant to cognition. Quite the contrary, the study of synaptic mechanisms and molecular neurobiology is making enormous strides at the most elementary biophysical stage of neuronal information processing in both learning and memory (Kandel, 2000), without which there is no cognition.

1

accommodate our capacity to act as free causal agents, albeit within physical and ethical constraints.

Cognitive neuroscience is beginning to explain our capacity to choose between alternatives of action – which includes inaction – and to extend our ability into the future to cause and to shape our future actions. Certainly this development requires substantial changes in our traditional ways of conceptualizing brain function. Among other things, this book is an attempt to explain those necessary changes. My purpose is to liberate liberty from intellectual limitations, while at the same demarcating the limits of both the brain and human liberty.

There is no persuasive semantic distinction between *liberty* and *freedom*. Some distinctions have been attempted on the basis of contextual usage in different cultures, but such distinctions are superficial and simply boil down to differences in etymology. The root of "liberty" is Latin, whereas that of "freedom" is Anglo-Saxon. In American English the term "liberty" may have gained historical and political currency following the American adoption of the principles of the French Revolution, of which "liberty" was one of the mottos.[2] However, the derivative words from "freedom," such as the adjective, can be more easily used without ambiguities than those from "liberty" to characterize the two most common applications of both words: freedom or liberty *from* and freedom or liberty *to*. In this book I use them without distinction. By doing so, I attempt to open the range of the discussion to bring in subjects like socioeconomics and politics, where one term is favored over the other.[3]

One of the most interesting developments in Western culture is the current convergence of philosophical thinking with neuroscience on the issue of free will. It is useful here to review briefly that issue from the point of view of modern philosophy. This will give us a better perspective on how neuroscience

---

[2] Thomas Jefferson may have had something to do with this, because before becoming President he had been Minister to France.

[3] At one time I toyed with the idea of entitling this book *The Neurobiology of Liberty* in a somewhat pretentious attempt to parallel it with *The Constitution of Liberty*, which is arguably Hayek's best socioeconomic book (1960).

approaches the problem of free will, which is my principal agenda.

Immanuel Kant (1724–1804) defended the existence of free will with ethical reasons (1993). To his rationalist mind, morality was inconceivable without free will. William James, a century and a half later, followed the same line of reasoning, but demurred on scientific grounds (James, 1956/1884). The main reason for his hesitancy was the formidable obstacle of determinism, mainly biological determinism. He ended up reluctantly declaring himself an indeterminist, with some tolerance for what he called "soft determinism," which admitted a measure of freedom and responsibility in human choices.

Biological determinism in its extreme form ("hard" determinism) is epitomized by the "demon of Laplace" (Gillespie, 1997) – that is, the idea that *if* we knew *all* the "initial conditions" of the universe, and had limitless computational power, we should be able to predict exactly *all* the behavior of an organism from cradle to death. In other words, we should be able to trace a line of causality through myriad facts and levels of complexity. This position[4] is inimical to modern neuroscience on several grounds, among them the complexity, variance, nonlinearity, and probabilistic nature of neural transactions, especially with respect to psychological phenomena.

The opposite of hard determinism is libertarian free will. This is frequently considered a dualistic (mind/brain) position. In it, free will would be some variant of Bergson's *élan vital* (1907), a kind of extracorporeal entity that infuses us with independence and freedom from physical laws. In recent times, some brain scientists have adopted dualistic positions akin to this one, where the entity is called mind or consciousness – the soul of yore – and endowed with will and control over the brain.[5] As of

---

[4] In 1814, a somewhat paradoxical position for Laplace, who subsequently became a pioneer of probability theory.

[5] To be sure, those scientists usually envision some kind of "port of entry" of that entity into the executive substrate of the brain. For Sir John Eccles (private correspondence with this author), that port of entry could be the prefrontal cortex, enlarged to incorporate the supplementary motor area (a portion of the frontal lobe's premotor cortex).

now, neuroscience does not effectively support any dualist point of view. Libertarians also generally oppose this view (Kane, 2011). But some neuroscience, as we will see, is compatible with qualified libertarianism.

Indeed, between those two extremes – determinism and libertarianism – there is a wide range of philosophical positions with which modern neuroscience harmonizes to one degree or another. Almost all of them come under the umbrella of *compatibilism* and have their origin in the philosophy of Thomas Hobbes (1588–1679) (1968). Compatibilism essentially maintains that free will and determinism are compatible, not mutually exclusive. To make that assertion, Hobbes based himself on the evidence that, in the absence of force or coercion, individuals have the ability to make choices in accord with their desires; in other words, to decide on a choice of action *if* there is no physical impediment to it. Generally, compatibilists admit some determinism but deem it irrelevant to human behavior. Many argue for free will on ethical grounds, invoking pragmatic and common-sensical reasons, such as the worthiness of reward or punishment. In this sense, they argue for responsibility more than for free will, though the two are intimately related.

In modern times, Frankfurt and Dennett are among the better-known compatibilists. Beyond their argument for compatibility, both offer fertile ideas for empirical neuroscience. Frankfurt (1971) claims that, in some instances, conflicts develop in a person between the desire to perform an act and the desire not to perform it. Giving the example of the drug addict, he ranks both kinds of desires by order of intensity or priority ("hierarchical mesh"). In the extreme case of the "wanton" addict, where the first-order desire to take the drug prevails in the complete absence of restraint, Frankfurt concludes lack of "personhood" and self-control. There is a plausible neural explanation for the conflict in the "go/no-go" of desired action, which is especially applicable to the addict: the competing prefrontal mechanisms of reward seeking and inhibitory impulse control (Bechara, 2005). In the failure of the latter lies probably the fundamental reason why in the addict free will falls hostage to the habit (Chapters 4 and 7).

Dennett anchors his concept of free will in evolution (Dennett, 2003). In his view, the will to help others (altruism), for example, is attributable to the evolutionary pressure of kin selection. As we see in the next chapter, freedom evolves *pari passu* with the prefrontal cortex, which at the top of the *perception/action (PA) cycle* relates the organism with the world of others; namely, with the human population.

Among Dennett's many ideas – some adorned with interesting neologisms – the one that seems most treatable by neuroscience is that of temporally staged decision-making. The idea has clear precedents in William James (1956/1884), its originator, and others (Mele, 2006; Poincaré, 1914; Popper and Eccles, 1977). There are numerous variants, but essentially it stipulates that a decision is arrived at in two stages. In the first stage, which may be triggered by random events, possibilities of action are considered with regard to probability of success, outcome, and consequences. Poincaré, the mathematician, had the important insight that some of the trigger events, as well as the process of evaluation itself, may be unconscious. In the second stage, actions are selected for the decision. Robert Kane (2011), a champion of modern libertarianism, limits the intervention of chance and indeterminacy to the very beginning of the first stage, while relegating to the individual what he calls the "ultimate responsibility" (UR). He takes a dim view of some two-stage models because, according to him, they do not respect UR enough; in other words, they are not libertarian enough.

All two-stage models of free will have the inherent problem of almost exclusively relying on feed-forward processing (following the direction of time) with minimal feedback, and only limited room for "changing one's mind." Based on neurobiology, I propose that the model of the PA cycle helps resolve that problem, at least partly. In this model, I place the possibility of chance events anywhere in the cycle; namely, in the external environment, the internal environment, or the brain itself. This implies that an action, and the decision(s) leading to it, can start, and conclude, anywhere in the cycle. It implies that the hypothetical "stages" of free will and decision-making are in effect collapsed, expanded, or alternated in a continuous re-entry of information – between the frontal and posterior cortices.

Also central to my argument and neural model is the notion that free will – that is, the freedom to take alternative actions – emerges from the intimate relationship between our brain and our environment in the PA cycle. That environment is largely within us, for it includes the internal representations of the world around us. It consists of our perceptual, cultural, and ethical knowledge, in other words, our "personal-world history" – internalized in our cerebral cortex.

The concept of internalized environment was first elegantly outlined in the sociocultural context by the Spanish philosopher José Ortega y Gasset in his 1914 essay (1961), and fleshed out by him in later works. Fred Dretske (2000) recently used a similar concept, directly addressing perception as a fund of acquired personal knowledge. Inspired by Dretske, and suggesting an idea similar to that of my cortical PA cycle, Murphy and Brown (2007) write: "A mental state is a brain-body event relevant to or directed toward a social or environmental context – past, present or future." More to the essence of their thinking and to the subject of this book, they write that mental causation – *ergo* a free mental agency – derives from *categories* of knowledge irreducible to sensory elements or "qualia." With it, they elevate willing causality to the level of what I call the *cognit*.[6]

It is a truism that with our brain we feel free to shape our future and that of others. Behind that truism, however, is the extraordinary evolutionary development of the cerebral cortex, and within it the prefrontal cortex in particular. It is with this knowledge, and after long years of studying this part of the cerebral mantle, that I feel emboldened to embark on this rescue of liberty in the brain. The mission is difficult and requires, above all, intellectual humility, because there are still large gaps in our knowledge. In this book, I attempt to reach and portray what

---

[6] This is not a capricious neologism. As I explain in Chapter 3, a cognit has the specific meaning of a cortical network, which *is*, itself in the aggregate, a unit of knowledge or memory with all its associated attributes. Although I use the word "representation" frequently in referring to a cognit, that word usage is somewhat loose and imprecise, and does not do full justice to the dynamic nature of the cognit – which is subject to change with learning, attrition from aging, etc. No piece of knowledge or memory ever *re-presents* anything exactly, as juries and judges know.

Hayek (1952) calls "the explanation of the principle." Here the principle to be explained is how it is that freedom emerges from the functional interaction between the brain and the environment, and what is the position of the prefrontal cortex in that interaction. This explanation of principle may be useful to the brain researcher, the natural philosopher, the jurist, and the medical professional.

It is not too early, however, for me to declare what the book does not do, because it cannot. It does not offer a precise explanation of the brain mechanisms at the cellular level behind the exercise of our freedoms. Nor does it offer anything resembling a computational model or algorithm of that exercise. Complexity, multivariate interactions, and nonlinearity are the main impediments to that explanation.[7]

Any advance in the cognitive neuroscience of liberty requires that we overcome five major hurdles obscuring liberty's positive, optional, and creative force. Above, I have already dealt with some of them from a philosophical perspective. No neuroscientist, I venture, will open this book without one or another of those hurdles in mind: (a) determinism; (b) reductionism; (c) "the central executive"; (d) the hegemony of consciousness; and (e) the hegemony of the "self." Here in this introduction I must address them, however briefly, for the reader to begin to appreciate the real source and power of freedom within ourselves, and the limits to that freedom. At the same time I will advance some concepts that are basic to my approach.

The theory of *determinism* (a) in human behavior applies to the brain the laws of thermodynamics and classical physics. In support of its underlying assumptions is a rapidly increasing mass of genetic, neural, and behavioral facts. With what we know and

---

[7] This should not mean to anyone, I trust, that the tenets of my model are based on mere intuition. On the contrary, I have made every effort to base every one of those tenets on the best available neuroscience, however fragmentary it may be on certain relevant subjects. In this respect, while my account may not contain uncritical statements, it does contain a measure of generalization or extrapolation. For example, with regard to the PA cycle, what is true for one sensory modality (e.g., vision), I assume to be true for others (e.g., audition and touch; the chemical senses, olfaction, and taste, are more problematic in this respect).

learn every day about those facts, we feel we are making our way ever closer to the mysteries of the human mind. Since everything in the brain, as in the rest of nature, has causal antecedents, brain science thrives in the hope that only further reduction will reveal those mysteries. For reasons that I will attempt to make clear in this book, that is a fruitless pursuit.

The first serious challenge to general determinism came with the advent of quantum mechanics. With it came the certainty of the uncertain (Popper, 1980; Prigogine, 1997). It is now established knowledge that, especially at the level of the very small, many natural events occur at random within wide margins of variability. Chance and probability have entered the physical world at the most elementary levels, and, at least on theoretical grounds, have fostered the concept that the world and the behavior of humans have become to a large extent unpredictable.[8]

At higher levels, those that really matter in the brain for cognition, we are not dealing with certainties, but rather with possibilities. Game theory, including the evidence that a competing player's strategy makes one's game risky and unpredictable, has added uncertainty to the results of our interactions with others (Glimcher, 2003; Holland, 1998). It is becoming increasingly clear that there is enormous variance in the natural phenomena that lead to, or result from, human behavior. Such variance, regardless of its source, contributes further uncertainty, although it also opens the organism to new possibilities and emergent functions, much as in evolution. Indeed, variance in the brain and in behavior, as in evolution, is what leads to options for selection.

Thus, both randomness and variability are now an integral part of neuroscience. This is especially true of research on the

---

[8] I say on theoretical grounds, because on empirical grounds there is an enormous distance between uncertainty at the subatomic level and uncertainty in human behavior and neural networks. That distance cannot be bridged with any kind of rational argument beyond the statement of analogy of principles at vastly different levels. In fact, it is highly disputable, though not inconceivable, that Heisenbergian uncertainty at the quantum level leads to behavioral or cognitive uncertainty by a direct causal path. Kane (1985), however, envisioned that path as a possible source of free will.

cerebral cortex,[9] where all major cognitive functions operate – attention, perception, memory, language, and intelligence. The variance that sensory physiologists encounter in the responses of cortical cells to external sensory stimuli leads them to attribute that variance to noise, accustomed as they are to consistency of response to stimuli with identical physical parameters.[10] In any case, nobody seems yet ready to recognize that, perhaps, among the "degrees of freedom" of statistical variance in the cortex hides one of the reasons for the freedom of the human mind.

Freedom is clearly not reducible to variance, in the brain or anywhere else. But variance, in a complex adaptive system such as the brain, is a necessary condition for plasticity, development, and emergence of new function, all of them conducive to the freedom of cognition and action from determinism. More than metaphorically, variance plays in cognition a role not unlike the one it plays in evolution (Chapter 2). There are three apparent reasons for this. The first is that selection among variants is not only what leads to the emergence of new traits in evolution but also what leads to new patterns of response in the brain. The second is that those patterns are biologically adaptive for the individual as well as for the species. The third reason is that, just as variance leads to changing adaptive relations of the genome with the environment, it also leads to changing adaptive relations of the brain with that environment.

Closer to the action, the role of variance is best illustrated by the prefrontal cortex. The main general function of this cortex is *the temporal organization of goal-directed actions in the domains of behavior, reasoning, and language*. The prefrontal cortex does not

[9] Failure to account for random variability often leads to the inference of chaos and to mischaracterizations of neural causality. Typically, the mechanisms and "specialized" functions of the association cortex have been inferred from *relative* differences in distributions of variance induced by an extrinsic variable. Neither mechanisms nor functions can be reasonably inferred from a partial range of their distribution as demarcated by the effect of any given extrinsic variable.

[10] They ignore the fact that the behavior of brain cells in primary sensory systems conforms to a Poisson distribution, the essential feature of any stochastic (random) process. In association cortex, a large part of the variance in the response of those cells to an external sensory stimulus is attributable to the "history" of that stimulus for the organism.

perform this function in isolation, but in close cooperation with many other cortical and subcortical structures. It sits at the summit of the PA cycle, deeply embedded in the circuitry of that cycle. In dynamic terms, this means that the prefrontal cortex is subject to myriad inputs from the external as well as the internal world. It also means that it sends vast numbers of outputs to efferent motor systems as well as feedback to input systems. Therein lies its crucial position in freedom and above determinism. My prefrontal cortex is not my "center of free will," but it is the neural broker of the highest transactions of myself with my environment, internal as well as external; that is to say, the highest transactions at the top of my PA cycle (Chapter 4).

At any given time, the specific prefrontal functions are guided if not determined by innumerable inputs in competition with one another, all of them of variable strength. Yet the output of the system is precise and consistent, in the form of a given selected action or series of actions in accord with a goal or set of goals that may be represented, at least in part, in the frontal cortex itself. The reason for this consistency of action despite variance of inputs is that the output is the result of competing averages and probabilities of input, which need not be fixed but can vary within certain ranges to produce the same output. The resulting action is goal-effective if, within limits, it conforms to the representation of the goal. For example, there are many ways to bring the coffee cup to my lips, depending on which muscle groups in my arm I contract in succession to do it. Given my initial position with respect to table and cup, the trajectory of my hand may vary greatly, while reaching out to, as well as bringing in, the cup, yet both actions will be effective if, aided by changing visual and muscle/joint sensory inputs, the end result is the cup against my lips.

The constancy of output despite variations of input obeys a fundamental principle first established in immunology but present in all complex biological systems (Edelman and Gally, 2001): *degeneracy*.[11] Because of it, several different inputs lead to

---

[11] The word is unfortunate, even if commonly used in immunology, for it implies destruction and entropy. Yet the concept is one of the most fertile in cognitive neurobiology. Degeneracy refers to the classing of inputs or

the same output. "Degeneracy" has the effect of categorizing actions out of the many that are possible in the presence of multiple variable inputs (this is what we mean by action constancy). Similarly, perceptual constancy results from categorization of sensory inputs also according to the principle of "degeneracy."

Take an example in which both perceptual and action constancies play a role: I spot a nice red rose in my garden, among many of the same or different color. They are all roses despite differences among them ("a rose is a rose … "). Perceptual constancy derives from the fact that, despite variations, they all have certain common characteristics (e.g., petal shape, fragrance, etc.). Now, I decide to cut that red rose for my lady. Action constancy comes into play: there are many ways to reach into the rosebush with the garden shears without getting hurt, and many places along the stem to cut the rose – though for the professional gardener there is only one. The end result will be the rose in the intended hands. The entire sequence illustrates the PA cycle ahead of detailed description in Chapter 4. (For illustration, here there is no need to bring in the emotional PA cycle, though it also enters my behavior and contributes inputs to it.)

Multideterminacy – that is, the fact that there are many possible causes of an action – does not mean that the action is "undetermined," but in practical terms it tends to mean the same. More precisely, as multideterminacy increases, it approaches indeterminacy; that is, possible causes multiply and any of them in particular appears to disappear as *the* cause. In terms of behavior and personal experience, the constraints on freedom diminish. The individual feels and, for all practical purposes, is more free. Options for input selection multiply as the number and ranges of inputs multiply. By the same token, options for action also multiply as competing goals multiply. Both increased inputs and increased outputs add up to more freedom for the organism.

In the search for causality of human action, the most serious obstacle is the currently fashionable fragmentation of cognition

outputs into general categories. Categorization is at the essence of all cognitive functions, especially perception. Objects and actions are classified in our mind by their common properties, and most importantly by the relations between properties.

into progressively smaller – and less relevant – neural components. This trend, of course, is the natural progression of *reductionism* (b). It has been, and will continue to be, immensely productive in science. In addition to being the golden rule of the natural sciences, reductionism has the attraction of any intellectual advance toward "ultimate causes," as is, for example, the attempt to reduce all chemistry to physics. Reductionism is almost an article of faith for any natural scientist, including the neuroscientist.[12]

Unfortunately, reductionism fails as a useful methodology to explore either causation or mechanism in cognitive neuroscience. Probably the most important reason is that the cognitive code is a relational code, irreducible to its parts.[13] The contents of any cognitive function are defined by relationships. Thus, a percept is defined by relations between sensory features ("qualia"), a memory by relations between associated elements of experience, a word by relations between letters or phonemes, the meaning of a sentence by relations between words, and so on. In every instance, the analysis of components leads inevitably to the disintegration or denaturalization of the object under study; in other words, it loses its meaning. Without noting a *relation* between them, the three letters *K*, *S*, and *Y* do not spell or mean anything.

The futility of that kind of analysis in the study of the brain/mind problem should be obvious. Yet its pursuit has led to the

---

[12] Here I am referring to methodological reductionism (in contrast to other forms, such as ontological reductionism). Thus in this instance I am referring to the possibility of acquiring new knowledge about the cognitive functions of a system, such as the cerebral cortex, by acquiring new knowledge about its parts in isolation. This is not a contradiction of the concept of emergentism – a frequently invoked opposite to reductionism – which claims the emergence of new functions from the aggregate of the functions of the system's parts (Zalta *et al.*, 2012). In fact, certain phenomena such as consciousness may well emerge from the aggregate of activated cortex. Further, certain forms of reductionism, such as "hierarchical reductionism" (Dawkins, 1986), are eminently compatible with an appropriate methodology to investigate the hierarchical organization of cognits or cognitive networks as discussed in Chapter 3.

[13] The word "code" throughout this book is used as a generic term for information, whether in cognition or in the cerebral cortex, and is similarly applied to the genetic code, but not to a legal or digital code. In the last chapter (Chapter 7), however, I deal briefly with *legal codes*.

spurious localization of memories in molecules, words in cortical spots, visual percepts in discrete portions of cortex, and emotional memories in discrete portions of the limbic system. What commonly leads to such errors is the finding that an experimental intervention (for example, a lesion or stimulation) on a small brain parcel can alter a percept, memory, or performance. If the location happens to be a node of heavy association in the neural network that associates the components of that percept, memory, or performance, the latter is erroneously inferred to lie there. The converse error is committed when a ubiquitous molecule or chemical – for example, a neurotransmitter – is identified as the processor of a given cognitive function or content, again in disregard of the relational cognitive code. Roger Sperry is purported to have said, appropriately, that any attempt to crack that code by molecular biology is like trying to understand a written message by studying the chemistry of the ink.

Evidently, what we pressingly need in cognitive neuroscience is a "floor" to causality, a ground base at the appropriate neural level. Reductionism under that level is irrelevant to cognition, and, as such, irrelevant to our quest for free will in the brain. In my view, that most basic level is the cognitive network of the cerebral cortex, which I call the *cognit*, the unit of knowledge and memory (Fuster, 2003, 2009). The concept of cognitive network or cognit emerges out of our current understanding of the basic principles of neurobiology, the connective architecture of the cortex, its physiology in behavior, and the latest findings of functional imaging in the human. Chapter 3 deals with the organization and dynamics of cognits. At present, I shall only outline their major characteristics. Also, I will explain why any reduction to the morphological or functional study of their parts, in isolation and out of the behavioral context, is not contributory either to cognitive neuroscience or to the neurobiology of freedom.

A cognit is a network of cortical cell assemblies or smaller nets representing, as a unit, an item of memory or knowledge (knowledge is semantic memory). That unit is made of sensory, motor, or emotional events experienced at, or nearly at, the same time (Fuster, 2009). As a result of that temporal coincidence or near-coincidence, those events are associated with one another by the strengthening of the contacts (synapses) between the cell assemblies or nets that represent them (Hayek, 1952; Hebb, 1949; Kandel, 2000). The appropriate adage goes like this: "Cells that fire together wire together." Thus, a cognit *is both* a neuronal network *and* a memory or item of knowledge, formed by the association of its constituent representations. With learning and experience, cognits grow and connect with one another, sharing nodes that represent common features. Consequently, in the cerebral cortex, cognits interconnect and overlap profusely, whereby a neuron or group of neurons practically anywhere in the cortex can be part of many memories or items of knowledge. The strength of the synapses within and between cognits varies widely, depending on such factors as selective attention, saliency, repeated experience, rehearsal, and emotional impact. The size of a cognit and its cortical coverage also vary within wide limits. The cognit is, by definition, a composite – not a minimum – unit of memory and knowledge.

Cognits originate and evolve in the course of life. Some expand as new memory or knowledge is acquired and synaptic connections are strengthened with it.[14] Others shrink and weaken from lack of use or aging, each factor accompanied by attrition of synaptic contacts. It is because of these changes that a cognit cannot be equated with a representation in the ordinary sense. Representation implies a persistence that the cognit does not have; in dynamic terms, with a cortical substrate constantly in flux, a cognit never *re-presents* anything.

Perceptual cognits – that is, cognits acquired through the senses, such as the memory of a televised tennis match – are distributed mainly in posterior cortex. Conversely, executive cognits, such as the rules of tennis, are mainly in frontal cortex. Perceptual-executive (sensory-motor) cognits, however, span both cortices, posterior and frontal – possibly also both cerebral hemispheres – linked by long nerve fibers through the corpus

---

[14] Temporal coincidence continues to be a critical factor in that strengthening of synapses is a result of new experience. Any such experience is accompanied by the retrieval of old experience by associations of context and similarity. In the process, there will be temporal coincidence between a retrieved cognit and the new experience, whereby new connections will be added to the cognit. New memory will have been formed on old memory.

callosum, the large commissure or bundle of fibers that connects the two hemispheres. One such perceptual-executive cognit, for example, would be the memory of my last tennis match.

Cognits vary greatly in size – that is, in number and cortical dispersion of their constituent neurons. Small cognits are nested within larger ones, all hierarchically organized, such that those representing concrete memories or items of knowledge are nested within, and hierarchically under, those representing more abstract or complex information. For example, the sounds, color, and shape of San Francisco's cable car are nested in the broader cognits of my last trip to that city and the concept of cable car. These are, in turn and in part, nested in the broader cognit for the concept of public transportation.

Because of the practically infinite combinatorial power of the 10 to 20 billion neurons or brain cells in our cerebral cortex, the breadth and specificity of our individual memories and knowledge are potentially infinite. The peculiarity of our individual memories resides in the specificity of neuronal combinations, although we all share networks for common knowledge (semantic memory) that must be at least topologically or isomorphically similar.[15]

At the same time, that nearly infinite combinatorial power of connectivity is the source of virtually infinite capacity for imagination and creativity; in other words, for the forming of new networks and the recombination of old ones. In Chapter 3 we discuss how that is possible. The essential point here is that the neural information for both perception and action is widely distributed in the cerebral cortex. The richer the past experience, the broader is the distribution of cognits in brain space; and thus the greater is the number of the available options, and the greater the freedom to select among them.

---

[15] The concept of isomorphism has a mathematical origin. It refers to the similarities between functions that relate different variables but share certain commonalities of relationship. Here, as in psychology, it refers to the similarity between perceived objects that have the same *relationships* between their constituent sensory features, regardless of differences in the elements themselves ("a rose is a rose, is a rose . . . "). A useful analogy is that of, say, two matrix-like lattices of rubber bands with identical connecting knots. Their isomorphic similarity is preserved despite the stretching or twisting of the lattices. Topology, in our context, refers to isomorphism in brain space.

The third hurdle (c) is the "central executive." The concept of a cerebral structure controlling all the complex, goal-directed actions of the human organism has long been attractive to cognitive neuroscientists. That concept grew largely out of the neuropsychology of the frontal lobe. It was commonly observed that humans with lesions from disease or trauma of the lateral surface of the cortex of the frontal pole or prefrontal cortex exhibited profound deficits in certain functions that cognitive scientists identified as "executive" or "supervisory," notably attention and working memory. Clinically (Chapter 7), the aggregate of symptoms from the frontal injury included, in addition to attention and short-term memory disorders, deficits in general drive, decision-making, language, and planning. That combination of symptoms was named the "dysexecutive syndrome" (Baddeley, 1983). By inference, the role of the *central executive* was attributed to the lateral prefrontal cortex.

From research on several animal species, especially the human, that designation appears entirely appropriate. Indeed, a multitude of experimental studies confirms that the prefrontal cortex exerts so-called executive cognitive control over a large variety of cortical and subcortical brain structures, to the effect of sharpening attention, maintaining working memory, making decisions, and organizing goal-directed actions (Fuster, 2008; Miller and Cohen, 2001). Therefore, many conclude, the prefrontal cortex is the seat of a cerebral superagency, such as the "central executive," possibly corresponding to the concept of a brain center of will and execution. The concept comes very close to endorsing a dualist position on the nature of the mind, physical on the one hand and mental on the other. From here there is only a short step to making special room in the prefrontal cortex for consciousness with its deliberative powers. By this reasoning, the "central executive" becomes a cover for a kind of "homuncular CEO" in the frontal lobe of the brain,[16] possibly in the prefrontal cortex, "delivering orders" to the rest of the brain and to the organism.

---

[16] This expression is a jocular extrapolation of the concept of "homunculus" – an upside-down distorted image of the human body (hands, face and mouth greatly magnified) – projected on the cortex to portray the distribution of the

Clearly, this picture is grossly misleading and a serious impediment to any discourse on the brain–liberty issue. The most obvious fallacy of the proposition is that it leads to an infinite regress. If we grant to the prefrontal cortex the role of supreme executive, the question is then which other "authority" or "controller" – cognitive entity or brain structure – the prefrontal cortex obeys; and the same question can be asked about that one, and so on *ad infinitum*. The problem is sidestepped, of course, by invoking a dualistic solution and some mysterious entity, such as the conscious ego, to govern the prefrontal cortex. But this dualistic solution is neurobiologically unsustainable.

The most plausible solution to the problem, in my view, is to attribute to the prefrontal cortex the role of the supreme *enabler* within the PA cycle (Chapter 4). The PA cycle, as we will see, is the circular array of cortical structures, and the circular processing flow through them, that govern the relationships of the organism with its environment. It is a cybernetic cycle, with feed-forward and feedback. The cycle does not need a central executive, for action can originate anywhere within it. At the top of the cycle, the prefrontal cortex enables and organizes action, exerting continuous control over posterior (perceptual) cortex, and the latter feeds continuous information to frontal cortex to control further action. Control is thus mutual, between posterior and frontal cortices, and action can be initiated anywhere in the cycle – that is, in the environment – in perceptual cortex or in executive cortex.

This helps resolve the controversy among neurophysiologists about the role of assorted cortical areas in intention, attention, selection, motor control, and decision-making. The most plausible answer is that all areas are part of the cycle and involved, at one time or another, in one or another of those aspects of voluntary behavior.

If we now add to the PA cycle the inputs from emotional structures of the limbic brain to both posterior and anterior cortices, we have both cortices, perceptual and executive, influenced by the realms of affect, motivation, drive, and instinct. As

---

sensory or motor effects of electrical stimulation of that cortex (Woolsey *et al.*, 1979).

we will see in Chapter 4, automatic and reflex behaviors do not need the cortical stages of the cycle. These can be enacted and coordinated at lower levels. Nonetheless, emotional inputs to perceptual and executive cognits undoubtedly contribute to their expansion and refinement.

Thus, the practically infinite combinatorial potential of cortical connectivity, the richness of potential encounters with the environment, and the panoply of human emotions undoubtedly constitute the fertile grounds for countless free options, though also constraints. Creativity, planning, imagination, and innovation thrive in those grounds, where the PA cycle engages the cognits of the past with those of the future in a continuous goal-directed dynamic interplay (Chapter 5).

No reasonable treatment of liberty in the brain is possible without dealing with the issue of *consciousness*. Here, I have two introductory and complementary goals. One is to question consciousness *per se* as an entity determining our behavior. The other is to emphasize how much unconscious knowledge does determine that behavior. Both goals require that I first deal briefly – if that is possible – with the thorny problem of the neural basis of consciousness.

Consciousness, our concern under (d), is not a function. Nor is it a causal agent. To give it either property is to immediately invite dualism of brain and mind. More accurately, consciousness is the subjective experience of a state of heightened activity of the brain – especially the cortex or part of it. It is that condition that evokes the subjective awareness of ourselves and of the cognitive and emotional functions our brain performs. Conscious experience is by definition a phenomenon or more precisely an epiphenomenon, in that it is secondary to the state and functions of the brain. In any case, it *does* exist, but it lacks operant characteristics or even an operational definition, other than by default – that is, sleep.

None of this negates the critical importance of consciousness as a resource to study the human mind and the human brain (Searle, 1997). They are inseparable, and through consciousness both are accessible to psychology, psychometrics, and cognitive analysis. By utilizing the experimental subject's or patient's consciousness and capacity for conscious attention, we are able to inquire into his mind, assess his conscious emotional experience, provide him with testing instructions, and measure his performance of any cognitive function; that is, attention itself, perception, memory, language, or intelligence. By our access to the individual's conscious attention we are able to assess how much that individual *feels* free to choose and to conduct his actions.

But it is the cerebral cortex that guides conscious attention, not the other way around. The cerebral cortex does not need a supervisory agency because it is inextricably embedded in the PA cycle, which continuously adjusts the organism to its environment, internal and external. Thus we do not need our consciousness to understand why we behave the way we do. Consciousness may not only be insufficient for that understanding, but also may be an impediment to achieving it; an impediment that the psychoanalytic method attempts to circumvent. Nor do we need an ethereal concept such as that of "universal consciousness" to understand why society behaves the way it does. All we need is our individual and collective cortices adjusting us, through toil, trouble, and circumstance to some sort of personal and social "homeostasis".[17]

This does not mean that we are automatons at the service of a rigid, predetermined cerebral cortex in its quest for adjustment; far from it. That cortex is neither rigid nor predetermined. In the first place, it comes to the world with enormous potential plasticity, some of it preprogrammed in the genome, but much, if not most, open to change and selection by encounters with the world. When I say plasticity I mean ability to increase the numbers of cells and connections between them. Above all, the cortex possesses infinite capacity to combine its architectural elements in countless cortical

---

[17] "Homeostasis" is a term coined by physiologists to designate the innate capacity of the organism to regulate its internal milieu by counteracting influences from the environment or the weather that can disturb its equilibrium (Bernard, 1927/1865; Cannon, 1932). The autonomic and endocrine systems, both under central nervous control, especially from the hypothalamus, serve to correct deviations from that equilibrium. Both systems intervene also to protect the individual from environmental stress (Selye, 1956). Inasmuch as the protection of the individual helps protect the social group to which the individual belongs, social stability would be a result of the aggregate of individual homeostases. The importance of homeostasis as the biological base of the PA cycle is discussed in Chapter 4.

networks to represent the world and to deal in new ways with the environment, both internal and external. Therein lies our cortex' potential for learning from its past and for shaping the future. And therein lies its potential for freedom, which is ours.

In the second place, always engaged in the PA cycle from cradle to grave, the cortex shapes its individuality, which is also ours. As we grow, we become progressively more conscious of ourselves, of our capabilities and limitations, and more conscious of our liberty and its constraints. We learn how much we depend on others, as others depend on us. But whatever we learn, we do not necessarily learn consciously.

Ninety-nine percent – to give it a number – of what we perceive in our daily life is unconscious. In fact it would clutter our cortex and our consciousness if it were not so. We transit through the world unconsciously "testing hypotheses" – that is, expectations – about that world.[18] Only if those hypotheses are disproved do we become aware of them and of their falsity, sometimes immediately, before we are capable of verbalizing the new or unexpected: something out of place in a familiar room, a significant three-digit change in our car's odometer, a new flower in the garden ... Then, the new or unexpected suddenly captures our conscious attention. Those are all telltale signs that we unconsciously process all the rest of what we perceive, innumerable details, out of awareness. Much the same can be said about our daily actions, most of them overlearned, practically automatic until the unexpected happens – as it may, for example, while we are driving in traffic.

If the PA cycle never ceases working and does not necessitate consciousness, it is reasonable to ask when exactly it begins to work in the newborn. Is it with the first perception or with the first action? The answer is probably with both at the same time.[19]

---

[18] The general idea that perception is a "top-down" interpretation of reality in accord with past experience comes from Helmholtz (1925). One of its most ardent supporters, in visual perception, is Richard Gregory (1970).

[19] We know that the newborn starts moving immediately after birth. But when does she start sensing? – let alone perceiving? That is a question that has long been debated by philosophers and psychologists since John Locke (Gallagher, 2005). Two things appear clear. The first is that the start of sensing differs

Later, in the child and the adult, the PA cycle will become progressively more "knowledgeable." Here again, some 99 percent of all actions will be unconscious. Surely there will be deliberate, well thought-out actions, and logical decisions that almost by necessity demand consciousness, or rather, highly active cortex. The choice of alternative actions, the solution to problems, and the clearing of ambiguities and uncertainties will tend to crowd routine behavior out of consciousness. Then as ever, some of the motives behind the action, some of its "subroutines," and some of the potential effects of these will be entirely unconscious. It has been shown that cortical activation antecedes even the intention to perform the most deliberate of willful actions (Libet, 1985).

By transferring freedom from a mythical entity for conscious and deliberate free will to the cerebral cortex, we are endowing the individual with more liberty, not less. For our cortex "knows" more than we think we know, and can "imagine" more than we think we can imagine. Our cortex stores a vast fund of past perceptual information, while our prefrontal cortex within it can recombine that information to produce an inexhaustible wealth of potential cognits of action. Individual freedom consists in the capacity for recombination of perceptual and executive cognits in the cortex of the healthy human being.

The self-awareness of liberty and free choice is a phenomenon of the cortical involvement in the cognitive operations of goal setting and choice, again not their cause. It is true that when cortical areas engage intensely in a cognitive function such as selective attention, working memory, or fine discrimination, consciousness is invariably present – as a direct result of cortical activation above certain levels of intensity. However, both

with sensory modality. Audition begins in fetal life, when the yet-to-be-born can apparently distinguish the mother's speech prosody (DeCasper and Spence, 1986). Music perception begins very early in life (Trehub and Hannon, 2006), perhaps even prenatally. The second thing is that all senses, for good development, have to pass certain critical periods of active exercise at the beginning of life outside the womb. Arguably, vision and touch begin *after* action (looking and actively touching). The neonate enters the world "palpating" it, with the mother's breast, in order to find the stimuli that through innate action will lead to bonding with the mother and the satisfaction of basic needs.

goal setting and choice are subject to influences that are uncon-scious. Thus, goals and choices may be biased to one degree or another by those influences. Nonetheless, the conscious experi-ence of liberty does not derive so much from the awareness of particular goals or actions as from the awareness of their poten-tial multiplicity.[20]

In conclusion, consciousness is a phenomenon of height-ened cortical activity in complex rational cognition and behavior. But consciousness *per se* is not essential to conducting that cogni-tion or behavior. Furthermore, much if not all of our cognitive activity, including our decisions to act and how to act, is biased if not determined by completely unconscious knowledge. Our lib-erty to act, and how we will act, is in fact enhanced by uncon-scious knowledge – barring pathological inhibition.[21] That unconscious knowledge includes a multitude of cortical cognits acquired by prior experience that guide not only rational deci-sions but also our emotional and moral conduct. They may inform our behavior by intuition or fuzzy logic, but in some instances they do it as effectively as the most deliberate rationality. They may include cognits of social behavior that augment not only our freedom but also that of our fellow humans.

Finally, there is "the self" (e); that is, the sense of the self as an autonomous entity "in" or "over" the brain. This is almost inevitably a Cartesian, dualistic view. In evolution, which is essen-tially a population process, the freedom of *the self* and that of society are closely interrelated. Each has its own PA cycle, so to speak, and social adaptation implies the harmony if not the

---

[20] It is easily understandable that an important new goal and its pursuit will be accompanied with full awareness by virtue of the intensity of the activation of the prefrontal cortex and its collaborating cortices. But, in that pursuit, it is the free cortex that leads to consciousness, not the other way around. It is our cortex that is free. Consequently, we feel free. Here there is a faint parallel of the Cartesian "*cogito, ergo sum*" (I think, therefore I am): I feel free, therefore I am – free.

[21] For one thing, liberty is enhanced by unconscious knowledge because such knowledge expands the fund of information that our choices are to be based on. Alternative choices thus multiply by the availability of that unconscious fund. On the other hand, the unconscious repression of that knowledge by psychogenic causes (as in hysterical disorders) leads to restricted choices and loss of freedom.

synchrony of the two. Hegel (2002) did not know Darwin's most important work, which was published nearly 30 years after Hegel's death. If he had, Hegel probably would have introduced in his social ideology Darwin's concepts on the dynamics of biological populations. Natural selection favors traits that are adaptive not only for the individual but also for the population at large. In fact the adaptation of the individual to its milieu is a microcosm of the adaptation of the population to that milieu, which is the dynamics of evolution. Natural law is the unwritten ethical code for the individual in the service of the population, and therefore is in the population's "interests" of survival and procreation. Consequently, Hegel's ideas of group cohesion and defense of kin are conceptual antecedents – or concomitants – of Darwin's ideas of biological population dynamics.[22]

Just as natural law imposes constraints on society for its own adaptive benefit, it imposes them on the individual for the same purpose (Chapter 7). Both are constraints on liberty, at least for the short term, but at the same time they protect liberty for the long term, to the benefit of both the individual and society.

The self is engaged in the PA cycle pursuing reward, praise, and adaptation to its environment, including of course, above all, the defense of life and limb. In those pursuits the self uses, consciously or unconsciously, all the options at the disposal of its brain in accord with urge, priority, and value. The liberty to exercise these options is not only condoned by society but also protected by it. Conversely, the individual self of the healthy citizen, wittingly or unwittingly, abides by natural law and respects its constraints, as well as those of common law.[23] At some point, however, conflict may develop between the two, individual liberty and societal liberty. The constraints of one may not jibe with the constraints of the other, or the short-term goals of one may not jibe with the long-term goals of the other. It

---

[22] When tyrants and demagogues use those ideas to promote a group – ethnic, national, religious, or other – at the expense of others, they lead peoples to oppression, misery, war, and untold human suffering.

[23] Whereas natural law consists of the laws of physical nature, including the behavior of social groups deriving from evolution, common law consists of laws developed by judges through the decisions of courts.

is largely to prevent conflicts between the individual and society that human institutions have evolved. What is more, human institutions, when they work correctly, expand the liberties of both the individual self and the rest of society.

How has human evolution made that possible? In large measure, it has done it through the enormous growth of the human prefrontal cortex. With it, two decisive events have led to the expansion of liberties. One is the great increase in the fund of knowledge and memory that the human brain can acquire and place at the disposal of action. The prefrontal cortex, at the apex of the PA cycle, can draw on countless cognits to shape language, thinking, and behavior. Some of those cognits are innate (Chapter 3), built in the sensory apparatus (sensory phyletic memory), which in the course of evolution has acquired extraordinary power of discrimination, and in the motor apparatus (executive phyletic memory), which has acquired extraordinary power of motor coordination. More inputs and outputs to and from the prefrontal cortex augment the options and freedom of the self in society.

The other decisive event that results from the expansion of the prefrontal cortex in the human is the "telescoping" of memory and knowledge into the future.[24] Natural selection implies that evolution is *postdictable*, not predictable. So is the human brain. But something marvelous happened with its evolution: the brain itself became a predictive or prospective organ (Chapter 5). The human brain retains from evolution, as a matter of fact, all of its reflex apparatus to adapt to the external and internal milieus and to correct for changes in both. But in addition it becomes capable of anticipating those changes and of preparing the organism for them. Whereas in past evolution the mammalian brain became adaptive by natural selection, the human brain, in addition, has become *pre-adaptive*.

And whereas in prior evolution the brain became capable of storing memory of the past, with the advent of the human

---

[24] In this context, "telescoping" into the future means projecting forwards in time the knowledge and memory presently extant in the cortex. It means what I call later (Chapter 5) "memory of the future."

prefrontal cortex the brain also became capable of making "memory of the future" (the expression is from David Ingvar, 1985). To be sure, there is already in nonhuman primates abundant evidence that their prefrontal cortex can anticipate the future by a few seconds or minutes (Fuster, 2008). Their working memory and their anticipatory motor set are preparations for future action.

But those animal capabilities are only a faint precursor of the capability of the human cortex to plan for the future. In the human brain, the prefrontal cortex, based on past experience, can help the individual to create the new and to make what is to come. That capability becomes potentiated and multiplied a thousandfold by the emergence of language with its future tense (Chapter 6), which makes it possible to encode linguistically the future and to bridge the time from perceived potential to reality and from imagination to creation. Further, the prefrontal cortex, singly or in alliance with that of other individuals, can help us imagine not only the self's future but also society's future. To wit, we have professional careers of many specialties, institutions of higher learning, libraries, spatial ventures, art galleries, concert halls, sports arenas, and means of transportation and communication.

Indeed, with language and prediction, the human brain has become capable of codifying for future action the evolutionary legacy of caring for others in the human population. Affiliation, trust, bonding, and responsibility have become institutionalized. The written word converts natural law into constitutions and codes of conduct. Institutions such as churches, legislatures, councils, academies, and universities assemble laws and knowledge of private origin and make them public for use by future generations. Here is where individual liberties are reconciled with social liberties (Chapter 7). Here also, under the midwifery of the human prefrontal cortex, democracy was born.

Because the brain is a physical structure, though a highly adaptive one, the first constraint to liberty is the brain itself. Here the limits come from the functional architecture of the immense conglomerate of cells and nervous pathways that make the brain a complex and open adaptive system, albeit with limited resources.

These resources vary from individual to individual as a function of genetic, developmental, and environmental factors that impact on such neural variables as cortical connectivity and transmission, synaptic strength, blood flow to the various cerebral regions, nerve-cell metabolism, and so on. To the extent that these variables, in turn, impact on cognitive and emotional brain functions, they will result in variance of liberty among subjects. On developmental grounds alone, for example, the child is less free than the adult.

Individuals are differently equipped for liberty on account of differences in cortical complexity stemming from genetics and life experience. The individual with a richly interconnected cortex, intelligent, well schooled, and with superior linguistic skills will have more options in life, and thus will be in principle more free, than an individual with a less interconnected cortex, mediocre intelligence, and faulty education. Of course, this does not mean that in a democracy under constitutional law their civic liberties should be unequal.

Other internal constraints on liberty can result from a host of pathological impairments of the cortex or other parts of the brain involved in the processing of visceral, perceptual, or motor signals (Chapter 7). The liberty of patients with extensive lesions of their prefrontal cortex is severely constrained in space and time. The frontal patient is a hostage of habit, incapable of innovation, and tied to the here-and-now. He confines himself to limited quarters and his mind lacks temporal perspective, either backwards or forwards.[25]

Then there is the loss of liberty that stems from disorders of the neural function of the basic biological drives of the organism ("biodrives"), either by abnormally enhancing one at the expense of the others or by substituting a new one for the others. A prime example of the latter is substance abuse (Chapter 7). The addict has created for himself a new drive as powerful as, or more

---

[25] However, if the lesion or disease process is circumscribed to the orbital or inferior frontal cortex, then the patient commonly presents a radically different picture: He is impulsive, uninhibited, and bereft of the elementary rules of ethics. As a result of his unconstrained, socially unacceptable "freedom," he is apt to run foul of the law.

powerful than, sex or hunger. Under insatiable craving he gears his behavior entirely to the satisfaction of his habit, to which he is ineluctably chained. The same can be said for gambling. Both drug addiction and gambling derange, as well as result from derangement of, the function of similar structures and chemicals at the base of the frontal lobes.

In peacetime the most important extrinsic constraint on freedom are human institutions. Included are all forms of legislation and ethical control of human behavior. To be sure, the constitution of a civilized country, which is the supreme law of that country, protects and indeed guarantees individual freedom for all individuals, but always within the framework of societal welfare. In this sense, constraints on individual freedom enhance societal freedom, which is the ultimate manifestation of the basic principles of natural law. Engrained in evolution, the principles of trust and affiliation ensure the freedom of the individual, the family, the community, the town, the nation, and humankind at large. Legislation institutionalizes those principles. At the same time, through education and example, those principles become incorporated in the cerebral cortex of the responsible citizen in the form of high-level abstract neuronal networks representing rules of moral conduct – that is, ethical cognits.

With this background introduction, our discussion can begin, but not without noting a peculiarity of my account that may surprise some readers. Although I do my best to build my argument in logical fashion from chapter to chapter, beginning with evolutionary and anatomical facts and ending with social considerations, I am also trying to make each chapter understandable in and by itself, without too much need to revert to previous chapters. Given the range of topics this book covers, I am anticipating the possibility that some readers may be more interested in some chapters than in others. With this in mind, and to add strength to my argument, throughout the book I allude to the basic premises of some key concepts, such as those of the cognit, the PA cycle, temporal preadaptation, and the hierarchical organization of all three.

2

Evolutionary roots of freedom

To give up the illusion that sees in it an immaterial "substance" is not to deny the existence of the soul, but on the contrary to begin to recognize the complexity, the richness, the unfathomable profundity of the genetic and cultural heritage and of the personal experience, conscious or otherwise, which together constitute this being of ours: the unique and irrefutable witness to itself.

Jacques Monod

It is virtually impossible to discuss the cerebral foundation of liberty without dealing with the evolution of the brain. The reason is simple: The capacity of mammalian organisms to modify their environment by choice and to adapt to it by chosen means has grown enormously with the evolutionary growth of certain parts of their brain, the cerebral cortex in particular. Most relevant to our present discourse is the cortex of the frontal lobes. It is indeed a remarkable fact with a touch of cosmic irony that the science of evolutionary neurobiology, which can only "postdict" but not predict, has unveiled in the prefrontal cortex of man the seed of his future, the capacity to predict and to turn prediction into action that will impact on that future and on that of human society.

The prefrontal cortex is the vanguard of evolution in the nervous system. Yet it is one of the latest cerebral structures to develop, in evolution as in the individual brain (Preuss *et al.*, 2004; Rilling, 2006; Schoenemann *et al.*, 2005; Sowell *et al.*, 2003). Language and prediction, the two most distinctively human functions that the prefrontal cortex supports, are anchored in the history of the species, as is the structure of the prefrontal cortex itself. In the human brain, the latter is tied to its evolutionary past and to the future it anticipates. Thus, while the human brain cannot predict evolution, it can predict the consequences of its actions, with them to predict and shape further actions in a continuous cycle, the perception/action (PA) cycle, which functionally links the organism to its environment. The prefrontal cortex is the highest structure in that cycle, which integrates the past with the future – however near or distant either is – in the course of behavior, language, and reasoning.

The PA cycle also has deep roots in evolution. In lower animals, earlier precursors of it mediate the adjustment of the organism to the surrounding world (Uexküll, 1926). The human brain, which sustains the PA cycle with the cortex, is the most complex adaptive system in the universe. It is an open system like all living systems (von Bertalanffy, 1950). As such, it is permanently in quasi-equilibrium, but also in constant exchange with its environment to maintain that equilibrium. Thanks to its prefrontal cortex inserted in the PA cycle, the human brain, unlike any other, develops a prospective temporal dimension. Thereby, it makes advanced long-term adaptive changes in its environment. Furthermore, language endows the human brain with the ability to record those changes, to codify them, and to institutionalize them.

In short, the prefrontal cortex confers on the human brain the capability to *predict* and, accordingly, to *preadapt*. Lower brains have a measure of that capability, as well as certain primitive forms of communication with conspecifics that may be the atavistic precursors of language. But the transition from the simian to the human in power of prediction and preadaptation, as well as communication, is so dramatic as to constitute a veritable quantum leap. All relevant variables (complexity, time, "vocabulary," and so on) increase by several orders of magnitude. Along with it, variability increases immensely, so do the options for choice among alternatives. In fact, those comparative increases over other species are so large that the argument about functional homologies between humans and animals, even the great apes, becomes well-nigh irrelevant. So does the discussion as to whether in evolution we are dealing with qualitative or merely quantitative differences in continua (Bolhuis and Wynne, 2009). With the advent of the human prefrontal cortex all the animal precursors of cognition – intelligence and communication among them – open widely to a future agenda.

This does not mean that the structure and workings of the animal brain are irrelevant to our understanding of the neurobiology of freedom. Quite the contrary; it is only in the brain of the animal, especially the nonhuman primate, that we can practically study the basic organization of knowledge, feelings, and values that give the human his or her freedom to make choices.[1] In the animal brain we can investigate the mechanisms of the PA cycle behind choice, planning, decision-making, and the temporal organization of behavior. All of them are functions in which, as we will see, the prefrontal cortex plays a critical role. Those mechanisms constitute the underpinnings of human liberty, creativity, and their myriad expressions.

Freedom, the capacity to choose between alternatives, emerges from the activity of cortical-cell networks of perceptual and executive memory, at the confluence of multiple converging inputs from past memory with multiple diverging outputs to future action. Freedom is a phenomenon of the brain's selection between those inputs and between those outputs for adaptive purposes. As a result of evolution and development, the cerebral cortex and freedom adopt in the human pivotal positions between an experiential convergent past and a divergent future of possibilities – and probabilities.

---

[1] To be sure, no animal is amenable to the study of the semantic aspects of language and, least of all, to the neural mechanisms at their foundation. But many animal species lend themselves well to the exploration of the neural mechanisms of the temporal organization of information that language shares with all other cognitive functions. Those mechanisms are not directly accessible in the human brain, even with modern imaging methods. Needless to say, only in the absence of stress or pain are cognitive functions testable in animals; this imposes strict scientific – in addition to ethical – constraints on animal experimentation.

EVOLUTION OF THE CEREBRAL CORTEX

Two approximate dates within wide uncertain ranges are especially relevant in the history of brain evolution: one 250 million years ago, and the other 250 thousand years ago. The first, in early Mesozoic, marks the appearance of the first mammals, the second the appearance of the last hominid, *Homo sapiens*. The brains of fishes, amphibians, and reptiles were – and are – covered by an evolutionally ancient cortex-like structure named the pallium (mantle). The pallium is divided into two components, the hippocampal cortex situated next to the brain's midline, and the piriform cortex, lateral to the hippocampal cortex (Figure 2.1). A third "pallium" will emerge between the two that in *Homo sapiens* will constitute 80 percent of the entire mass of the brain: the neocortex.

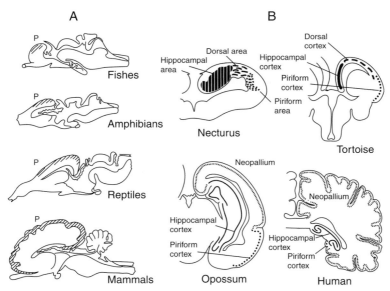

Figure 2.1 Evolutionary development of the cerebral cortex.
A: Lengthwise sections of the brains of four classes of vertebrates. *P*, pallium, generic name for cortex, both old and new (phylogenetically). From Creutzfeldt (1993). *B*: Crosswise sections of the brains of a primitive amphibian (*Necturus*), the box tortoise (*Cistudo*), the opossum (*Didelphis*), and the human being. From Herrick (1956), modified.

The neocortex or neopallium, the "new" cerebral cortex of the mammalian brain, remains physically wedged between the two ancient cortices, the hippocampus and the piriform cortex. The developing neocortex crowds the hippocampus toward the midline and the piriform lobe (piriform cortex and amygdala) toward the lateral underside of the brain. In later mammals, the neocortex grows heftily, pushing the two ancient cortices toward each other in the middle of the cerebral hemisphere. These two ancient cortices, even in the mammalian brain, preserve some of the functions they perform in primitive species: the sensing of life-sustaining signals, such as taste, olfaction, and spatial orientation. Additionally in primates, the hippocampus is involved in the acquisition and retrieval of memory, while the amygdala is involved in emotion, endowing memories with feeling.

In the course of evolution, the neocortex, among all brain structures, increases the most in size, especially in primates. That evolutionary growth of the neocortex is exponential, out of proportion with the growth of other structures. Further, the volumetric expansion of the neocortex occurs concomitantly with the differentiation of its cellular architecture, culminating in the human brain with a relatively large size and marked lamination of its cellular structure (six layers of neurons of different sizes, shapes, and densities). These changes, embedded in the human genome, appear to be the result of selective upregulation of gene expression[2] relative to nonhuman primates (Preuss *et al.*, 2004). Through those changes, and concomitant genetic mutations, humans have evolved mechanisms that allow them to overcome the physical constraints that impede the course of their own evolution (Krubitzer, 2009). Among the changes are those that take place in cortical architecture. Clearly, the evolutionary growth and differentiation of the neocortex has much to do with the increased ability to adapt to the environment and with

---

[2] Upregulation refers to the increase in the capability of a gene to express cell products (e.g., specific proteins) in response to internal or external stimulation, as, for example, an immune antibody to a new virus or an antitoxin to a new chemical agent.

the prolongation of life. In the human brain, that cortex has developed a large number of specialized areas to respond to all manner of sensory signals as well as to execute all manner of skillful movements.

In brain evolution, the greatest neocortical expansion takes place in areas called "of association," which serve the higher cognitive functions; that is, those functions that deal with knowledge and memory. Naturally, they deal as well with the neural transactions between the organism and the environment that depend on those functions. In the human brain, there are two separate cortical regions with areas of association. One is in the posterior part of the brain, extending over large portions of the parietal, temporal, and occipital lobes (PTO region), which contains networks of knowledge and memory (cognits) acquired through the sensory systems. Those networks or cognits serve the highest aspects of cognition, including perception, language, and intelligence. The other associative region is the prefrontal cortex, the association cortex of the frontal lobe, which serves the executive aspects of cognition, especially the temporal organization of actions in the domains of behavior, language, and reasoning. This "executive" cortex develops maximally in the human brain,[3] where it occupies nearly one-third of the totality of the neocortex (Figure 2.2).

Especially relevant to the development of the distinctive cognitive prerogatives of the human in language, planning, and

---

[3] Primarily on the basis of morphological imaging data (Semendeferi et al., 1997), it has been argued that the prefrontal cortex does not evolve more, in proportion, than other cortical areas. Whereas this may be true volumetrically for the entirety of the frontal cortex, it does not take into account the fine structure of cells and fiber connections that characterize the prefrontal cortex per se. In the primate, anyhow, the frontal region that association nuclei of the thalamus innervate, which we call the prefrontal cortex, considerably exceeds in size the region they innervate in the posterior – perceptual – cortex (Jones and Leavitt, 1974; Walker, 1940). Further, on cytoarchitectonic grounds, the prefrontal cortex, which roughly corresponds to what Brodmann (1909, 1912) called the regio frontalis (that is, all frontal areas minus areas 4 and 6), constitutes, by his calculations, 8.5% in the lemur, 11.5% in the gibbon and the macaque, 17% in the chimpanzee, and 29% in the human, of total cortex. On that basis alone, it seems legitimate to speak, figuratively, of an evolutionary "prefrontal explosion" in the human.

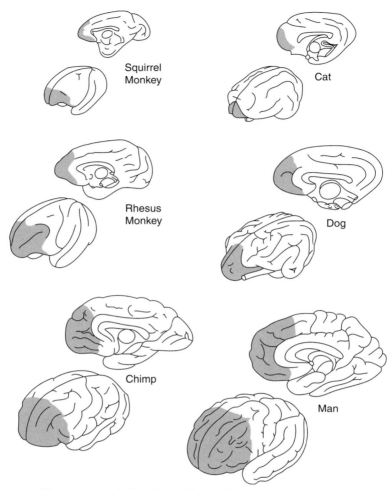

Figure 2.2 Relative size of the prefrontal cortex with respect to total cortex in six animal species (marked by *shading* of external and internal hemispheric surface). PTO, parieto-temporo-occipital association region (posterior association cortex).

the exercise of freedom is the evolution of connections between prefrontal neurons and those of other cortical areas. Those connections, together with the neurons they link, constitute the essential components of the neural infrastructure of cognitive networks, and thus of all the cognitive functions of the cerebral cortex.

The most rapid and efficient connectivity in the brain is that consisting of fibers surrounded by myelin,[4] which constitute the bulk of the subcortical white matter and of the corpus callosum, the large commissure that connects the cortices of the two hemispheres together. It is the white matter, more than the gray – cellular – matter of the cortex that increases the most in evolution. That is a clear indication of the vast expansion of the connective potential to form neural networks, which the human cortex requires in order to deal with the complexities of the world around it.

Among all the connective tracts with which the human brain is endowed, probably none is more important for cognition than the one that links, in each hemisphere, the posterior (PTO), perceptual, cortex with the prefrontal, executive, cortex: the superior longitudinal fasciculus. The connections within that tract are bidirectional; in other words, they run in both directions, some PTO to front and others front to PTO. They constitute the backbone of the PA cycle, connecting posterior and frontal cortices reciprocally in tandem function. They will become essential for all kinds of temporally structured behaviors, where perception will guide action, and vice versa, through the environment. Most importantly, they will be essential for the spoken language in dialogue, where the environment includes the interlocutor (Chapter 6).

INDIVIDUAL DEVELOPMENT OF THE CEREBRAL CORTEX

An old idea, first promulgated in 1899 by Ernst Haeckel (1992), is that ontogeny, the early development of an individual, recapitulates phylogeny, the development of the species. Indeed, many features of the individual nervous system of the human appear to develop in the same sequence they followed in the course of evolution as a result of natural selection – that is, during the development of earlier animal species. Such features include,

---

[4] Myelin is a white substance made of proteins and lipids that forms a sheath around the rapid-conduction fibers (axons) of the brain. It is indispensable for proper cortical integration and coordination.

for example, the prefrontal cortex, which develops late in evolution and does not develop fully until the third or fourth decade in the life of the individual.

Haeckel's recapitulation idea is basically flawed in one important respect. Whereas natural selection follows a passive process based on random genetic variance and mutation, ontogeny follows an order established by biological clocks that determine gene expression and molecular-enzymatic change – jointly with environmental influences from point of conception onward. Nevertheless, Gould (1992) attempts to reconcile the two trends, phylogenetic and ontogenetic, by proposing the concept of "heterochrony." Heterochrony would simply signify the change, in the development of the individual organism, of the relative rate and timing of appearance of characters already present in ancestors. In other words, ontogeny by its own clock would compress, extend, and retime the *results* of evolution.

The concept of heterochrony would legitimize the prediction of ontogeny based in part on the postdictable evolution of traits, but that would still leave that prediction subject to the uncertainties surrounding lineage and ancestry in evolution. In any event, it would be wrong to deny or obscure the evidence that the development of the human brain to adulthood entails the development of social traits already present in the behavior of most animal populations. Among those traits are the inborn tendencies to affiliation, trust, group protection, and hierarchical social structure. Consequently, it is fascinating to study brain development in the attempt to glean how it relates not only to the development of cognitive functions that are distinctly human, such as prediction and language, but also to the development of social dynamics already present in ancestral populations. Both issues bear on the roots of freedom.

There is an added incentive to study the ontogeny of the brain from an evolutionary point of view. It is now increasingly evident that, just as in the evolution of species and traits, in ontogeny the development of the brain's features and functions is the result of dynamic interactions between the elements of biological populations: gene populations, neuron populations, synaptic populations, network populations, and nerve fiber populations.

The neonate comes into the world with the structure of the cerebral cortex practically complete, with all its principal elements in place. The neocortex, the "new" cortex in evolutionary terms, is already characterized by its laminar structure, the presence in it of the major types of nerve cells, synapses, and other contacts between cells, as well as the major excitatory and inhibitory chemical neurotransmitters.[5] In quantitative terms, however, certain fluctuations occur over time in the relative amounts of those elements. There are periods of exuberant production of neurons followed by periods of attrition in their numbers. The same may be said for synapses and other elements of cellular architecture. From the beginning, however, there is a gradual and more or less continuous increase of fiber connections between cells in most all layers of the neocortex (Figure 2.3). This increase in connectivity persists into adulthood and is most manifest in the myelination – covering with myelin – of long fiber connections between cortical areas. This translates itself into general increments of cortical white matter even in the presence of some relative decrements in gray matter.

The age-related increase in cortical connectivity is critical for cognitive development, and, therefore, for the development of free will. Connectivity is essential to a relational code, such as the code of cognition and of the *cognits* of memory and knowledge.[6] Cognits are defined by *relationships* between elements (neurons or assemblies of neurons) that represent discrete components of a memory or item of knowledge (Chapter 3). By virtue of the combinatorial power of connections, an also discrete number of neuronal assemblies can encode, by combination and permutation, an almost infinite number of different items of

---

[5] The most important excitatory neurotransmitters are glutamate, norepinephrine, serotonin, dopamine, and acetylcholine (Siegel, 1999). The concentration of each of these varies somewhat from area to area. By far the most important inhibitory transmitter is the ubiquitous gamma-aminobutyric acid (GABA).

[6] A study of brain connectivity by reliable neuroimaging reveals the age-related enhancement of cortico-cortical connectivity in children performing cognitive tasks, such as listening to stories (Karunanayaka *et al.*, 2007).

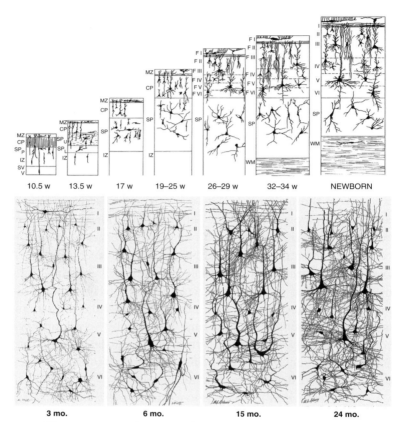

Figure 2.3 Development of neurons in the human cortex. *Top:* Prenatal period, from 10.5 weeks to birth. From Mrzljak *et al.* (1990), with permission. *Bottom:* Postnatal, at 3, 6, 15, and 24 months. From Conel (1963), with permission.

memory or knowledge. The same can be said for the cognits and the relationships between them, which can be part of larger cognits. In fact, it is that combinatorial power of connections that gives us the individuality of our memory and of our actions.

The existence of more synaptic connections than neurons can provide the executive cortex, especially the late developing cortex, with enormously diverse inputs and outputs. Thus the prefrontal cortex can thereby give rise to – i.e., organize – an immense number of alternative actions. Given that cortical connectivity increases with age at a higher rate than brain mass, it is reasonable to conclude that the options ("choices") of both inputs to and outputs from the executive cortex also increase with age at a very high rate. The same is true for freedom, which is in essence the capacity of that cortex to selectively favor or bias inputs and outputs.

The best direct evidence of the age-related increase and reinforcement of cortical connectivity is the age-dependent myelination of long cortical nerve fibers. We have known for over a century, since the seminal work of Flechsig (1901), that around the time of birth cortical myelination follows a certain chronological order, which can be discerned by histological fiber-staining methods (Figure 2.4). The first to myelinate are the sensory and motor areas of the cortex. From then on, myelination takes place in progressively higher areas of association.[7] The last areas to fully myelinate are those of the posterior and frontal association cortices (*white* in Figure 2.4). Thanks to modern scanning methods, we now know that the prefrontal cortex does not reach full myelination until the third or fourth decade of life (Sowell *et al.*, 2003). The implications of this fact are profound, especially as they relate to cognitive maturity and, of course, freedom of action and responsibility for it.

Assuming that the degree of myelination is related to neural maturation generally, and assuming further that neural maturation is related to psychological maturation, it is reasonable to speculate on the age-related neural constraints of psychosocial development. For example, it seems more than just possible that much of the turmoil of adolescence is caused by an imbalance between the two sides, emotional and cognitive, of the PA cycle. On the one side is the input from emotional centers under the onslaught of massive hormonal changes; add to that the exigencies of gratification in the presence of still immature principles of behavior. On the other side is an immature prefrontal cortex

---

[7] The staining of myelin in anatomical specimens of the cerebral cortex is not a simple matter. It is a laborious technique subject to errors, some of which have been pointed out by seasoned neuroanatomists as possibly having distorted Flechsig's original observations. Nonetheless, whereas some quibble about the precise order of myelin formation as portrayed in Figure. 2.4, there is general consensus on the conclusion that the process commences in primary sensory and motor areas and continues through the association cortex.

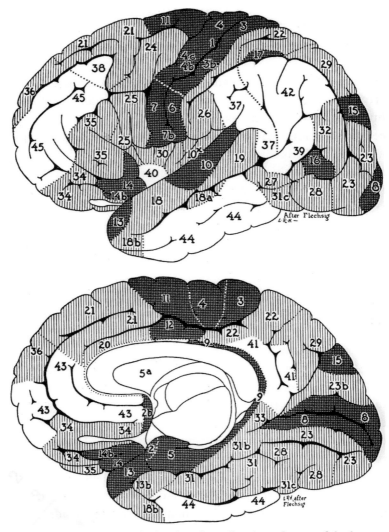

Figure 2.4 Numerical order of myelination of areas of the human cortex, according to Flechsig. Primary sensory and motor areas (low numbers, *in black*) myelinate first; association areas (high numbers *in white*) myelinate last. From Bonin (1950), modified.

ready for physical action without the capacity, yet unavailable, for reasoning or good judgment. The result is self-oriented and self-adjudicated liberty with minimal responsibility, characteristics of the typical teenager.

By age 20, freedom has in most individuals acquired a social dimension, and with it the social responsibility that constrains, or rather complements individual freedom, is nearing its adult plateau. The third decade of life calls for sharp cognitive decisions on one's future. By then, full maturity is reaching the highest areas of cortical association. With it the brain reaches the peak of inventive capacity and imagination. With the maturation of the prefrontal cortex in particular, language and the capacity to predict expand, and with them the capacity for social planning with common purpose. Those capacities will lead to decisions at higher level, together with more freedom to lead others to greater enterprises – educational, scientific, artistic, legislative, sporting, and so on. It is the time when careers get started, superior studies undertaken, and plans made for emotional, professional, or social associations with others.[8] With further cortical maturation, more elaborate, complex, and abstract cognits are acquired and consolidated in the cortex as part of the individual's experience. These cognits include, among others, principles of altruism and social justice.

NEURAL DARWINISM

The brain is essentially the organ by which the animal, through sensing and acting, adapts to its environment. As such, the brain develops modes to adapt to that environment that are similar, if not identical, to those that guided evolution. A principle of development that applies to ontogeny as well as evolution is natural selection. To be sure, natural selection works for growing individuals in different ways than for growing species. But its

---

[8] Nonetheless, it is somewhat simplistic to ascribe the acquisition of any given social trait to narrower chronological age spans. In the first place, any phenotypical trait at any age is the result of the interaction of genetic factors with environmental factors. There is individual variance in both sets of factors. Environmental factors intervene at different ages depending on internal conditions, such as hormonal levels. That interaction, in turn, leads to changes in social interaction. To this we have to add the imponderables of individual differences in nervous and hormonal maturation. The result is a long and complex series of PA cycles between the individual and society that defy precise chronological bracketing.

adaptive results are similar, and to some extent parallel and synergistic.

Something radically new, however, takes place in the human brain that is unprecedented in prior evolution. Largely on account of the extraordinary evolutionary growth of its prefrontal cortex, the human brain "opens" to the future. Selection is no longer between items of information or action that have occurred in the past or are to occur in the immediate future. The cerebral cortex of the human has become predictive. With that change, selection can be made between *anticipated* options of percept and action to occur in the future. Caution is needed here, however. The anticipating agent is not consciousness, the "ego," or some other subjective entity. It is the cortex itself, which by predicting becomes preadaptive. Our will is as free as our cortex is free to select future actions and prepare for them.

It is as if human development had forced a Copernican shift on evolution, from the past to the future – a shift, nonetheless, that does not change the basic principles of selection, variance, and probability that move evolution under the umbrella of adaptation. There are, however, two new principles that appear with the human's prospective adaptation: teleonomy and affordance, which I shall discuss later.

Under the title *Neural Darwinism* (1987), Edelman proposed a new theory that applies evolutionary principles to the individual brain. His theory of neuronal group selection (TNGS) relates to the formation or modulation of brain circuits as a result of the sensory contacts of the organism with its environment. Originally, the cortex and its link to the outside – that is, the thalamus – come into this world with a genetic endowment of what he calls a primary repertoire of interconnected neuronal groups in the two structures. Through interactions of the animal with the environment, and the neurobiological mechanism by which "cells that fire together wire together," a secondary repertoire of cell groups will be formed. This secondary repertoire will emerge at the expense of those cell groups not selected, which will wither away – in correlation with the observed postnatal attrition of cells and synaptic contacts. The selected groups will self-reinforce their connections by circuit re-entry – output returning as input. In this manner perceptual experience will be acquired and registered in thalamic-cortical circuitry. A similar argument can be applied to the dispersed neuronal groups of the cerebral cortex, which, if they fire together, will wire together into cognitive networks. Re-entry is the universal consolidator and activator of those networks.[9]

Regardless of the precise role of genetics in phylogeny and ontogeny, the fact remains that in the nervous system certain principles apply to both. These principles generally apply to the adaptation of all biological organisms to their environment and are unmistakably present in both phylogeny and ontogeny. They include variance, selection, and probability. In the human organism, with its prospective properties, we have to add teleonomy and affordance (below).

Variance is the essential precondition of evolution. It is in response to variance, whether in random gene mutation or in environmental change, that natural selection occurs. Traits, features, competitive advantages, and so on are selected by nature (note the passive voice) to adapt the organism to its environment; the adaptation occurs at the level of the population of the species – indeed, evolution is a population phenomenon – with the end result of furthering survival and procreation. Much of the selective adaptation, of course, takes place in the nervous system.

Variance in the nervous system, at the interface of the organism with the environment, also serves selection and adaptation in the individual. Here, however, the selection – say, between sensory inputs and between actions – is active – that is, from the organism outwards. As in evolution, the selection is adaptive, but now the organism exercises it actively on the world. Evolution has in fact given the individual the means to do it by itself. As in evolution, selection serves the adaptive ends of the population, beginning with brain cells and circuits and extending to the social order.

[9] The Darwinian aspects of the TNGS can be criticized by the same argument that distinguished the role of evolution from that of ontogeny in the formation of neural structure. Even Gould's concept of heterochrony does not quite reconcile the two. Thus, in the defense of neural Darwinism, the latter has been simply referred to by some as a metaphor of the evolutionary process. Nobody disputes, however, the critical importance of re-entry in the structural and functional development of the cerebral cortex (Edelman, 1987).

Selection takes place in all the interactions of the brain with the milieu, both internal and external. It serves the related purposes of economizing resources and increasing efficiency. On both counts, selection works on all percepts and all actions. In those two domains, selection performs two separate but synergistic adaptive functions: (1) categorizing and (2) discriminating.

Perception is the categorizing of the world that surrounds us (Harnad, 2005; Hayek, 1952). We perceive, that is, categorize objects by virtue of their common features and the relations between their parts (next chapter). The identity of an object stays the same despite wide variations in size or other features of its parts, provided that the relations between some of those parts stay the same ("a rose is a rose is a rose," despite differences in color, shape, size, or fragrance). This is the fundamental psychological principle of perceptual constancy, which says that we perceive an object as the same regardless of variations in size, perspective, color, shape, and so on.

In our daily life we continuously perceive – mostly unconsciously – the objects and events around us by classifying those objects and events into categories, and by matching them to previous experience – that is, by matching them to established cognits in our cortex. Conversely, we distinguish and discriminate between objects and events as we concentrate on their individual features (a yellow rose is different from a red rose). Categorizing and discriminating are tandem functions in the establishment of sensory order in our cortex (Hayek, 1952). They guide not only our ordinary life but also our scientific endeavors. Deduction and induction, generalization and analysis, depend on them.

The two selective functions of categorizing and discriminating also operate on the side of action. Now the categorizing principle is the purpose or goal of the action. Many possible movements can lead to the same outcome. We may call this function "action constancy." At the same time, large goal-directed movement is composed of small subcomponents to attain different subgoals on the way to a major goal (Bernstein, 1967).

Clearly, the categorizing of either perception or action in the nervous system cannot be accomplished without something akin to the principle of *degeneracy* of Edelman (Edelman and

Gally, 2001). In essence, degeneracy refers to the fact that in the brain, as in other complex systems, multiple inputs can lead to the same output.[10] No organism could survive without it. Degeneracy, or something like it, is at the root of perceptual and motor constancy.

The cerebral cortex is permanently in a state of internal change, yet that change tends to equilibrium at some point in the future. The billions of neurons concomitantly active in the vigilant cortex, whose electrical activity is characterized by "desynchronized" rhythms,[11] would bombard sensory and motor centers with such a diverse flow of impulses that those centers would easily be led to chaos. In the absence of degeneracy, in other words, in the absence of the capacity to generalize across inputs or outputs, no stable perception or action would be possible.

In the state of *attention*, a cognitive function that is selective by definition, selection is evident in the two components of the PA cycle, perception and action. Attention could rightfully be considered the mother of all cognitive functions. It selects certain percepts, memories, motives, and actions at the expense of all others, which are suppressed and inhibited (Fuster, 2003). But again, this happens with or without consciousness, though consciousness is a constant *phenomenon* in the most demanding selections. It happens as a result of the internal dynamics of the cortex, without the need for a central executive. Certainly, the prefrontal cortex serves attention, but merely as the mediator of selective perception or action. Any control from this cortex over attention – and over other cortical regions – derives exclusively from its dynamic involvement in the PA cycle (Chapter 4).

In the human brain, selection – especially selective attention – reaches into the future. The cerebral cortex selects perceptual and executive cognits *for* goal-directed prospective action, while other less relevant cognits are inhibited. Here evolution

---

[10] Conversely, in sensory discrimination and in discriminating action, one input, depending on certain features of it, can lead to different outputs.

[11] "Desynchronization" is a characteristic of the cortical electroencephalogram (EEG) in the awake state. It probably reflects the re-entrant activation of multiple cognits, each at its own frequency range or "spectral fingerprint" (Siegel *et al.*, 2012).

has endowed the human brain with the ultimate cortical apparatus to do that prospective selection, in the full sense of the word "ultimate": the prefrontal cortex. It is with the prefrontal cortex that the human brain acquires its freedom to set goals and purposes.

In science, teleology is a dirty word. It is also a logical incongruity, because it implies the temporal inversion of causality, which is just about the worst possible anomaly in scientific discourse. Yet it is extremely compelling to attribute to the prefrontal cortex a teleological function. Things appear to happen in that cortex *because of* a future event, whether that event is a course of future action, a goal, a reward, or the answer to a request from somebody. Is a future event the cause of present action? Here the laws of physical causality would seem to be turned backwards and upside down.

That is just an appearance, however. With the advent of the prefrontal cortex, goals and purposes have entered the agenda of the brain. On close examination, the teleological paradox dissolves before our eyes, because the cause of future action is firmly anchored in the past. That past, in the brain, consists of evolutionary and individual memory in the form of established drives and imagined cognits of the future; it is the "memory of the future" (Chapter 5). A better word for that kind of teleology is *teleonomy* (Monod, 1971), which, in essence, is a critical dimension of liberty, perhaps in effect its most decisive dimension. Teleonomy has been identified with life, as its future preservation is the first objective of life itself.

Out of the "night of evolutionary time," *Homo sapiens* emerged, the end result of countless interactions of countless organisms with their environment. At the crux of those interactions was a long and silent cycle of mutual influences between genes and "environmental demand." By a process that we do not understand, and probably never will, the brain of *Homo sapiens* ("knowing man") acquired the means to foresee and foretell the "demands" of the *Umwelt* (the world around) and to change them in order to better adapt to it during his life and that of his descendants. The PA cycle grew in complexity. Surely there is a rudiment of it in other primates, but no more than a rudiment (next section). With the human brain, the temporal period of the cycle increased by several orders of magnitude. So did the complexity of the agent, now the brain itself, and the complexity of the environmental information it was able to handle, and to predict. The prefrontal cortex developed as the supreme neural predictor at the top of the cycle.

Language is an immense elaboration of animal communication. It also emerged from the expansion of the prefrontal cortex with its temporal organizing properties. Language became a marvelously suited means of closing the PA cycle between the brain and the environment in the service of the self and others. With language, the human brain became capable of formulating probabilities of future causality, to bias favorably those probabilities with logic (Greek, *logos*, word) for the benefit of the self and others, and to record changes, both past and projected into the future. Language adds another decisive dimension to freedom (Chapter 6).

The psychologist Gibson (1977) coined an interesting term, *affordance*, which fits perfectly in the human PA cycle, especially in its future perspective. Affordance is a quality of an object or environment that allows a subject to perform an action. Thus, affordances are action possibilities that the world offers to the individual. I think the term and its definition are useful here, but that definition should be expanded, as the human being is capable of *creating* affordances and of projecting them on the environment. New affordances can thus emerge from perception of the environment in the light of prior experience – that is, in the light of established cognits. The invented new cognits, projected on that environment, can thus be incorporated in the PA cycle and guide the action to the adaptive manipulation of its objects. Affordances, therefore, are another means by which the prefrontal cortex can imagine ("memorize") future action. Affordance is yet another decisive dimension of freedom. The human being is unique in that it can freely create his or her own affordances. As we will see in the corresponding chapter (Chapter 6), language is an extraordinarily fertile creator and vehicle of affordances. The prefrontal cortex, the most advanced product of evolution in the human brain, is the supreme enabler of both language and affordances.

THE TWO TEMPORAL FACES OF LIBERTY

Just as Janus the Roman god had two faces, one looking backwards and the other forwards, liberty has two temporal perspectives, one looking to the past and the other to the future. The analogy has been aptly applied to the conscious experience of time, which has been called "mental time traveling," between the past and the future. Now, applying it to liberty requires some explanation.

Of course, we are not free to change the past, for the past is "done." But the Janus analogy is valid with regard to freedom because of the simple fact that, while we are not free to change that past, we are free *to choose* parts of that past to make informed choices for the future. Further, a chosen action is not only based on prior experience, but it also engenders new experience to inform future choice, thus completing the PA cycle.

In effect, however, the lion's share of prior experience at the base of our freedom to make choices is not exclusively our own, but belongs to the entire human species; it is made of our sensory and motor systems. That common "experience" is built in the genome and finds its expression in the physical anatomy of those systems. For that reason, I call the structure of those systems "phyletic memory." It is genetic memory in the form of the nervous structures and mechanisms that are essential for ecological adaptation. Phyletic memory includes the peripheral receptors of primary sensations and the generators of elementary movements for nourishment and defense.[12]

It should be apparent therefore that the term *phyletic memory* is more than a figure of speech, in that the memory it carries in its very structure is the collective experience of the species in dealing with the physical environment. It can be legitimately called memory because it consists of "stored" information that, after

---

[12] To call the sensory and motor systems "structural memory" makes sense only in evolutionary and ontogenetic terms. Surely it is fundamentally genetic memory in the sense that the structure of those systems is encoded in our genes. Even before birth, however, it is subject to environmental influences upon the phenotype of those two systems.

critical neonatal periods of "rehearsal,"[13] is retrieved and utilized with every act of perception or overt action. The primary sensory and motor cortices are part of that memory and comprise the indispensable interface between evolutionary and individual memory.[14] It is through the functioning of phyletic memory in those cortices that individual memory, perceptual and executive, is formed and deposited in the cognitive networks (cognits) of the cortex of association. Liberty rests on the potential selectivity of those individual associative cortices, and it is logically constrained by sensory or motor handicaps that affect their phyletic base.

In any event, it is the cortex as a whole that makes the choices that are the essence of individual liberty, not an extra-cortical or extracorporeal entity that we can identify as a choosing, deliberating, and willing *I*. The *I* is nothing other than the cortex, selecting between inputs, some from the past and others from the present, in order to select outputs of adaptive action.[15] Thus, individual selection is no longer the natural selection that served the population in evolutionary time; however, the cognitive choices of the individual crucially depend on that phyletic history.

The selective cognitive networks of the cerebral cortex are constantly under the influence from another store of phyletic memory situated deep in the interior of the cerebrum: the

---

[13] During certain critical periods shortly after birth, the sense and motor organs have to be utilized to become fully functional from then on. Animals that through those periods have been deprived of visual or auditory stimulation become permanently impaired, visually or auditorily, because of faulty cortical development (Hensch, 2004).

[14] The primary motor and sensory cortices, while being the lowest and most basic levels of phyletic cortical memory, are not the lowest stages of inherited evolutionary sensors and effectors in the central nervous system. Arguably, we have to descend to the spinal cord and to the nuclei of the autonomic nervous system in the brainstem to find them. For it is in these structures where lie the centers of reflex activity that regulate the most primitive, innate, defensive, and nurturing mechanisms with which we adapt our organism to the internal and external milieus.

[15] Each cortical choice is the result of a massive process of computation of inputs from many sources upon the association cortices, and ultimately the prefrontal cortex. An important point here is that the prefrontal cortex enables and mediates the action within the PA cycle, but is not the sole generator of that action.

emotional or limbic system or brain. The limbic system consists of an array of interconnected neural masses and nuclei of ancestral phylogenetic origin that critically intervenes in the implementation of instinctual drives and emotional responses of the organism to the environment, internal and external. The foremost components of the limbic system are the hypothalamus, the amygdala, and the hippocampus. The first two are implicated in all instinctual behavior (feeding, sex, flight, defense, and aggression), as well as in the acquisition, maintenance, and retrieval of emotional memory – that is, the memory of likes and dislikes, love and hate, reward and punishment, pleasure and pain (Denton et al., 1996; Hess, 1954; Pessoa and Adolphs, 2010). The hypothalamus and the amygdala are also directly or indirectly connected with the autonomic nervous system and hormonal systems, which play important roles in visceral control and emotion (Buijs and van Eden, 2000).

The hippocampus is a transitional ancestral structure situated between the limbic brain and the neocortex. It is anatomically a portion of ancient cortex, folded onto itself and tucked in the middle of the cerebral hemisphere on each side. In lower mammals, it performs vital functions in olfaction, touch, and spatial navigation.[16] In primates, especially the human, the hippocampus plays a critical role in the acquisition, consolidation, and retrieval of memory of any modality (Squire, 1992).

Adjacent to the limbic brain are the basal ganglia (Ariëns Kappers et al., 1960), a conglomerate of neural structures, also of early phylogenetic and ontogenetic development, that critically intervene in voluntary, reflex, and automatic motility. Connective loops that link the motor cortex, the cerebellum, the thalamus, and the basal ganglia mediate the timely execution

---

[16] It has always been somewhat of a mystery why the hippocampus of rodents is so critical for these three functions, whereas the human hippocampus is only marginally involved in them. The reason, in my opinion, is because the hippocampus of the rodent (which is the most advanced cortex the rodent has) is in charge of the three functions inasmuch as they are essential to the animal's survival, whereas in the human, those functions have migrated to higher cortex for more flexibility and range of adaptation to a more complex environment.

of voluntary – as well as automatic and well-rehearsed – motor sequences (Alexander *et al.*, 1992; Kreitzer and Malenka, 2008).

In conclusion, those internal parts of the brain, together with primary sensory and motor cortices, in the aggregate, constitute the cerebral ground layer of phyletic memory. That structural memory, including predispositions to action in the basal ganglia, is the primordial neural apparatus for adaptation to the environment. That environment includes the internal milieu, which was selected in evolution to fulfill the most immediate exigencies of survival and procreation of the species.

Freedom will rest on that fund of evolutionary experience, while remaining also constrained by it. For, no organism, including the human, can surpass the limits imposed by the sensory and motor capabilities it inherits. In other words, that heritage – after critical postnatal periods – limits our senses to light, sound, touch, olfaction, and taste within certain ranges of frequency, intensity, and chemical composition. It also limits the range of angle, direction, and bearing of each of our joints and limbs. Thus, considering the genetic endowment of our motor systems, there are physical limits to the actions we can execute with those systems. This remains true even after full development and physical education.

Freedom will not only rest on, but also emerge from, that primordial structural memory of sensory and motor systems, visceral control systems, and emotional systems. The most immediate conditions permitting its emergence are the variance and plasticity of those systems, and, most critically, the cognitive networks of the cortex of association. In the individual human, those systems and networks will provide the essential inputs to the PA cycle, which moves us from one choice to the next, from one decision to the next, and from one objective to the next. The aggregate of those inputs constitutes the experience, phyletic and personal, on which liberty is based. It is the major share of the retrospective aspect of liberty.

How free are our choices of retrospective memory? They are, and must by necessity be, only *relatively free* because they are not free of physical and psychological constraints. Regardless of those constraints, our freedom depends on, and is directly related to, the availability of alternatives, whether we are aware of them or not. We experience freedom even though – and in part because – we are unaware of the degree to which those alternatives steer our actions. This is not a blanket endorsement of determinism. On the contrary, having decoupled cortical choice from consciousness, freedom asserts its independence. Determinism is tempered in the variability and randomness of a complex adaptive system such as the human cerebral cortex.[17] But here the concept of "cortical choice" needs to be qualified.

Choice implies alternative. But the alternatives of information that reach the cortex to literally inform action do so with different degrees of intensity (synaptic strength) depending on a variety of internal and external states or circumstances. Some alternative inputs will be in conflict with one another; others will potentiate each other. The inputs that prevail in the decision to act will be the probabilistic result of competition or summation of synaptic "weights," which will sway the cortex to one action or another. Probability here is to be understood in the Bayesian sense, in this manner applicable to the state of the evidence or knowledge contained in any given set of inputs.[18] Ultimately, the weight of each input on a decision will be "determined" according to an estimate of probability based on prior knowledge and bearing on the synaptic weight of that input.[19]

As we have seen, alternatives of input will arrive in the prefrontal cortex from many sources, some cortical and others subcortical. Alternative sources of input will multiply if the

---

[17] The concept of *open* adaptive system was first proposed by von Bertalanffy (1950), the father of "general system theory" (GST), to account for the dynamics of organisms – biological and sociological – that tend to equilibrium or steady state in the face of perturbations. They do it by use of self-correcting feedback, among other mechanisms. Clearly, that cybernetic concept applies to all self-regulation in the nervous system, and of course the PA cycle.

[18] Bayesian probability, as distinguished from "frequential" probability, is the logic based on uncertain statements about a hypothesis and liable to change by the acquisition of further data (Jaynes *et al.*, 2003).

[19] The expression "synaptic weight" is meant here to encompass not only the strength of present or potential electrochemical transactions at the membranes of nerve cells, but also the numbers of axon connections and other input fibers arriving at those cell membranes.

actions informed by those inputs are complex and high in the hierarchy of the PA cycle. By contrast, inputs of subcortical origin, at the foundations of phyletic memory, will be simple and straightforward, such as the urge to eat, fight, or mate. They will arrive to the cortex by fiber paths funneled through the orbital prefrontal cortex, which collects information about rewards with biological "valence." Rarely, except in a sociopath, will those impulses come to the cortex unaccompanied by inputs from cortical networks representing social, ethical, and esthetic principles. Hence the formalities of dining, sport competition, and courting.

Those natural impulses will come to our cortex also accompanied by inputs from the cognitive networks that store our episodic and semantic memory. Those too will be subject to internal "competitive bidding" in the higher levels of the PA cycle. Consider, for example, the many inputs that, in addition to hunger, inform our choices of restaurant and menu: personal experience, counsel from friends, cost, means of transportation, parking availability, ethnic-food preference, and so on. All will weigh on the choices.

In sum, on the retrospective side of liberty are the inputs to the orbital prefrontal cortex from the internal milieu and its limbic sources. Concomitantly, inputs from the cortex at large converge on the cortical lateral convexity of the frontal lobe, conveying to it information from the cognitive networks of knowledge, personal memory, and social values. The prefrontal cortex will reconcile and prioritize those inputs before each decision. Completing the PA cycle, the prefrontal cortex will also reconcile and prioritize the consequences of each action for further action. The reconciling and prioritizing will be done in and by the cortex itself. Those operations will take place in a multivariate and probabilistic environment of synaptic connections of widely differing and variable weights. It is the relative internal configuration of those weights with respect to one another that will lead to one alternative of action or to another. The root of the decision, therefore, is to be found in all its antecedents and the relative synaptic weights of each of their respective neural foundations.

EVOLUTION OPENS MAN AND WOMAN TO THEIR
FUTURE

Inseparable from the retrospective aspect of freedom is its prospective aspect, which will be further discussed in Chapter 5. The two are two sides of the same coin, namely, of the dynamics of the PA cycle, which by definition has a past and a future alternating with each other. Both are anchored in phyletic memory, from which the selectivity of individual human cognition flows. Arguably, action precedes perception, in phylogeny as well as ontogeny. Just as evolution selects from genetic variance "actions" that are adaptive for the population, the human infant enters the world palpating it to select certain "adaptive" stimuli within it. It is by haptics – active touch – that the newborn finds the mother's breast. Crying, which is another phyletic action, will rapidly join haptics in the PA cycle of infant nourishment.[20]

With the evolution of the cerebral cortex in general, and the prefrontal cortex in particular, the PA cycle of the human begins early in life to work at higher levels of complexity for the benefit of the individual and, eventually, society as well. Liberty will emerge from the expansion of both the fund of alternatives of information available to the cortex and the alternatives of action to which that information can lead.

Among the alternatives of action, none is as relevant to liberty as those that evolve in the fields of cognition most characteristic of the human being: planning and language. Here we have to address a question that often arouses endless controversies. Are there precursors of planning and language present in the animal kingdom before man? The most immediate – and least controversial – species to query in this respect are the great apes.

A way to assess the ability to plan behavior is to examine the ability to use tools, since tool use invariably implies a certain sequence of personal actions that is reasoned, goal-directed, and

[20] Later, "babbling" and the rudiments of language will be incorporated in the PA cycle between the child and the environment presided over by the mother (Chapter 6).

not innate. For several years around the time of World War I, Köhler (1925), a noted gestalt psychologist, studied meticulously the reasoning potential of chimpanzees in a colony of such animals he maintained on one of the Canary Islands. One of his smartest subjects, Sultan, learned to stack boxes on which to stand and to use poles to reach high-hanging bananas. From this Köhler concluded that the animal was able to reason to some degree and to use intermediary objects to attain spatially distant goals.

Whether Sultan planned actions or used tools in the strict sense of these words has been extensively debated. It is unquestionable, however, that the animal was capable of a degree of prospective and purposive reasoning. It is also unquestionable that he learned or had the intuition to use "tools" to attain his goal. Lower primates are capable of doing both, though to a lesser degree. Later studies, furthermore, have shown that the great apes are capable of cognitive "time-traveling" and foresight, as they can display sequential actions to reach goals that are *distant in space and time* (Osvath and Osvath, 2008). The argument that all those operations are the result of associative learning is idle, because there is no foresight or tool use of any kind without some degree of prior associative experience. In fact there is no liberty to act reasonably one way or another without prior empirical knowledge of context and consequences.

Thus, there is rudimentary planning and foresight in the earlier primates. However, because humans exceed those capabilities by many orders of magnitude, it has been mistakenly argued that those capabilities are the exclusive patrimony of our species. Similar arguments and counterarguments have been made with respect to language, albeit usually with more vehemence on both sides. The most obvious question in this respect is whether the vocalizations of nonhuman animals qualify as evolutionary precursors of language. The answer is yes, insofar as those vocalizations consist in means of communication between conspecifics, like language. Another, more relevant, question is whether animals possess some primitive form of language. The answer here is definitely no, as animals, while able to communicate with symbols, cannot communicate with logical reasoning, which is an essential attribute of language.

With language and the enormous expansion of the cerebral cortex that goes with it, comes the unique tool that more than any other allows humans to fashion their future: speech. This is the supreme maker of affordances, *à la* Gibson (1977). It is not a coincidence of nature that that "ultimate tool" (Greenfield, 1991) develops together with a region of the frontal cortex that is heavily involved in tool making and utilization.[21] Nor is it coincidental that the entirety of the frontal cortex, where that area is located, serves not only speech but also, more broadly, what Lashley (1951) called the "syntax of action." Indeed, by speech, evolution comes around to furthering an unwritten "purpose" of the evolution of the species: the freedom to ensure its own survival. For it is by the written word that the human race codifies the liberty of its progeny.

CONCLUSIONS

Our freedom and ability to shape our future are the ultimate offspring of the extraordinary evolution of the human brain. Both freedom and creativity have their most recent evolutionary root in the prefrontal cortex, the latest domain of the cerebral mantle to attain structural maturity, in evolution as in individual development.

Critical for both human prerogatives, freedom and future, is the rich connectivity that develops between prefrontal cell populations, as well as between them and those in other cortical regions. Because of the inherent synaptic plasticity of that connectivity, cognitive networks (cognits) will be formed by life experience in the associative cortex, which will codify the memory of the individual and inform his decisions to reach his goals (Chapter 3).

Freedom flourishes with the capacity of the cortex to choose between memory networks and between action networks in the pursuit of chosen goals. In all instances, the pursuit of a goal takes

---

[21] The area in question includes Broca's area and a large portion of the premotor cortex, both adjacent to each other in the frontal lobe of the left or dominant cerebral hemisphere.

place within the dynamics of a PA cycle that runs through the posterior cortex, the prefrontal cortex, and the environment, and back to the cortex in a circular fashion until the goal is reached.

In parallel with that cognitive cycle and interacting with it, a deeper and older cycle processes emotions and instinctual urges through the limbic system. The orbital prefrontal cortex is an integral part of that cycle, which feeds emotional and instinctual influences into the cortex at large. Because reactions to those influences are biologically rooted and weigh heavily on our decisions, the limbic system constitutes the most primordial evolutionary root of liberty in the human brain.

Liberty, in general, has two major components with opposite temporal perspective; the first is the ability to choose experience from the past, and the second is the ability to choose the future based on the chosen past. The two alternate in tandem with each other under the prefrontal cortex, which integrates past with future at the top of the PA cycle (Chapter 4). The most essentially human is the second, the capacity of the prefrontal cortex to predict events, as well as to select, decide upon, plan, prepare for, and organize goal-directed actions in the immediate or distant future (Chapter 5). Among those actions is spoken and written language, the truly unique patrimony of our species at the service of all our freedoms and our creative power (Chapter 6).

3

Anatomy of cognition

Traveller, there is no path,
The path is made by walking.

Antonio Machado

New cell processes are formed that are capable of improving
the suitability and the extension of the contacts, and even of
forming entirely new relations between neurons originally
independent.

Santiago Ramón y Cajal

Cognitive neuroscience is the neuroscience of what we
know, which encompasses all our memories and everything we
have learned since we were born. It deals with the mechanisms by
which our brain acquires, stores, and retrieves knowledge. It
deals also with the brain mechanisms that drive cognitive functions – that is, the functions by which we use knowledge in our
daily interactions with others and the world around us: attention,
perception, memory, language, and intelligence. Most importantly, cognitive neuroscience deals with the mechanisms by
which our feelings and emotions influence every one of those
functions.

Because our liberty depends on what we know and how we
use it, any neurobiological treatment of freedom and creativity
has to address the cerebral store of knowledge and the brain's
capacity to steer that knowledge and its functions in our choices.
Indeed, liberty is all about choice, not only about the ability to
choose a goal, and the actions to get to it, but also, critically, the

ability to choose the information in our memory and in our senses that will shape those actions. In the brain/liberty debate, that choice of information at the core of the PA cycle is commonly lost. Here we cannot elude it, because, figuratively speaking, blind vision leads to blind action, both curtailing our freedom to choose. We bet on the horse as we choose and weigh in our mind what we know about that horse and its jockey, their odds to win or lose, the records of competitors, our own betting record, the conditions of the racetrack, and so on. The reasons behind those choices of relevant information are not necessarily conscious, as they may hide behind intuition or "gut feeling."

This chapter deals with the anatomical seat of the information on which choices are made, which constitutes in a very real sense the anatomy of freedom. We can start the analysis with two assumptions that border on the truism and for which there is overwhelming empirical evidence. First, insofar as it is constantly open to new information, the capacity of our brain's cognitive store is huge, practically infinite, vastly greater than that possessed by any known computer or biological system, including the genome.[1] Second, the contents of that cognitive store are constantly changing, day and night, for as long as we live. They change even in our sleep, because even then the strength of neuronal contacts, which in the aggregate constitute the store of our memories and knowledge, is changing by consolidation or loss.

We can legitimately call that cerebral store, with all of its contents and functions, *the mind*. At any given time, however, most of that "knowing mind" is unconscious; that is, we are subjectively unaware of its knowledge and of what our mind is doing with it. Consciousness is a quality or state of the working

---

[1] The immense capacity of the human brain's cognitive store is a direct product of two related facts. One is that the cognitive code is a relational code: Items of memory and knowledge are essentially defined by relationships – between physical properties, between sensory qualia, between events, between symbols, and so on. The other fact is that those relationships consist of associations between nerve cells. In the human cortex, even a limited number of neurons – 10 to 20 billion – can be associated in infinitely different ways. Thus, the infinite capacity of cortical cognition derives from the infinite combinatorial potential of cortical cells. That potential rests on the rich evolutionary endowment of connectivity with which the human cortex comes into the world and which life experience will enlarge by many orders of magnitude.

mind that is only present – though operationally not essential – in conditions of relatively high mental activity. High mental activity means high activity of the cerebral cortex, whether it is in vigilant alertness or in selective attention, both of which, by necessity, are accompanied by conscious awareness, even though consciousness *per se* is not the agent. The cortex is.

Indeed, our mental store of knowledge is essentially the cerebral cortex. That does not mean that there is no knowledge elsewhere in the brain. In fact there is much. For example, some "motor knowledge," that is, so-called procedural memory, habit, or motor learning, is stored in subcortical structures such as the basal ganglia.[2] We learned to ride a bicycle with full use of our cortex. After we had learned the skill, however, the cortex was no longer needed for it. Only under exceptional circumstances does the cortex retrieve again the stored knowledge to modify it in some way (for example, a very sharp turn of the road, or a flat tire).

Guided by the findings of neurologists and psychologists who studied the effects of lesions of the cerebral cortex in humans and animals, many scientists of the nineteenth and twentieth centuries embraced the general assumption that knowledge and memory are localized in a cortical map of dedicated modules, a kind of cognitive quilt or mosaic of knowledge. Each "module" within it would be dedicated to one or another category of knowledge or memory. Given that certain elementary sensations and movements could be localized in discrete modules of primary sensory or motor cortex, it was thought that cognitive contents, although more complex, could be likewise allocated to comparable modules of the association cortex. Indeed, observations in humans and animals suggested cortical modules for visual perception, for language, for spatial memory, for auditory

---

[2] All motor skills are acquired at first by full use of the cortex, especially the motor and premotor cortex of the frontal lobe. After a skill has been learned, it no longer necessitates much of the cortex, as the latter relegates both the storage and the performance of the skill to the basal ganglia. This frees the cortex for new learning. Neuroimaging studies illustrate well the progress of the organization of cortical and subcortical regions in the process of acquisition of a motor skill (Grafton *et al.*, 1994; Ungerleider *et al.*, 2002).

perception, for working memory, and so on.[3] This approach, however, runs into a number of theoretical and practical problems, some of which are insurmountable and seriously challenge the credibility of cognitive maps of any kind. Predictably, quasi-phrenologies of this sort have been lately on the wane. It is not the case, however, that modules do not enter cognition at some point. To the contrary, they are essential in the lower cortical stages of cognition – namely, in primary sensory and motor cortices. In higher stages, however, as in the cortex of association, modules "dissolve" into networks by virtue of the essentially associative nature of cognitive information in that cortex.[4]

Although the ideas of localized cognition were long suspected to be untenable, it took a long time for the most plausible alternative view, the cognitive network model, to take hold. At first, it began to open its way empirically almost by default, as Karl Lashley (1950), a Harvard psychologist, failed to find in animals any discrete memory deficit from any discrete cortical lesion. Somehow, he thought, memory and knowledge had to be "distributed." Other psychologists (Hayek, 1952; Hebb, 1949) theorized that percepts and memories consist of widely distributed cortical networks. They were soon joined by computer scientists and by experts in artificial intelligence. Some of these postulated so-called connectionist models of cognition that, based on network notions, accommodated fairly well cognition in language (Fodor and Pylyshyn, 1988; Marcus, 1998; McClelland and Rumelhart, 1986; Myers, 1967).

---

[3] There are two major reasons for the spurious allocation of different cognitive functions to discrete areas of the cortex – reminiscent of nineteenth-century phrenology. One reason is the variability of the strength of association between the cell assemblies that constitute a cognit or cognitive network (next section). Most methodologies miss the presence of relatively weak but functionally active associations forming a penumbra around the core of a cognitive network. That penumbra is probably the physiological basis for the recall phenomena of "priming" and "tip-of-the-tongue." The other reason is that such networks overlap extensively with one another, sharing nodes in common of more or less solid association.

[4] Cajal, in 1894, was probably the first to publicly postulate the synaptic character of associative memory in the cerebral cortex, as well as the reticular – network-like – character of memory (Cajal, 1894, 1923). As exemplary of the formation of memory networks, he referred to the establishment – by synaptic usage – of motor habits and skills; in other words, executive memory.

The physiology of cognitive networks, however, has not been substantiated until the last two or three decades. Its main support comes from the fields of behavioral electrophysiology and functional imaging (for review of the relevant research, see Fuster, 2009). According to the now most plausible network models, knowledge and memory are contained in an immense array of overlapping, interactive, and widely distributed networks of interconnected neurons of the cerebral cortex.[5] The networks are formed by life experience and constitute the substrate of all cognitive functions. Attention, perception, memory, language, and intelligence all use the very same networks. The next section describes the essentials of such networks, which I call "cognits." The description is a little long because its subject is key to my reasoning on freedom and creativity. Cognits, past, present, and future, are the material on which our cerebral cortex makes its choices, and we make our choices.

THE COGNIT

The *cognit* (the term introduced by me ten years ago [Fuster, 2003]) is a piece of knowledge or memory in the form of a distributed network of neurons of the cerebral cortex. That network represents one of myriad possible facts or experiences of mine, the individual. They may range widely in content, from an early childhood memory to a recent memory: from our first ski lesson to yesterday's lecture, from the multiplication table to the relation between mass and energy, from botany to our garden party a year ago, from the cost of our house to that of the bus ride, and so on – the list is infinite. Some memories are linked to others, "holding hands" through tenuous or strong connections in cortical gray matter. Some are within others, like matryoshka dolls.

---

[5] That the internal functional architecture of the cerebral cortex essentially consists of a vast network of interconnected neurons is a truism. It is evident on cursory examination of the microscopic structure of the cortex. This fact has given rise to innumerable models of cognition based on networks that operate in series or in parallel. None of these models, however, contain the basic features of the model that I employ in this chapter: its relational – associative – structure, and the overlapping, interactive, hierarchical, and node-sharing characteristics of its networks (Fuster and Bressler, 2012).

Some are emotionally "neutral"; others carry emotional connotations. All carry literally our existential self at the time of their experience or acquisition, or even in expected future time.

Each cognit – namely, each memory or item of knowledge (knowledge is also memory, essentially *semantic memory*) – is defined *structurally* by a network of cortical neuron assemblies that has been formed in life experience by the coactivation – that is, simultaneous activation – of smaller networks or neuron assemblies that represent the component features of that memory or item of knowledge. At the root of cognit formation are two basic biophysical principles illustrated in Figure 3.1. They were theoretically proposed long ago by the Canadian psychologist Donald Hebb (1949) and subsequently verified in invertebrate animals and in the mammalian cortex. Both principles say, essentially, that cells that are in touch with one another and fire together will strengthen their contacts (synapses), such that later they will transmit impulses from one to another easier than before.

Most important for the formation of associative memory is the principle that Hebb called sensori-sensory association and I call *synchronous convergence* (Fuster, 1995). It says that when two inputs converge at the same time on the membrane of an output cell, they induce changes in that membrane to the effect of lowering the threshold – i.e., facilitating synapses or cell contacts – for future transmission of either input through the output cell.[6] That is the foundation for the associative nature of all memory and all knowledge. As I said, the two Hebbian principles are unified in the adage, "cells that fire together wire together."

As cognits self-organize in the brain with life experience; as their associative paths proliferate, they grow into the association

---

[6] The principle of synchronous convergence is practically identical to that of Hebb's "sensori-sensory association" (1949, p. 70). Here it is expanded beyond sensory systems to include converging inputs from other than sensory sources, such as other pre-existent cognits. Note that an input or sensory stimulus need not be strictly and constantly defined in the same physical terms or mental content to be associated with another. Similar stimuli or inputs will do the same, more or less well. Here, at the neurobiological level, we find the explanation of the dictum by the philosopher James Mill (1829) that resemblance is a special case of co-occurrence, and thus a special case of what he called "synchronous order."

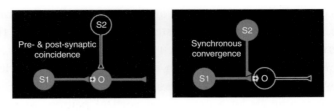

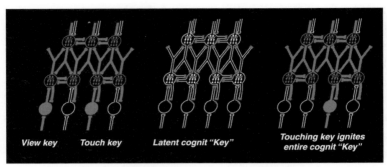

Figure 3.1 *Top:* Two basic principles of memory formation in cognitive networks (cognits). According to the first principle (*left*), when two cells in a chain (S1 and O) fire repeatedly together, the synaptic membrane of the output cell (O) will be modulated to transmit impulses more easily (+) from one cell to the other. According to the second principle (synchronous convergence, *right*), when the input impulses from two cells (S1 and S2) arrive at the same time in cell O, the membrane of the latter will be modulated to transmit more easily (+) inputs from either S1 or S2. *Bottom:* Formation and evocation of a cognit extending from the sensory up to the association cortex. The cartoon simplifies all the major modes of cortico-cortical connectivity (feed-forward, feedback, convergence, divergence, and lateral). *At left,* I experience the sight and touch, together, of my house key. *In the middle,* the cognit "key" consists of a network of cell assemblies linked together by facilitated synapses (*in red*). *At right,* the touch of the key in my pocket evokes the entire cognit, including the visual image of the key.

cortex. There they form more complex memories and items of knowledge, becoming progressively both more general and more abstract. In that cortex, the convergence no longer takes place between sensory inputs only, but also between pre-existing cognits aroused by sensory stimuli or stimuli from other sources – e.g., emotional, visceral. Thus, as they are made, cognits will find their niche in a cortical hierarchy that goes from the concrete sensory memory in the lower association cortex at the base to the abstract piece of knowledge in large expanses of the higher association cortex, where inputs from many sources converge.[7]

Accordingly, the cognit "apple," for example, consists of a network that associates by prior experience the neuronal representations of certain sensory or semantic qualities, such as the color red (or green or yellow), the spherical shape, a given flavor (taste and smell), and a word or symbol. Those qualities are in turn represented by smaller cognits – that is, smaller networks, in or near cortical areas of sensory association. Thus the cognits of knowledge, such as "apple," are interconnected also by experience with overlapping cognits of personal memory such as a visit to Uncle Vincent's apple orchard. Because the two types of networks – knowledge and memory – are thoroughly intermeshed in experience and in the cortex, it is practically pointless to attempt to separate them, either in the mind or in the brain. In knowledge as in memory, some cognits are nested within others of larger size. For example, the cognit "apple" is nested within the categorical cognit "fruit," and the visit to Uncle Vincent is nested within the broad categories of personal journeys, vacations, family visits, or events of the season. So are their respective networks in the cortex. Further, knowledge networks are nested in memory networks, and vice versa.[8]

It follows from these considerations that the size and complexity of cognits vary enormously. Some, such as an autobiographical memory, unite items of great variety, extending over several contiguous or noncontiguous cortical areas. Others contain discrete information, sensory or motor, and are circumscribed to small cortical areas. The content of these smaller networks may

---

[7] Therein lies the apparently paradoxical correlation between abstraction and complexity. Because abstract cognits are made of many instantiations of singular experiences, an abstract cognit that characterizes the commonalities of those experiences will maintain nested within it some or most of them. These smaller, singular, cognits will add at least latent or subjacent complexity to the abstract, hierarchically higher, cognit.

[8] For these reasons, the neural structure of memory is essentially identical to that of knowledge. The only property that differentiates memory from knowledge, in the brain as in the mind, is the presence or absence of associations with self, personal map, and calendar.

be simple and concrete, like the face of the clock, yet embedded in larger networks that detail assorted events in our life, with their cognitive and emotional associations.

Several general conclusions or corollaries stem from this broadly outlined state of affairs. One is the sheer complexity of the cognitive structure of the cerebral cortex. Another, which is a consequence of that one, is the difficulty of localizing memories or knowledge within it, because cognits and their networks are widely distributed, overlap extensively, and are thoroughly intertwined, sharing network nodes of association with one another. Yet another conclusion is the immense variety of potential inputs to our cognits, and thus to the freedom of our cortex to choose between them. This is a good place to be reminded that freedom consists not only of the capacity to select actions, but also of the capacity to select the information that will guide those actions. Choice serves freedom on both sides of the PA cycle, perception and action.

In the foregoing, surely the reader has already noted an apparent ambiguity. Are cognits represented *in* networks or *by* networks? My contention is that they are both, or more precisely, that cognits *are* networks. Here the subjectivism of conscious knowledge is more of a hindrance than a help to our understanding. Part of the problem resides in the word "represent" with all of its derivatives, which is highly misleading in the context of neural networks, because it implies subjective mental constructs without tangible neural substrate. Moreover, aside from the fact that the networks – that is, cognits – are constantly changing, and therefore do not *re-present* anything exactly as it ever was (a problem for judges and juries), they and their contents are most of the time completely unconscious.

The concept of complex, interwoven, and widely distributed cognitive networks may suggest that there is absolutely no topography to cortical knowledge. This is incorrect. We know that discrete lesions in animals and humans impair some aspects of knowledge or memory *more than* others. In the next section, from those data plus functional data, I will attempt to sketch some general cortical topography for different kinds of cognits.

In summary, a cognit is a cortical network formed by the strengthening of the contacts (synapses) between neurons and neuron assemblies widely dispersed in the cerebral cortex. Which neuron assemblies belong to a given network depends on the nature of the stimuli that have simultaneously or nearly simultaneously coactivated the cortical assemblies that form the network. Further, one important point is that those stimuli will concomitantly activate – by association – the pre-existing cognits (sensory, motor, or both) – formed in the past by the same stimuli or others like them. Thereby the new stimuli will enlarge or otherwise modify old experience. In other words, new cognits will enlarge or modify old ones. In this manner, new knowledge will supplement, complement, or replace old knowledge, and new discriminations will be made on old knowledge, all as a result of the network dynamics of new experience.

A fundamental fact of neurobiology, already mentioned in the previous chapter, is that, for the consolidation of memories (cognits) in the neocortex, the hippocampus, which is a portion of ancient – limbic – cortex, as well as other parts of the medial temporal lobe, notably the amygdala, plays a crucial role. Without those structures, new memories cannot be consolidated;[9] also, to some extent, old memories are hard to retrieve. Without the amygdala, in particular, memories and knowledge are deprived of the consolidating and retrieval power of affect and emotion.[10]

---

[9] The role of the hippocampus and surrounding structures in the acquisition of memory was first discovered in H.M., an epileptic patient who, for the successful treatment of his condition, had the inner portions of his temporal lobes, including the hippocampus on both sides, surgically excised. After the operation, H.M. suffered from anterograde amnesia; he was incapable of acquiring any new memories of events, dates, identities, faces, and so on (Scoville and Milner, 1957). By contrast, the evocation of the memories of events having occurred before the surgery was relatively intact. The generally accepted interpretation, now reinforced by other cases, is that the hippocampus and surrounds are essential for the consolidation of new memory, presumably in the neocortex (Squire, 1987, 1992). A more general conclusion is that the retrieval of memory is also to some extent disrupted by hippocampal lesion. This inference stands to reason inasmuch as acquisition always implies a degree of retrieval. New memory invariably elicits old memory, which it will expand and modify.

[10] The amygdala, like the hippocampus, is an evolutionary derivative of ancient cortex (Chapter 2). It consists of a roughly spherical conglomerate of nervous nuclei situated right in front of and adjacent to the hippocampus. In almost all mammals in which it has been investigated, the amygdala has been found embedded in brain circuits implicated in emotion and the evaluation of

From the interactive architecture of cortical networks it follows that a neuron or group of neurons can be part of many networks or cognits – that is, of many memories or items of knowledge. The strength of a cognitive network, and thus its cognit, is determined by several variables, among them primarily synaptic strength, which includes both the robustness and the number of synapses at the connective links of the network. These links contain neuronal assemblies or "netlets," smaller networks that codify in their anatomical structure subcomponents of the larger network. Further, each link can be a nodal component of many cognits. Take, for example, a connective node codifying the color red: it can be part of the cognits codifying fire, apple, rose, blood, sunrise, ink, and debt. It is not yet possible to ascertain if, in the context of any item of knowledge, the red is codified by one node or, more likely, several.[11] In any case, the entire arrangement of interconnected nets with common nodes is reminiscent of connectionist models and their applications to language, where symbols or words act as nodes (Fodor and Pylyshyn, 1988; Myers, 1967).

An important concept to emphasize here is that the stored cognitive code of knowledge as well as memory is an anatomical code, defined by relations in brain space, not a temporal code.[12]

---

sensory signals (Le Doux, 1992; Phelps, 2004). Those circuits include the orbital prefrontal cortex and the hypothalamus. It seems appropriate to remark that these circuits, in a figurative sense, add emotional color to our percepts and actions, and thus add zest or deterrent to our choices of either.

[11] The degree of defining power of a feature in a given cognit depends on its functional "centrality" in the network; in other words, it depends on the importance of the feature for defining the cognit. It is an expression of the synaptic strength with which the feature is anchored in the cognit. Thus, for example, redness is more of the essence of, and better associated with, the cognit "blood" than with "debt"; the association of redness with the latter or with financial deficit is much more symbolic and peripheral to the definition of the cognit. Depending on the context, of course, the color red is more or less associated with executive cognits also: for example, stop the hemorrhage, extinguish the fire, or balance the budget.

[12] Strictly speaking, the words "information" and "code" refer to precisely defined data and their analysis, whether the data are mathematical, symbolic, or both. Both words are almost inseparable from information and communication theory, as introduced by Shannon in the mid twentieth century (Shannon and Weaver, 1949). Out of that context, and of its legal or ethical connotations, the word "code" is used in a variety of other contexts (neurobiology, computer science, genetics, cryptography, and others). Here, both words, "information" and "code," are applied to cognitive, mental information, as contained in cognits and utilized in neural transactions.

That anatomical code is "written" in the cortex by synaptic strengths between related neurons. It is, therefore, a relational code. The code becomes functional, physiological, and displayed in time when it is used in a cognitive function such as working memory,[13] perception, language, or the acquisition of further knowledge. Thus, essentially, we retain retrievable knowledge in the measure in which our cognits "glue" together neurons with sufficient synaptic strength.

The synaptic strength of a cognit depends on the solidity with which it was formed – that is, the synaptic strength of its network. That in turn depends on the synaptic – "etching" – force of the experience that formed it, including the saliency of the stimuli and/or actions that elicited the experience, its repetitions, and its emotional impact. We remember best the vivid sensory experiences of emotional events. Sometimes only one experience, if strong enough emotionally, leaves an indelible, precise memory of the event ("flashbulb memory") and the context in which we learned of it. Most everybody remembers what he/she was doing when learning of President Kennedy's assassination, for example.[14]

To some degree, every neuron in the cortex is connected, directly or indirectly, with every other one. The entire cortex can thus be considered one global network permanently open to segregation and enhancement by the internal or external milieu. That global network contains or can contain every conceivable cognit defined by a pattern of connectivity in it. Thus every cognit is to some degree potentially connectable to every other. Furthermore, the synaptic strength within a cognit is far from

---

[13] As, for example, in Fuster and Bressler (2012).

[14] A personal note: I learned of the event in my Munich apartment – while a visiting scholar at the Max-Planck Institute. Not long ago, I was relating to a group of University of California, Irvine students my experience of hearing about the event on the evening news from a roundish, white radio on the windowsill of my bedroom. I recounted to them the vividness with which I remembered all details: the voice and words of the German newscaster, the marble stand under the radio, the snow falling in the dark by the streetlamp – even the hot bands of the radiator tubes on my legs. After the seminar, a probably incredulous young student darted out to check the internet. She came back to tell me, with a semblance of concession, that "it was pretty cold that evening in Munich."

uniform, and so is the magnitude of its changes over time. Most easily retrievable are those parts of the network that are most firmly established in terms of synaptic strength. Most forgettable are those most feebly established that way.

Cognits have their preferred cortical domains in and around nodes of heavy concentration of the associations that define them. In the next section I discuss the general location of the principal categories of cognits according to "origin" – perception or action – and hierarchical level. In theory and in practice, however, it is difficult precisely to demarcate the physical boundaries of any given cognit. One reason is that those boundaries are diffuse. A cognit's most defining connections are strong, as they originated with strong stimuli and powerful inputs – and possibly also emotional color. Its periphery, however, consists of a penumbra of associations that link the cognit with more distant contents, in terms of synaptic strength as well as cortical reach. Nonetheless, those peripheral connections may assist the recall of memory when the central connections, for whatever reason, fail.[15]

Time and disuse weaken the synaptic links of established cognits, but not uniformly; some links are more resilient than others, depending on such factors as personal relevance or emotional load, but also possibly depending on other, imponderable, factors. Consider the common, often painful, experience of forgetting the name of a person we see again after many years. Unaccountably, we "block" on that name. Instead of facilitating the task of dragging it out of our unconscious, our conscious and anxious efforts seem to sink it further. Note, however, that, in a calm moment, the name may pop up spontaneously. Note also, more interestingly, that we may be able to pry that name out of the unconscious by evoking other aspects, however distant, of that person's cognit, such as the context of our first meeting, or by

---

[15] In those weak or virtual connections resides the potential for rehabilitation of a damaged cognit. Tenuous or merely virtual connections can be strengthened, or even created anew, in that reservoir of plasticity that is the synaptic penumbra of a cognit. Indeed, cognitive rehabilitation rests in large part on the strengthening of weak associations and the creation of new ones in that penumbra that we may consider a large component of the "cognitive reserve" of the individual.

running in our mind through the letters of the alphabet in search of the name's first letter, or by mentally reviewing a list of common acquaintances. What we are obviously doing, often successfully, is to "fish" with peripheral associative links for the name of that person in the connective penumbra. Given that the most direct and presumably strongest link failed because of poor connection, we try others with weaker synaptic strength. Those are alternate routes to the unconscious. But the unconscious is not a place in the cortex or elsewhere in the brain. The unconscious is the inactive, feebly active, or inhibited state of cortical networks.

Brain disease and old age weaken synapses within and between cognits, but again not uniformly. "Use it or lose it" becomes in these conditions more of an imperative than under normal circumstances. Conclusive evidence is not yet available in this respect, but common sense dictates that exercising any cognitive function that activates our cognits is going to make them more resilient; hence the conventional wisdom of mental exercises, solving puzzles or learning a new language. Physical exercise has also been found effective to enhance cognition (review by Ratey and Loehr, 2011), perhaps by enhancing brain blood circulation, among other things.

A CORTICAL GEOGRAPHY OF MEMORY?

To cortical cognition, the precept that says, "a place for everything and everything in its place," applies only faintly. As I have noted, cognits have diffuse borders. Then we have to contend with their overlapping and interactive properties, which greatly complicate the picture of their localization in the brain. There is, however, a certain topographic order, a certain diffuse and broadly defined pattern that allows us to identify, albeit only approximately, the cortical domains of different cognitive networks in the human cortex. At the very least we can identify the cortical areas in which those networks are in heaviest concentration. That topography is determined by two factors that will guide our ensuing discussion: the origin of any given cognit and the generality or level of abstraction of the information it contains.

In this discussion it is imperative, again, not to attempt to distinguish between the neurobiology of knowledge and that of memory. The only difference between the two is that memory has more connections than knowledge with personal experience and with events tagged by personal time and place. But even the most autobiographical of memories is deeply infused with semantic knowledge (names, town, title, kinship, physical illness, social group, season, and so on). The memory of my last visit to Monticello is intertwined with my semantic knowledge of Jefferson and the Declaration of Independence, and, of course, the concept of personal freedom.[16] This intertwining of subjective memory and common knowledge emphasizes the heavy interconnections between knowledge and memory cognits. It also points to the heterarchical character of much memory, which contains material of different hierarchical levels.

In any event, there are in our cortex two general categories of cognits defined by origin and composition: two categories of memory in the broadest sense of the word *memory* (Figure 3.2). The first category is made up of *perceptual* cognits, mainly distributed in the posterior part of the cortex (parietal, temporal, and occipital – PTO for short). It covers all the cognits that have been acquired through the senses. This includes all sensory experiences and all that has been learned through them, all schooling and all social experiences – in sum, all our memories and knowledge acquired through any of the five senses. At the lowest, most basic level, it includes the feature analyzers of the sensory cortices, which I call "phyletic sensory memory."

The second category of memory comprises the *executive* cognits – in other words, the knowledge and memory of action, of doing things, acquired by the organism through its experience of acting upon the environment and other human beings.[17] Executive

---

[16] Without disregard for my emotional feelings toward liberty or the person that accompanied me on that visit.

[17] The most elementary carriers of executive information to the frontal cortex consist of proprioceptive sensations – that is, sensory inputs from joints and muscles, and "efferent copies" of movement (Gallistel, 1980). Cortical inputs come from higher executive cognits representing higher categories of action. They all contribute to the formation of schemas of action in the frontal cortex.

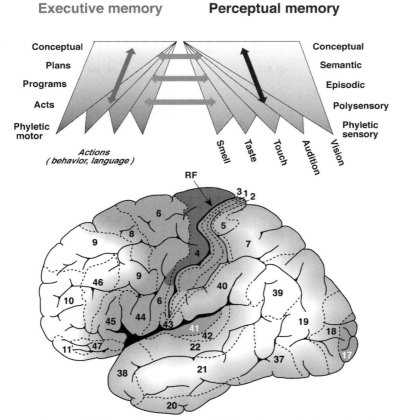

Figure 3.2 Organization of cortical cognits on the lateral surface of the left hemisphere (areas numbered as per Brodmann's cytoarchitectural map). The *lower* figure hints at the hierarchical organization of perceptual cognits, from primary sensory areas (*dark blue*) and motor areas (*dark red*) to posterior (PTO) and frontal association cortices (*white*), respectively. The upper figure, with the same color code, further schematizes the organization of areas, connectivity, and cognit categories. Abbreviation: *RF*, Rolandic fissure.

cognits are mainly distributed in the anterior, frontal parts of the cortex. At the lowest, most basic level of this – executive – cortex, lies the primary motor cortex, which is in charge of coordinating the simplest movements. These primitive movements are innate and a product of evolution. For this reason, I consider the motor cortex "phyletic motor memory."

Admittedly, it is highly unusual to call physical portions of the cortex "memory," but I believe it is eminently reasonable and serves our argument well by upholding the continuity between evolutionary memory and personal memory. Both these forms of memory are thus placed on the same structural – and functional – continuum. As I have said in the previous chapter, the structural aggregate of sensory and motor cortex is a form of memory acquired by our evolutionary ancestry to adapt to the environment; it is a highly adaptive form of memory that comes with the human genome. Following birth and certain periods of "rehearsal" (critical periods), the sensory and motor cortices that constitute that phyletic memory are ready to be "recalled" (reactivated) with every elementary sensation and movement of the body.[18] In sum, those cortical sensory and motor structures are part of the "memory of our species," which contains all the sensory-motor adaptive power that the neonate comes into the world with. It is on top of that ancestral genetic memory that all the perceptual and executive cognits of the individual will be formed.[19]

Beyond primary cortices, the rest of the neocortex, where individual memory will be formed, is the cortex of association, for many years presciently called that way ahead of the evidence. It harbors the cognits of personal memory, which are made of the associations of everyday life. As they arrive in the brain simultaneously, the stimuli carrying new memories and items of knowledge – perceptual or executive – are immediately associated with one another. At the same time they join previously established cognits. They are drawn, so to speak, to those older cognits because of associations of similarity or other common traits.

---

[18] If a neonate is not exposed to sensory stimulation of a given modality during a critical period of days or weeks, that infant will remain permanently unable to properly process information of that modality (Funnell and Wilding, 2011; Gallagher, 2005).

[19] The maturation process of the memory substrate, however, consists not only of a gradual increment of elementary structure, but also of the pruning of that structure (Low and Cheng, 2006). Neurons, axons, and synapses that are not used are eliminated from an early exuberance of them. That attrition results from the selection of those elements that the growing organism utilizes at the expense of those that it does not.

Thus the new knowledge enters the cortex of association and finds its place in it, where by affinity it will join old networks. That new knowledge will be consolidated under the agency of the hippocampus, but the entire process of knowledge and memory acquisition will be largely autonomous, taking place by self-organizing association. New paths will open up by usage, much as they do allegorically in Machado's poem and theoretically in Cajal's quotation, which are both at the head of this chapter.

That etching of new knowledge on old networks, however, does not occur in the brain following arbitrary paths. Nor is the ultimate place of settlement of each new arrival arbitrary. The new arrivals follow fiber tracts that course through the networks of the cortex, stepping from area to area, from sensory and motor areas to the highest, most richly interconnected networks of association cortex. Interestingly, those tracts follow the order in which the various areas develop, in evolution as well as in the individual brain (Chapter 2). Through convergent and divergent fibers, the pathways of memory lead to successive areas of asso-ciation in the higher cortex: one set of fibers for each modality at first, and then into areas that associate stimuli of different modal-ities. The sensory-perceptual pathways for taste and olfaction terminate in neocortical areas near the primary cortex for those two modalities, at the base of the frontal lobe, and near the limbic brain, above the junction of the temporal and frontal lobes. However, the pathways for the other three modalities, vision, audition, and touch, course through wide associative areas of lateral cortex that collect inputs from all modalities, as well as emotional inputs. Motor-executive pathways flow both ways: (a) from the top down – that is, from high prefrontal areas of associ-ation to motor cortex – and (b) conversely, in the form of a counter-flow of connections from the bottom up, from motor cortex to prefrontal cortex.[20]

---

[20] Whereas the general processing of motion descends from the prefrontal cortex to the motor cortex for the execution of action, the upward counter-flow connections from the bottom up are essential for two reasons: (a) to acquire executive memory in the high associative cortex (prefrontal) in the form of executive cognits, and (b) to monitor executive performance at every step as it proceeds to its goal (Gallistel, 1980).

In their progression toward higher associative areas, the sensory and motor pathways visit areas that contain cognits of increasingly complex and abstract information. The new incoming information (sensory stimuli and feedback from motor action) will thus "latch on" to existing networks at the corresponding levels of complexity or abstraction. At each of those levels the new information will complement or modify pre-existing cognits. As a consequence of these processes, cortical levels of increasing cognitive complexity and/or abstraction will be stratified and hierarchically organized above primary sensory and motor cortices. These processes take place almost continuously, not only as we experience the events of our everyday life but also in the acquisition of the skills that we decide to master.

Figure 3.2 portrays schematically much of the above and illustrates the general organization of cognits of perceptual and executive memory in the human cerebral cortex. As the two hierarchies develop upwards, the figure (upper diagram) indicates the progressive overlap of information from different modalities of sensation or movement. The hierarchical ascent of the formation and deposition of memory toward higher and broader associative areas leads to progressively more abstract cognits: from cognits that represent concrete sensations or movements to those that represent broader perceptual memories, rules, and plans of action. Thus, in the posterior cortex, there is a gradual transition of perceptual to unimodal and polymodal memory, to episodic memory, to semantic memory, to perceptual concepts and knowledge in the higher association cortex. Conversely, in the frontal cortex, there is a gradual transition from the representation of motor acts in the motor cortex to the representation of acts defined by goal and trajectory in the premotor cortex; and further – in the prefrontal cortex – to action plans and programs, as well as conceptual executive cognits – broad concepts of goal-directed action.

The vertical bidirectional arrows (*blue* and *red*) in Figure 3.2 symbolize the general gradients of perceptual and executive memory formation, processing, and organization in the cortex. The arrows also symbolize the fiber pathways that serve those three functions. Some run bottom-up and others top-down. As they form with daily life, cognits take their place in the hierarchy by order of complexity and abstraction of content. Many, however, make connections at various levels, as they represent material of different degrees of complexity. For this reason, many cognits are *heterarchical*, structurally and functionally. This is also the reason why, for example, episodic memory is so difficult to disentangle from semantic memory.

The horizontal arrows (*green*) symbolize the connectivity (superior longitudinal fasciculus) between the two hierarchies and the directions of information processing in the acquisition and behavioral utilization of cognits. All the symbolized connectivity in the figure is of critical functional significance, for it constitutes the infrastructure of the PA cycle, which is vital to the exercise of human liberty. I am sure the reader has noted my persistent use of organizational parallelism between perception and action at all neurobiological levels of the cortex. One of my principal motives is simple: I wish to make clear that in the brain there is no freedom of action without freedom of information; no executive memory, past, present, or future, without perceptual memory, past, present, or future.

FREEDOM OF INFORMATION IN THE CEREBRAL CORTEX

Perhaps I have gone into more detail than necessary to describe the distribution of memory and knowledge in the cerebral cortex. My reasoning on doing this has been that, in the brain, as in the real world, intelligent choices of action are preceded by intelligent choices of information. Similarly, in a democracy, choices are supposed to be made freely in the "marketplace of ideas," as John Stuart Mill and Oliver Wendell Holmes had in mind.[21] I suggest that in our cerebral cortex there is a free "marketplace" of cognits, whose participants I have attempted to outline in this chapter.

---

[21] John Stuart Mill, in his book *On Liberty* (1859), was probably the first to use the expression.

Our cerebral cortex is an immense repository of information about ourselves and the world around us. The richness of the cortex' cognitive content lies not in the presence of myriad minute locations or structures – neurons, molecules, or cell assemblies – for storing a corresponding myriad items of information, as in a computer. Instead, that richness derives almost exclusively from the fact that, as I have said, the cognitive code is a relational code, and so is the cortical code. The richness lies therefore in connections and connective potential. Here, a clear analogy with language will epitomize what a relational code means. I use language as I could use music or some other form of sequential expression.

The alphabet has a limited number of characters. By combining – that is, relating – those basic symbols with one another, and by adding pauses, spaces, and punctuation, we can construct an infinite variety of linguistic expressions in multiple languages. Is there any doubt in anybody's mind that the reduction of language to those elements would be a wrong-headed way to analyze language? Yet, surprisingly, this reductionism is the way some approach the problems of cognitive neuroscience. In the case of the neuroscience of language, the proper approach, of course, is to search for the neural correlates of the gestalts – that is, linguistic cognits – that those symbol combinations form. It is the analysis of those correlates by functional, electrical, and imaging methods. It is the analysis of the disruptions that brain lesions produce in the understanding and expression of language (aphasia, agraphia, agnosia, and so on), as Geschwind masterfully did in his papers on what he felicitously called "disconnexion syndromes" (Geschwind, 1965a, 1965b). In sum, it is the study of the physiology and pathology of the relational code of language. Chapter 6 will deal more specifically with the role of language in liberty.

Without the necessity to specify how phonemes or morphemes are represented in the brain, which we cannot yet do with present methods, it is perfectly reasonable to think that they constitute small cognits or networks of unspecified dimensions. It is equally reasonable to think that they organize (i.e., self-organize) between and among themselves into larger cognits that define words, and these in turn into yet larger cognits that define sentences. My point here is that, in the cortex, relational power makes for enormous economy of codification within cortical space. By comparison, the codification power of a computer is minuscule. Not so in the case of the internet, however, which approaches the codifying power of the brain by virtue of the fact that its relational code is immensely distributed (below).

To understand how choices of information and action are made in that immense relational archive that is the human cortex, we have to make two difficult but indispensable shifts in our thinking. The first is to transfer the role of "free chooser" from the ego or the *I* to the cerebral cortex. The second shift is to divest the ego or the *I* of the self-consciousness of its choices; in other words, to make consciousness to a large extent "optional." Both shifts are necessary to understand the epistemology of liberty in the brain. That does not mean that free will and consciousness should be deprived of any role whatsoever in deliberate action. It does not mean either that when we make decisions the cortex is completely on "autopilot." It does mean, however, that the cortex has the capacity to make reasonable and intelligent choices among untold items of information within itself. It also means that a large number of those choices, however decisive, are unconscious, at least in part. That means, in turn, that we are not consciously aware of the reasons for much of our behavior. This does not make our behavior unfree or predetermined. It simply expands the latitude of our options to include an enormous fund of hidden knowledge under the guise of such subtle psychological resources as "priming," "intuition," or "insight."[22] In contrast to psychoanalytic theory, here the unconscious removes constraints to freedom, instead of adding them.

In our daily life, every act of perception is a choice, an unwitting choice, but a choice all the same. It is a choice between each percept as one category of knowledge and others, between one cognit and others that are not identical but related to it by

---

[22] As some investors and entrepreneurs do unconsciously in their predictions, however erroneous these may turn out to be. Here it is almost obligatory to mention John Maynard Keynes, an advocate of intuition, who is supposed to have been more successful as an economist than as an investor (Davis, 1994; Nasar, 2011).

similarity, discordance, or association. Perceiving is thus a constant testing of assumptions about the world and the objects in it, a constant unconscious matching of each object with our internal cognit or "hypothesis" of it (Harris, 1970; Hayek, 1952). We "choose" (perceive) one object if it meets our expectations. And then another, and another, all day long. This goes on with all myriad objects around us. Only when an unconscious "choice" does not meet our expectation, when our assumption is proven "wrong," do we become consciously aware of it. For example, I enter my study, my usual workroom, and experience the sudden sensation that something has changed in it since yesterday, without at first being aware of what it is. After careful scrutiny, I discover it: somebody consulted my atlas overnight and replaced it on the wrong shelf. Think of how many assumptions (percepts) I tested unconsciously on entering the room before I, my cortex, experienced that something was amiss in that room!

By now it must be clear to the reader that my view of the neuroscience of perception differs considerably from those inspired by the empiricist philosophy of the mind. Yet this philosophy underlies practically every modern treatment of perception in the brain. Encouraged by the finding of sensory-feature maps in sensory cortex, especially for vision, the neurophysiologist often ventures to extend to the associative cortex the same mapping principles that obtain in early cortical processing stages, only now for more complex configurations of vision, touch, hearing, or spatial arrangement. He now searches for more complex cortical maps to accommodate more complex physical features integrated at higher levels of a hierarchy of sensation, a hierarchy always defined by the physical parameters of the stimuli. So far, this chase of perception up the sensory ladder has been rather fruitless. The trouble with this methodology is basically twofold, theoretical and experimental.

Theoretically, the problem with the empiricist view of perception lies primarily in the simple fact that a percept carries history – in addition to sensation – and, without taking this fact into account, neither its psychology nor its physiology is comprehensible. A legion of psychophysicists and philosophers has been stressing the point for many years without effectively penetrating brain science. We not only remember what we perceive, but also perceive what we remember.[23] Perceiving is classifying the objects of the world into categories defined by relationships within them previously established by experience in our nervous system; in other words, into cognits. Cognits have history by definition. At their root is the history of the species or phyletic memory of sensory cortices, which "interprets" the physical aspects of a perceptual cognit. *All* the perceptual "interpretation" of an object is based exclusively on the history – experience – of that object in our individual life. Thus, consciously or unconsciously, we are free to pick and choose in the vast archive of our knowledge and memory, which are distributed and interconnected in our cerebral cortex much as collective knowledge is in cyberspace.

Experimentally, for the physiologist, the trouble with the empiricist view of perception lies in the evidence that, beyond the primary sensory cortex, the reactions of neurons to complex stimuli generally become loose, feeble, and subject to "top-down" influences, attention among them. The sensory specificity of any associative cortical field becomes elusive. Many of those fields respond more or less well to many stimuli of one or several modalities.[24] These findings are not in agreement with a neural map of perception based only on physical features of sensory stimulation. They are in agreement, however, with a widely distributed array of interactive and overlapping cognits with the loose constraints defined in previous sections. In any event, the demonstration of a more or less specific reactivity to a given complex stimulus anywhere in the cortex always leaves the lingering suspicion that Bacon's problem of induction has not been overcome in that situation, that a "black swan" has not yet been found. In other words, the most effective stimulus has not been found – and thus not tested – for the part of the cortex we are probing.[25]

[23] Among the most eloquent proponents of this point of view are Helmholtz (1925), Boring (1933), and Hayek (1952).
[24] I have treated this premise as crucial for my reasoning on the distribution and interactivity of cognits (Fuster, 2009).
[25] The problem of induction in science is excellently treated by Popper (1980).

In our seamless interaction with the environment, choices are not limited to perception but naturally also extend to action. We engage in a steady stream of actions and reactions in the PA cycle, continuously adjusting and readjusting to our environment and to the changes in it, many of these changes induced by ourselves. When I say "ourselves," I mean our brains, and when I say "environment," I mean not just the external environment, but also the internal environment or "milieu" of our body as well, including the "circumstance" *à la* Ortega (our history and our culture). Most of our interaction with those environments is automatic and completely unconscious, involving mainly subcortical parts of the brain; thus the cortex remains unencumbered and free to do other things, like thinking or imagining.

As behavior, reasoning, or language becomes complex, and as more and more unpredictable or adjustable elements surge from the environment, more and more of the cortex enters the PA cycle and, with it, also a state of heightened consciousness. But note that most of the interactions, now involving much of the cortex, still remain unconscious. Unconscious choices expand; with them, liberty does too. For liberty does not need conscious choice. Nor do the reasons for choice need to be conscious. As I said before, unconscious knowledge in the form of intuition in fact adds liberty to our choices. As behavior, reasoning, or language becomes elaborate and deliberate, much liberty (and some of its constraints too) derives from a massive, unconscious, and relentless search of information within the cortex. In our waking day, both perception and action are constantly informed by that steady – "Google-like" – search by the cortex within itself.

This brings us to computers, which have memory too, and whose business is to manipulate that memory. In fact they do it much faster than we can, even though we are much smarter than they are.

OF BRAINS AND COMPUTERS

Is there a computer metaphor for human memory? In principle, the analogy based on memory configuration and access seems extremely poor, because human memory, unlike computer memory, is relational and content-addressable. However, the analogy with the internet and a search engine like Google is very appropriate. Let us see why.

In the previous sections I have described in simple, non-computational terms a well-supported conception of the making and organization of the structure of knowledge and memory in the cerebral cortex. My primary purpose has been to present to the reader the network nature of that structure, its role as the store of information acquired by experience, and its potential for making that information available to cognitive functions. The main objective of this chapter has been to highlight the neural substrate of a mental faculty that is often ignored in the liberty debate: the capacity to choose, to select, the conscious or unconscious information that is to inform our free actions.

Before closing this chapter, I should like to deal briefly with the more or less obvious computer metaphors of cortical cognition. Computer memory is addressed by means of a binary code that points to the exact location in the hard disk where the memory is located. Even RAM (random-access memory) – a form of digital "working memory" – is addressed that way, and placed in a temporary disk store. In the cortex, however, the information is *addressed by content*, by association. One of the essential properties of a cognit is that it can be retrieved by a sensory stimulus, or another form of input, by association. The activation of one of the cognit's associated components thus leads to the retrieval of the others, which follow like the tangled cherries out of the basket. Further, the computer ordinarily processes information in series, whereas the cortex can do it also in parallel on a massive scale.[26]

Moreover, I have said in passing that the cerebral cortex has much greater capacity of information storage than any regular computer. I could have added that the brain has more storage capacity than any system of interlinked computers. This would not be true, however; to wit, the internet, which also works with a relational code. In fact, because of this, the analogy between cortical cognition and information in the internet is quite

---

[26] Some modern computers, however, can process information in parallel, like the cortex.

compelling. Let us briefly focus on the similarities between the two, having in mind their possible relevance to liberty of choice.

Indeed, both the internet ("cyber-cortex") and the cerebral cortex use a relational code that transcends and overrides their basic binary codes of bits or cell spikes. In both internet and cortex, the relevant code is one of relationships between units of information or knowledge.[27] Language contributes many units of information to both brain and internet, although in the case of the brain the units (cognits or modules) can be more elementary – for example, simple sensations – than words or symbols. As in the cortex, the capacity of the internet to encode by relationship is practically infinite. Here that capacity derives from the combinatorial power of millions of computers and the information within them. Also as in the cortex, units of information, or network nodes, can be part of many informational networks (webs), some intersecting with, or nested within, others.

Think of the choices you make when you navigate through the internet for whatever reason, even if what you do is idle "surfing." Those are really free choices *of your cortex*, which, attached to the internet by an extra set of connections, expands its existing database with additional cognits, or modifies those already in its possession. People who marvel at the power of the internet do not quite realize that it does what their cortex has been doing all their lives with every perception, every recall, and every mental calculation.

In functional terms, however, there is a fundamental difference between the cortex and the internet. It is true that in both the cortex and the internet the information is addressable by content, not by assigned local address. In the cortex, however, the information is self-addressed, by association, whereas in the internet it is addressed by human brains manipulating search engines from millions of individual computers.

What do I mean by the associative self-addressing of information in the human cortex? I mean, simply, that for any human cognitive function, such as attention, perception, language, or

---

[27] Except e-mail, of course, which through the internet sends information to specific addresses.

intelligent performance, the cortex can address within itself the cognits that are necessary to that function at any given time. A sensory input may, at that time, carry new external information, but this information, in order to be useful, must be interpreted by, and incorporated into, the cognits it activates in our brain. Take the sudden smell of smoke at home: It will immediately activate by association the cognits that are relevant to appropriate defensive action. The smoke will not only be sensed but also perceived – that is, placed by our brain in the context of past experience – thus entering the PA cycle. This will lead to a search for the source of the smoke, and that search to the possible discovery of fire, and that discovery to the fire extinguisher and/or the emergency phone call, and so on. Each act in the series will be guided by a perceptual cognit self-addressed by the cortex within its immense array of cognitive networks.

I have chosen a simple example of behavior that could be conceivably automated by machines to illustrate how, even in behaviors of this kind, the cortex addresses memory content mostly by itself, whereas automated systems do it by external signals – through sensors. Furthermore, regardless of signal source, the latitude for selection of inputs and outputs, in terms of number, signal parameters, thresholds, and informational volume, is infinitely greater in the cortex than in servo-machinery, whereas the constraints of the latter are infinitely greater. The machine – though man-made after all – may be faster and more exact than the brain to do what it is designed to do, but its options will always be more limited than those of the cortex of its inventor or operator. Even the memory buffers or RAM of the computer cannot approach the range of conceivable contents in cortical working memory.

In any event, whereas the individual computer cannot match the human brain in storage capacity, the internet, linking together many individual computers, can. In fact the internet serves as a massive cerebral cortex to supplement our own and adds enormous dimensions to its capacity to select information for guiding our actions. It is also true, however, that the internet can bias our liberty by injecting the emotions of others into our choices. In that sense the internet serves the demagogue's intent of influencing those choices, which may thus become prejudiced and not completely free.

CONCLUSIONS

In neurobiological terms, our liberty consists of the capacity of our cerebral cortex to select between alternatives of goal-directed action and the information to guide it. The choosing agent is the cortex, not an immaterial agent controlling it. Conscious free agency is a phenomenon of the high activity of the cortex in the computation of choice, decision, planning, and creating. All these processes are based on pre-existent information in the cortex itself or elsewhere in the brain, including the substrate of biological drives.

Cognitive information is acquired and stored in a web of distributed, intermeshed, and overlapping networks, named cognits, which are units of knowledge and memory addressable by content, unlike computer memory. They are formed by life experience in the cortex of association on a foundation of phyletic memory ("the memory of the species") – that is, the structure of primary sensory and motor cortices. By mechanisms of synaptic modulation, notably synchronous convergence, life experience generates those networks or cognits, which constitute structural patterns of association between neurons representing the more elementary aspects of perception and action.

Cognits overlap and intersect extensively, sharing nodes of heavy association constituted by cell assemblies that represent common features of different cognits. Perceptual cognits are hierarchically organized in the posterior cortex, and executive cognits in the frontal cortex. The two hierarchies are interlinked at all levels by reciprocal fiber connections, which are part of the structural foundation of the PA cycle, essential to the exercise of liberty and the subject of the next chapter.

4

The perception/action cycle

The constancy of the internal milieu is the condition for free and independent life.

Claude Bernard

Brains differ from computers in a number of key respects. They operate in cycles rather than in linear chains of causality, sending and receiving signals back and forth.

Dennis Bray

Our capacity to choose between alternatives rests on the dynamic interaction of our brain with the world around us and within us. Whether our choices are guided by preference (freedom *to*) or aversion (freedom *from*), they are immersed in the continuous functional engagement of our nervous system with the internal and external environments. The most profound biological root of liberty is *homeostasis* – that is, the set of physiological mechanisms by which the organism adapts to its environment and maintains its internal stability.[1] Some of these mechanisms create stability, whereas others protect it. Homeostasis, we might say, is the phyletic memory of physiological adaptation. And liberty, we might also say, is the elevation of the adaptive principles of homeostasis to serve the cognitive-emotional stability of the individual in society and the world at large.

---

[1] The concept of homeostasis was introduced in France by Claude Bernard in 1865 (Bernard, 1927) and in America by Walter Cannon (1932), both stellar physiologists.

Thus, liberty, like homeostasis, implies a continuous "dialogue" of the organism with "the other," animate or inanimate. More precisely, it implies a multitude of simultaneous interactions of the self with the environment, the latter to include the internal environment of the body. Without those interactions, liberty makes no sense and has no agenda – that is, literally no choice – because liberty closely hinges on the effects of environmental events on the self and on the present or *anticipated* impact of the self on the environment. As the relationship self/environment develops with evolution to include human choice, something most remarkable happens: The relationship expands enormously in its time scale, especially in its future perspective, as does the span of the environment it covers. All that is a direct consequence of the extraordinary development of the human prefrontal cortex and the perception/action (PA) cycle it serves.

Here it needs to be emphasized that, in the human, the time scale of the adaptive interaction self/environment extends mightily into the future of the life of the individual. With it, choices and decisions multiply to reach forwards in time, to take effect or to produce their effects in a future that extends to days, weeks, months, years, or decades. Thus, what began with the immediate reactions of the sea anemone to small perturbations of the marine environment has grown immensely into the long-term planning of *Homo sapiens* with a greatly extended PA cycle. That cycle operates in an infinitely more complex environment. Liberty has evolved to support it, to protect it, and to give it a future – in other words, to make it *preadaptive*.

BIOLOGY OF THE CYCLE

Deep in the mammalian brain, between the two cerebral hemispheres – that is, in the diencephalon or "brain in-between" – there is a structure named the hypothalamus – because it lies under the thalamus, the major relay station for sensory pathways on their way to the cortex. The hypothalamus harbors a collection of tightly packed nuclei[2] devoted to the regulation of a large variety of basic physiological functions, such as temperature, heart rate, response to stress, and endocrine functions ranging from body metabolism to growth, ovulation, lactation, blood sugar, and so on. Some of the visceral hypothalamic regulation is exerted through the so-called autonomic nervous system; some is exerted through the secretion of substances acting directly or indirectly upon a score of endocrine glands (for example, pituitary, thyroid, gonads, and adrenals). Without fail, every one of the regulatory functions of the hypothalamus, which for good reason can be called the *organ of homeostasis*, makes use of chemical or neural *feedback* to correct and stabilize the internal milieu. Homeostatic mechanisms are, therefore, servomechanisms operating with regulatory feedback.

In addition to its role in the regulation of the homeostasis of the internal milieu, the hypothalamus plays a crucial role in the satisfaction of basic drives – namely, feeding, sex, flight, and aggression. We have to marvel at the number and complexity of the regulatory and instinctual functions orchestrated by such a small structure as the hypothalamus. Of great significance is the fact that the four instinctual functions mentioned above have a "*purpose*" that extends beyond the organism into the external environment, presumably serving not just the individual but also the defense and propagation of the species. The Swiss physiologist W.H. Hess, who studied in great detail the hypothalamus, had the insight of calling "teleokinetic" the instinctual movements elicited from several hypothalamic points (Hess, 1943). The prefix *teleo-* is as appropriate to denote movement upon or toward the external environment as to denote action upon or toward the future.

If here I have mentioned a number of hypothalamic functions, however broadly, it is to emphasize the presence, already in a lower brain structure, of the basic features of the brain's adaptive

---

[2] These nuclei are aggregates of nerve cells that have direct effects over the visceral outlets of the autonomic nervous system and over the hormonal glands. All their functions are broadly adaptive, in that they ensure the adaptation of the organism to its internal and external milieu. They are of critical importance in the expression of emotion.

interaction with the environment. The hypothalamus is an "open" system (von Bertalanffy, 1950), which tends toward equilibrium without ever perfectly reaching it. But it already has the basic features of a complex adaptive system as well, including control with feedback, which is an essential aspect of the cybernetics of any regulatory system. That primitive system, however, does not have freedom, for it operates reflexively, with limited options and within the narrow constraints of the functions it controls. Even the instinctual functions, though "teleokinetic," go straight to their goal, unswerving, like arrows to their target.

Almost a century ago, the prestigious biologist Jakob von Uexküll (1926) revealed in lower animals the origins of what, at the level of the cortex, I call the PA cycle: A flow of environmental signals gathered by sensory systems shapes the actions of the organism upon the environment; these actions produce environmental changes, which in turn generate new sensory input, which informs new action, and so on. This circular flow of information operates in the interactions of all animal organisms with their environment.

Working on the comparative biology of a broad variety of species, von Uexküll further remarked on the critical emergence, in higher species, of internal feedback from brain structures that organize movement to structures that organize sensation. That internal feedback, he noted, counters the direction of the external sensory-motor feedback of the universal cycle operating in all species, which normally runs from the environment through the brain and back to the environment. His language has a certain archaic patina of nineteenth-century naturalism, but his observations are exceptionally lucid and, as we will see, critical to the anatomy of liberty. In sum, von Uexküll showed that in higher organisms, including the human, the motor system sends controlling signals to sensory systems. Now we know what was not known in his time: that at all levels of the structural hierarchies for perception and for action, there are nervous pathways running from motor structures to sensory structures, and thus in a direction opposite to that of the main cycle. What are those pathways doing that run from motor centers to sensory centers, apparently "against traffic"?

That question intrigued researchers for several decades, until neuroscience found the answer to it in the prefrontal cortex. This cortex sits at the highest executive level of the PA cycle, which is the extension to the cerebral cortex of the cycle formulated by von Uexküll. Indeed, the prefrontal cortex is the origin of pathways that carry what Hans-Lukas Teuber called "corollary discharge," made of nerve impulses *that prepare* sensory structures of the brain for the anticipated consequences of prospective motor action (Teuber, 1972). Thus the corollary discharge prepares the subject for the action in anticipation of its effects on the environment. It is a function with a future perspective, a preadjusting function. Another function, also with a base in the prefrontal cortex and a future perspective, consists of the forward correction of misperceptions through better adjustment of sensory structures for anticipated input (Wolpert, 1997). Yet another is the "cognitive control" of perceptual attention, with a seat in the prefrontal cortex, which controls activity in posterior cortical areas (Miller and Cohen, 2001). Finally, there are the recurrent paths from motor to sensory structures of the cortex that maintain working memory for anticipated motor action.[3]

All those recurrent modes of "backward" connection from motor to sensory structures in the PA cycle, somewhat paradoxically, serve the future-oriented functions of attention, error correction, anticipatory preparation, and working memory. The latter is a state, rather than a form, of short-term memory that by definition has a future perspective, as it prepares the organism for the action it has to perform in the near future. Thus, all kinds of internal motor-sensory feedback impinge on the future dimension of our liberty, as they anticipate and prepare us for the consequences of every choice we make. When the choice is important, literally decisive in one way or another, the internal controlling feedback runs through the cerebral cortex.

---

[3] The recurrent or re-entrant pathways and functions referred to in this paragraph have been anatomically confirmed, in the human as well as in non-human primates (reviewed in Fuster, 2008).

THE CEREBRAL CORTEX IN THE CYCLE

The future dimension of our liberty, of our freedom to choose, plan, decide, or create, rests squarely on the prefrontal cortex and allied cortices. Freedom is impossible without a firm anchor in cognition to inform our choices, plans, decisions, and creations. That indispensable fund of cognition – that is, of knowledge – consists of our personal history and our interpretation of current reality in the light of that history, all of it in a complex array of cortical networks. We perceive the world through that fund of pre-existing knowledge, through that multitude of perceptual and executive cognits that represent it. As we freely move through that world, we – our cortex, that is – automatically, unconsciously, "consult" that fund of knowledge in order to construct successful actions and reactions.[4] Bernstein (1967) placed a component named the "comparator" at the center of his model of "action-perception cycle." In my view, that "comparator" is the cortex, especially the prefrontal cortex.

Also embedded in our history are our feelings, values, and emotions. As we shall see later, they enter the PA cycle also. Their neural influences on the cycle originate in the limbic system or "emotional brain," with the hypothalamus at its base; included in that system is the lower part of the prefrontal cortex, the cortical port of entry of those influences, which lies directly above the orbit – for that reason called the "orbital prefrontal cortex." Limbic impulses flow from that system into the neocortex and attach themselves to cognits as these are formed, imparting to them the emotional attributes they elicit. They will "color" the newly formed cognits with emotional associations, which will be revived with the reactivation of any cognit in the measure of the strength of those associations with it. It is those associations that make our memories pleasant or unpleasant, and indeed "memorable."

---

[4] Ortega y Gasset called that aggregate of personal history the "circumstance" of the individual, his internalized world, a kind of internal environment encapsulating all personal experience and value systems (Chapter 1). Thus the PA cycle courses not only through the external environment but also through that internal one, which really defines the personality: "I am myself and my circumstance" (Ortega y Gasset, 1961).

As we evolve as a species and as individuals, the PA cycle reaches full development and gains maximal flexibility to accommodate human liberty – that is, our freedom of choice. The various cortical regions, it will be recalled, are stacked in developmental and connective order to house two hierarchies of cognits or cognitive networks: one in the posterior cortex mostly for perceptual cognits – acquired through the senses – and the other in the frontal cortex mostly for executive cognits – acquired through action.

In both hierarchies, perceptual and executive, the stages or levels of cognition are only coarsely separated, as they are vertically straddled by many heterarchical cognits – made of networks linking neurons of different levels.[5] Further, the two hierarchies, perceptual and executive, are profusely and reciprocally interconnected. There are two principal reasons for this, one structural and the other dynamic: (a) to wire together perceptual-executive cognits, and (b) to serve the PA cycle in operation. Figure 4.1 represents the global scheme of the cortical stages of the PA cycle with their interconnections. Note that at all hierarchical levels of the cortex – as in the spinal cord and brainstem at the sensory-motor base of the cycle – there are lateral reciprocal connections between corresponding perceptual and executive levels.[6]

Before we consider in dynamic terms the major connectivity in the cycle, we must deal with two general considerations of its organization. One is its hierarchical structure, which corresponds to

[5] Heterarchical cognits are pervasive throughout the cortex, reflecting the psychological reality that the bulk of our knowledge and memory is heterarchical. This means that in the cognitive fabric of our cortex, cognits of different hierarchical levels are intermixed to form large items of knowledge and memory. Thus, items of common knowledge at various levels of abstraction are associatively connected with personal memory. Of course, the strength of the interlinking connections may vary widely, and change over time. That is why the vividness of the component memories or knowledge, as well as the ease of their evocation, may vary widely from time to time. The weak links are the first to fail in normal aging and, markedly, in dementia.

[6] All the connectivity symbolized by arrows in Figure 4.1 has been substantiated in the nonhuman primate by histological methods (review in Fuster, 2008); in the human, it is being further substantiated by tensor imaging technology (Le Bihan et al., 2001). Reciprocal connectivity, at any level, can serve any function that requires re-entry, such as working memory, control feedback, "corollary discharge," and self-monitoring.

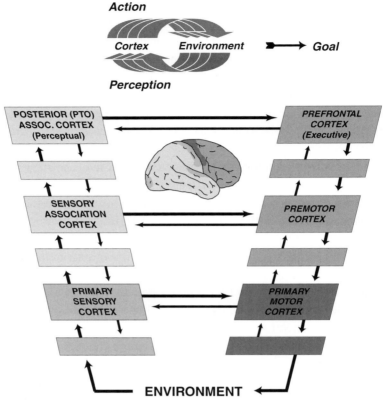

Figure 4.1 Dynamic flow of activation through the cortical hierarchical stages of the PA cycle in the pursuit of a goal. Unlabeled rectangles stand for intermediate areas or subareas of adjacent, labeled, areas. Large arrows – clockwise – indicate the main flow of the cycle. Small arrows – counterclockwise – indicate feedback flow.

the hierarchical organization of the cognits that participate in it (Chapter 3). Here it is essential to consider that perceptual networks feed into executive networks at all levels. At high levels, the cycle mediates the high-level transactions between conceptual cognits of perceptual and executive memory or knowledge. Conversely, at low levels the cycle mediates the lower-level transactions between more concrete cognits, which are nested within the higher ones.

The second, related, consideration is that multiple PA cycles can be active simultaneously at different hierarchical levels, the lower serving the higher: There are many cycles working in parallel, even though each one works separately, in series, to attain its particular goal. Each cycle has a perceptual or memory base in the cortex, each with its sector of the environment, each with its objective, which may lie in the short or in the long term.

Cycles with a minor or subsidiary goal serve others with overriding goals. For example, our daily morning routines before we go to our workplace consist of a series of successive acts (showering, dressing, having breakfast, driving, parking, and so on), each with its cycle, its environment, its means, and its goal. They all serve a larger cycle whose objective is to show up for work on time, after proper hygiene and in proper attire. That larger cycle of getting to work, and the subsequent cycles of performing the obligations of our job, are in turn subsidiary cycles of several larger cycles that include providing for our family, earning a vacation, and pursuing the goals of our career or profession, all working in parallel with different time frames. All have feedback to anticipate and correct future behavior. Note that each cycle implies a measure of freedom and choice on the brain side of the cycle, in the perceptual as well as the executive sector.

Note also that many of those PA cycles consist of habits that are triggered or parsed by discrete environmental stimuli (e.g., alarm clock, traffic signals) or more or less pressing internal urges (e.g., appetite). Those habits do not necessarily engage enough of the cortex to be conscious. That frees the cortex for more intense activity to serve the larger cycles and their goals with attention, deliberation, and logical reasoning. In any case, at times that are for whatever reason critical (e.g., pending decision or the need to formulate a plan), a PA cycle involves large cognits of perceptual and executive cortex in the pursuit of its goal.

Before further analysis of the PA cycle, we have to ask ourselves a pressing question: Given that there are so many, practically an infinite number of potential PA cycles in cortical circuitry, is there a situation where they are all at rest, even if they are not currently in use driving language, reasoning, or behavior to its goal? The answer is, probably, no. Even in sleep, the cortex is active, albeit down to minimal levels. External sensors and motor effectors are shut off, but it has been shown that memory consolidation continues even then,[7] and some hints of reasoning and creation take place also in sleep (Chapter 5).

In the resting state, when a subject is allowed idly to free-associate his thoughts, we have known for a long time that the cortex exhibits a certain level of elevated electrical and metabolic activity. This basic activation in idle rest is maximal in the prefrontal cortex, for which reason David Ingvar, the discoverer of the phenomenon, called it "hyperfrontality." Ingvar assumed – and inferred from subjective reports – that, in that state, the subjects were imagining actions of various kinds, consciously anticipating "simulated behavior" (Ingvar, 1979). Thus, at rest, the frontal cortex, the "efferent" region of the cortex, appears to be a silent "free-wheeling agent," doing subliminally many things but overtly none.

Modern functional imaging reveals that the prefrontal area activated at rest is but a portion of a large network that extends into the parietal and medial cortex (Fox and Raichle, 2007). That presumed "default network," at rest, would be in spontaneous pre-activity, as if waiting for input to process. It is as if, in attentive vigilance, that extensive cortical area, which comprises perceptual and executive cognits, were in a permanent state of primed activation, ready to set in motion one or another PA cycle. Those cognits are presumably open to many inputs and give exit to many outputs, ready to handle a stream of circular processing between the organism and its environment. In sum, the wake cortex is a wide-open system ready to receive and to give out information in a permanent state of preadaptation.

Now that we have immersed the entire cortex in the PA cycle, at the interface between the organism and its environment, it is instructive to reflect on the writings of certain cognitive scientists and philosophers who construe cognition, in its entirety, as precisely the dynamic relation between the two that my PA cycle embodies. Indeed, the PA cycle appears to constitute the essence of what some have termed "embodied cognition." In no other way, it seems, can we interpret the philosophical

---

[7] A well-controlled study (Born *et al.*, 2006) shows that the learning of certain cognitive tasks is consolidated during sleep, especially slow-wave sleep (SWS), with electroencephalographic waves in the 0.5 to 2 cycles per second range.

position of Noë (2004), who views perception as active sensing, the exploration and "palpation" of the world against a background of prior knowledge about it. The PA cycle is nothing other than the "extended mind" that Clark (2008) postulates – an extended mind that incorporates logical reasoning into the cycle. With a more hierarchical view, evidently in tune with the tenets of this book, Barsalou (1999) envisions perception as the categorization of sensory instantiations, and places, at the top of the perceptual hierarchy, the abstract categories of perceptual symbol systems, just as I do in the higher levels of the association cortex. In sum, the theoretical formulations of Barsalou, Noë, and Clark find a fitting accommodation in the neurobiology of the PA cycle as presented in this chapter.

CYCLE DYNAMICS: ENTER EMOTION

What are the inputs, the stimuli, which in the state of more or less relaxed vigilance arrive in the cortex to set a PA cycle in motion, and to keep it active? They are potentially infinite in number. Some come from the internal environment, the body or brain itself; others from the external environment, through the senses. In different admixtures and intensities, they converge on the cognitive apparatus of the cerebral cortex from myriad potential origins. Freedom and choice begin right there, for the cortex exerts choices on that constant stream of information arriving to it in waking hours.

The choosing and evaluating by the cortex goes on all the time even in the absence of any need for decision. Many of the choices take place subliminally – that is, unconsciously – at low levels of cortical activity. This deserves repeated emphasis because free will is generally assumed to imply consciousness, when it may not. Furthermore, an unconscious choice is commonly supposed not to be a choice at all, but a biologically predetermined fact without options. These two assumptions ignore the fact that the organism makes decisions based on probabilistic data, in the face of ambiguity, complexity, and uncertainty. They also ignore the power of intuition – that is, the unconscious use of intelligence to assess urgency, relevance, priority, and risk. Many of our decisions come out of our gut feeling, based on a broader and sometimes more reliable database than the one we have in conscious awareness. That does not make our decisions less free or more deterministic. Choices go on in our brain all the time, whether we are aware of them or not. Awareness does not make them freer. In fact, the conscious awareness of a set of options may constrain freedom by limiting the availability of others.

The choice of the information to make a decision to act or not to act, or to act in one way or another, is a prerequisite of freedom of action, and in fact it is part of it. Thus, our first task in trying to understand the neurobiology of freedom is to identify that information in terms of the categories of inputs with access to the cortical PA cycle.

In the first place, there are the inputs from the external environment that come to the cortex in the form of stimuli from the various sense organs – for vision, audition, etc. That sensory information is not only sensed but also instantly perceived – consciously or not. In fact, without perception, it is useless to our free organism; that is, it is to no avail without its immediate interpretation in the light of prior experience.[8] Every possible or conceivable sensory stimulus has a "history" by virtue of its relationship or similarity with other stimuli we have experienced in the past. There is nothing absolutely "new" for us "under the sun." That means that all perceived external stimuli activate by immediate association an array of perceptual cognits. These cognits will become available to the rest of the cortex for selection and, if they warrant action of any sort, will enter the PA cycle.

Then there is the information available to the cortex from the internal milieu. This information is basically of two kinds: (a) the value or motivational significance, biological or ethical, of external stimuli; and (b) the urgency or need to satisfy a biological

---

[8] Here is where the empiricist's explanation of perception badly fails. Sensation alone is meaningless to the organism, literally. All perception, without exception, requires immediate, automatic, "top-down" interpretation of sensation. Most of the time that interpretation is an immediate "given" founded on prior experience, and completely unconscious. That immediacy of perception is essential to cortical physiology, if nothing else for economy of serial processing, which is needed for attending to anything.

drive or to obtain a secondary reward or reinforcement of behavior, such as money.[9] Internal information of these kinds can, by itself, set the PA cycle in motion and keep it – together with its subsidiary cycles – continuously in that state until the satisfaction of an innate primary need. Of course, internal motives act more as sources of "bias" than as options for choice. That "bias," however, may actually have overriding or "veto" power and transform itself into the only option to choose, and thus to unleash or block a PA cycle. In any event, an internal impulse from the world of emotion or a moral imperative may not qualify as a choice *per se* but certainly as an item of information of deciding importance. The essential point here is that a choice of information can bias or determine an action (or non-action), and liberty resides in that choice as much as in the choice of consequent action.

The third source of inputs to the choosing cortex consists of the conclusions resulting from deliberate thinking. These inputs originate in the cortex itself. Deliberate thinking (system-2 thinking) (Kahneman, 2011) is the process of reasoning, in and by the cortex, with the goal of solving a problem or, more generally, of reaching the "truth," the "good," or the "best." That includes, of course, the analysis of risks and benefits from a prospective course of action (Kahneman and Tversky, 1979). The reasoning process constitutes an internal PA cycle in itself, which may serve other cycles of higher order. It is important here to recognize that, because of the close relationship between thought and language, that process of internal deliberation will involve language and semantics in addition to reasoning, and thus, most assuredly, the prefrontal cortex of the left hemisphere.[10]

There are two other reasons, related to language (Chapter 6), why the prefrontal cortex is critical in deliberate thinking about

[9] Money, in the psychological literature, is considered a secondary or "conditioned" reinforcement of behavior inasmuch as it is instrumental for obtaining primary reinforcements, such as food or shelter. For many people, however, money is just about the only driving motive, even after all basic needs have been satisfied.

[10] Functional imaging methods show that the prefrontal cortex, especially on the left, is prominently activated by the retrieval of semantic information (Tulving *et al.*, 1994), which is essential for reasoning and language, and by reasoning itself (Kroger *et al.*, 2002).

prospective action: One is the predictive character of that process and the other the probabilistic nature of its outcome. It takes the prefrontal cortex, with its executive cognits – past and future – to make probabilistic assessments of current information as well as the future outcome of its use. It takes the prefrontal cortex, above all, to integrate information in the axis of time, in the process of planning as well as in the action itself (Fuster, 2001).

The concepts of deliberate thinking and reasoning, however, indicate two mental faculties that are important but non-essential to my present argument. One is consciousness and the other rational logic. It is true that our internal deliberation is most likely to be carried out with our full awareness of most all the premises and conclusions of our rational thinking. But it is our cortex that conducts the deliberation with itself. It is not our consciousness *per se* that does it, nor our state of awareness, which is nonetheless an obligatory byproduct of that deliberation by virtue of the cortical activity it requires.

The other component of deliberation that is not essential to my argument is rational logic. It is true that rationality is indispensable for the objective assessment of prospective actions and their consequences. But it is also true that the outcome of our deliberation, what the cortex is given for choice(s), is not only the result of totally rational and objective logic. Very likely, it is to some degree biased by influences from affect, emotion, and ethics of which we are not aware. Yet neither this bias nor the absence of full awareness makes the choice of information by the cortex un-free – that is, exempt of alternatives – even though that choice itself may not be free of belief or prejudice.

In summary, before and during a PA cycle there is a constant barrage of information arriving in the cortex from internal and external sources for choice and evaluation. Some of it is conscious, some unconscious. Whether conscious or unconscious, in terms of synaptic strength some of the information is weak and some strong.[11] Only some of it may at any given time attract

---

[11] Strength of information is determined by the strength of the connections that define it. In other words, the strength of an item of information, which from any internal or external source is accessible to the choosing and deciding cortex, is

and sustain our complete attention. In any case, all of the information available to the perceptual side of the PA cycle at any given time will be subject to cortical computation for weighing alternatives; that is, for weighing synaptic strengths, as well as for informing the action sector of the cortex – namely, the prefrontal cortex and lower frontal cortices. That computation in the complex cognitive system of the cortex is not only multivariate but also probabilistic.

By "multivariate" computation I mean the computation of information coming from many sources and of variable strength. By "probabilistic" I mean that the neural computation of multiple variables is based on internal assessments of probabilities, and so is the information passed on to the action sector. It is helpful to view the entire process as one of concurrence and competition, where some variables weigh more than others on an output vector of probability.[12] Some variables are synergistic, whereas others are incompatible. Some items of information may be so strong that they will tip the balance heavily in their favor, in "winner-takes-all" fashion – with veto power over alternatives. Naturally, they will impact with commensurate probability on the choice of action, which can be, for example, a 911 call, a sudden trip after family loss, or a message of congratulation.

---

based on the synaptic strength of the pathway(s) in which that information is stored in the cortex and through which the cortex has access to it. That strength can vary in time and depend on many factors. Among those factors are the following: (a) the intensity and saliency of sensory stimulation, (b) the biological significance of that stimulation, (c) the strength of a drive associated with that information, (d) the synaptic solidity of the cognitive net or cognit representing the information, and (e) the urgency of the reaction that the information may call for from the organism.

[12] The sheer complexity of the computation, and its essentially multivariate character, make the computational modeling of the process prohibitively difficult. Too many imponderable variables make the analysis in the real brain equally difficult. My treatment of the subject with regard to liberty can be productive only in the search for neural principles, not necessarily quantitative algorithms; in any event, the latter can only be nonlinear – and liable to future imponderables. Whatever those principles and applicable algorithms may be, they must conform to Bayesian logic. This is the branch of logic that applies to decision-making and to the inference of probability of future outcome (Jaynes et al., 2003). It uses the knowledge of prior events to predict future events; in this sense it falls within the "enabling" physiological purview of the prefrontal cortex.

Whatever PA cycle is active at any given time, the cortex will treat the external feedback from the effects of the action on the environment in the same manner as other inputs. Thus that feedback will be used to monitor and to inform further action. Every step of the way, corrective measures, changes, even reversals, may result from internal and external feedback on the perceptual side of the cycle. This will maintain the action on course until it reaches its goal.

Freedom has a heart that beats to the tune of our desires, our fears, our biological needs, our family, our beloved, our beliefs, our community, and our nation. That heart is the inner world of emotion. Its neural base is in the lower and middle portions of the brain. Like the substrate of cognition, the substrate of emotion is amply distributed, this one mainly in subcortical regions. It has two major components: the sensing or feeling of emotion, and emotion itself, which, as the etymology of the word indicates, has a "motor" element. The sensing and feeling component resides in the limbic brain, the orbital prefrontal cortex, and the receptors and nerve endings of the autonomic nervous system, scattered throughout the viscera and their ducts. The "e-motional" cerebral substrate resides in the same structures, mainly in their output or "motion" side – that is, their output side – which modulates emotional expression, blood flow to the skin and other organs, and the drives of instinctual (phyletic) origin – sex, flight, feeding, and aggression.

Just as there is a PA cycle for cognition mainly in the cortex, there is a "sensing-emoting cycle" mainly in limbic structures. Curiously, in a similar manner as we have debated causality in the PA cycle, some psychologists of the last century, notably William James, debated causality in the emotional cycle. Their debate included, for example, the discussion about whether we cry because we are sad, or we are sad because we cry. William James (1890) theorized it was the latter. All emotional feelings, he proposed, are generated by the activation of autonomic and visceral effectors in reaction to emotional experiences.[13] In modern

---

[13] Simultaneously and independently, the Danish psychologist Carl Lange did the same (1887). That is why the theory has been named the James–Lange theory of emotion.

times, Damasio (1996) has advanced a germane hypothesis: that the neural sensors ("somatic markers") for emotional response reside in limbic and orbitofrontal locations of the brain. From their activation, emotional feelings would emerge, as well as important neural influences bearing on decision-making.

In my view, the argument about emotional causality is as moot as the argument about cognitive causality. In neither the cognitive PA cycle nor the emotional PA cycle is there a true constant origin: Sensing or acting may begin on one side or the other of the cycle. The emotional cycle, however, is faster because in its lowest levels it controls homeostasis, the state of physiological near-equilibrium of the internal milieu, where action-reaction, as well as feedback, is immediate. The hypothalamus is there largely in control.

At higher levels of emotional control, however, the two cycles intersect each other. The interaction occurs most clearly in the prefrontal cortex, between the orbital and lateral portions of this cortex. Emotional outputs, through the orbital cortex, have access to the PA cycle at the level of the lateral cortex, which they modulate; and vice versa, outputs from the latter modulate the emotional cycle. In other words, emotion is in both loops. The interaction between both would actually translate into reciprocal neural influences at the root of the interplay of emotion with reason in the PA cycle. Figure 4.2 depicts cortical and subcortical inputs and outputs of the PA cycle, some of them connecting the cognitive to the emotional cycle. This connectivity has profound implications for social behavior.

Is there an instinct for liberty? It is difficult to argue for it in the strict sense of the word "instinct," which implies an innate, genetically transmitted drive of the organism. It is easier to argue, however, for a deep-seated drive for independence. Both the independence of free action and the independence of the avoidance of harm or oppression favor a stable and predictable environment or territory. Liberty thrives best in that environment. Therefore, we should reflect on the neural implications of the close relationship between liberty and territory.

Humans, like animals of many other species, are intensely territorial (Ardrey, 1966; Lorenz, 1963). Like them, humans

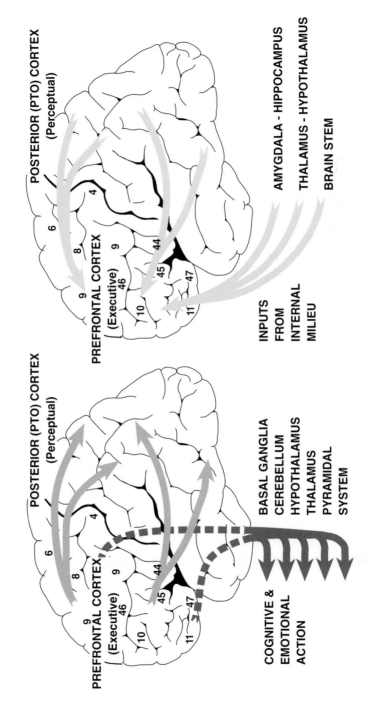

Figure 4.2 Inputs (*blue*) and outputs (*pink, red*) of the prefrontal cortex at the top of the PA cycle.

choose, demarcate, and defend their territory, often with tenac-
ity. Some humans make acquiring living territory their major
endeavor in life. Naturally, our home is our elementary living
territory. But even the homeless are territorial, as they compete
for public space. The protection of one's territory can lead to all
kinds of conflicts, from disputes between neighbors to the legal
contest of the public appropriation of land. Nations go to war to
defend their borders or to expand their territory. Throughout
history, bodies of water and high mountains have been used as
natural defenses of territory. When these proved insufficient,
walls and castles were erected.

Liberty and territory go hand in hand. We defend both of
them keenly, sometimes with passion. The reasons why the two
are so closely related and why we defend them with such fervor
are quite apparent when they are considered in anthropological
terms, at the individual level as well as at the societal level. They
become obvious when considered in the light of our neural model
of cognition.

Indeed, a stable living territory is a precondition for max-
imum freedom of the cortex to select information and to act on it.
Here I use the term "living territory" in the broadest existential
terms, to include home, workplace, marketplace, and the other
human beings with whom we live, work, or do business; I include
them all as integral part of our living environment. It is not too
much of a stretch to include our body as a part of that living
environment for freedom and for expressing ourselves;[14] in fact,
it is the part of that environment that we protect above all others.
Liberty thrives when our cortex deals with a world that is thoroughly familiar, predictable, and trustworthy. "Familiarity," a
word that I use here to denote both intimacy and dependable
knowledge, is necessary for the cortex to utilize most freely its
fund of knowledge. When our environment becomes strange,
unpredictable, or untrustworthy, our liberty is threatened,

---

[14] The members of most string quartets play sitting down. Once, Arnold
Steinhardt, first violin of the Guarneri Quartet, told me that they did it mainly
in deference to the cellist. Then, pointing to his heart, he confided that he
preferred to play standing, as he did as a soloist, because the additional bodily
movement gave him more freedom of emotional expression.

because our pre-established cognits fail to match that environment. Uncertainty about "existential" space becomes a constraint
to liberty for as long as it persists. Only with time, by test and
retest, can the new home, the new boss, or the new broker be
admitted into our living territory. With increasing trust, our
liberty grows as that territory becomes stable and predictable.

Our cortex must be free not only to move in a familiar
territory but also to protect it from intrusion. The "territorial
imperative" includes the defense of our living territory. That
too protects our freedom, as the intruder, whether animate or
inanimate, also curtails our freedom to act in a familiar, unencumbered environment. Hence, if necessary, the PA cycle, which
is normally attuned to that environment, must gear itself to
defend it from the intruder. That requires mobilizing cognitive
resources either to expel the intruder or to adjust to it, again by
test and retest with repeated feedback along the way.

None of this contradicts the incontrovertible fact that freedom can also thrive by expansion of the known territory, especially if the expansion takes place into the unknown. In effect, the
expansion of that territory is at the foundation of scientific discovery and the exploration of nature. But note that both entail the
expansion of established knowledge by doing precisely what perception does all the time unconsciously: to prove and refute
assumptions – that is, old and new cognits. Furthermore, unless
progress and exploration require a radical paradigm shift, they
advance along established parameters. In any case, no one can
dispute the intellectual or physical territoriality of the scientist or
the explorer. He stakes and defends his territory with the same
passion with which we all stake and defend our home, our family,
and our possessions. I am arguing that in every case, by asserting
our territory, we assert our liberty and that of those we love.
Basically, we do it – within the PA cycle – by protecting and/or
enhancing our cognitive resources, the vast universe of cognitive
cortical networks that we have accumulated in the course of our
life. We do it, as I reason in the next chapter, by providing both
knowledge and freedom with a future perspective.

The linkage of liberty with territoriality can be traced
through the history of mankind. It permeates the history of

nations, and is one of the foundations of patriotism. Statesmen of all kinds have exploited the human longing for liberty to rationalize territorial defense or expansion. Unfortunately, sometimes one people's liberty is another people's bondage. Almost inevitably, the expansion of the living territory of a nation (*Lebensraum*) has led to the invasion of another. In some instances the territory of an entire nation (e.g., Poland in World War II) has shifted or shrunk geographically as a result of the territorial ambitions of flanking totalitarian empires. Demagogic tyrants, defending a populist philosophy of one kind or another, have led nations to enormous territorial travesties and human tragedy, often under the pretense of protecting both territory and liberty. It is not difficult to envisage the "collective cortex" of a people manipulated by demagoguery, which is the language of emotion, into a giant PA cycle that promotes its liberty by the oppression or enslavement of another people.

In any event, there is no denying that the protection of societal liberty and territory is necessary to protect the liberty of the individual. Democracy is actually founded on a collective PA cycle that, for the liberty of all, runs through the people, its legislators, and the ballot box.

FREEDOM IN THE CYCLE

We all experience situations in which we have little or no choice. Indeed, in such situations, we may be obliged to take the one and the only option, which may be life-saving. But, barring total servitude or imminent danger, most of the time in civilized society we are and feel free to choose between alternatives. To be sure, there are limits to our freedom, not the least the need to make responsible choices. Nonetheless, our liberty, however relative, is very real. The question is, who are our free selves? It has been my contention on this point that our free self is our cerebral cortex. Now, after our discussion of the PA cycle, we must refine that definition.

Ortega y Gasset (1961) claims that we are inextricably bound to the world in which we live. In his book *Meditations on Don Quixote*, he makes the point that we are children of our time and of our culture ("I am myself and my circumstance"); that our choices are to a large extent determined by what surrounds us or, more precisely, by our intimate communion with our world and with the world of others.[15] The determinism of the mind and its myriad expressions dissolves in the uncertainties, variability, and continuous reciprocity of the PA cycle at the core of that communion.

Here, to transpose Ortega's reasoning to the brain, the cortex cannot be dissociated from its milieu, internal and external. The choices that our cortex makes are completely embedded in the PA cycle, and can impinge on any of its parts. In that manner, consciously or unconsciously, we choose our guiding memories and principles, our venue and means of expression, our friends and mates, our goals and rewards. In this scenario we do not need the utilitarian view of an autonomous and controlling "substance" somewhere in or out of the brain, a center of free will making plans, decisions, or choices for us. What we possess to do those things is a cerebral cortex with enormous resources within itself, almost always ready and able to interact with its environment for benefits that the organism can share with that environment. Here, in a harmonious communion with nature and "the other," there should be ideally no place for egotism, envy, or greed. But this is not an ideal world, and these are moral matters that we will have to deal with, in the context of the brain, in another chapter (Chapter 7).

At the initiation of behavior toward a goal, as in the course of it, stimuli from the internal and external environment are processed – serially or in parallel – through the cognitive stages of the posterior cortex, which contain perceptual knowledge and memory in their networks. The output from each processing stage is sent further up for continued cognitive processing, and at some point to the executive hierarchy for the processing of appropriate action. That action causes changes in the environment, which generate new sensory input, which in turn will be

---

[15] Marías, 1970. In the same book, as if envisioning the role of the prefrontal cortex in that relationship, Ortega in 1914 noted that "the future that awaits us is not any future, it is *our* future" (my emphasis).

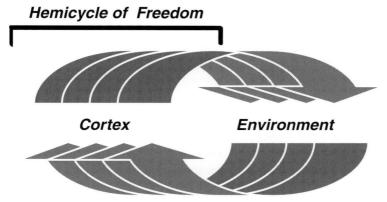

Figure 4.3 The hemicycle of freedom. Choices are made in the cortical compartment (bracketed) of the PA cycle. In the perceptual cortex (blue), the choices are between alternatives of experiential information (memory and knowledge). In the executive cortex (red), the choices are between alternatives of action.

processed to inform further action. And so on until the attainment of the goal or objective of the behavior. At each stage of processing there is feedback (counterclockwise arrows in Figure 4.1) to serve corrective control and future processing. Where is liberty in that scheme of things?

A PA cycle can start anywhere: in the internal or external environment, in the posterior – perceptual – region of the cortex, or in its frontal – action – region. Liberty, that is, the capacity of our cortex to make choices between alternatives, has its seat in both regions, posterior and frontal, because in them is where the perceptual and executive choices are made by the cortex itself at the start and on every turn of the cycle. Consequently, it is justifiable to name the aggregate of both cortices the *hemicycle of freedom* (Figure 4.3).

If the behavior is automatic or well rehearsed, the processing can be shunted to lower levels of the nervous system and need not encumber the higher cortex. If the behavior is, however, novel and complex, with ambiguities or uncertainties, then the higher association cortex (PTO and prefrontal cortex) must engage in the processing. This cortex becomes essential when the behavior is discontinuous, and working memory is required to integrate the behavior across time gaps. Recurrent connections between prefrontal and posterior cortex, at the top of the cycle, mediate the reverberation of their networks to retain working memory online, ready for use (Fuster, 2008; Fuster and Bressler, 2012).

Complex, goal-directed behavior can mobilize several PA cycles in the cortex, either simultaneously or sequentially, as that behavior may contain a number of intermediate goals. Further, some behaviors may be interrupted for long periods of days, weeks, or longer. Under such circumstances, in the pursuit of the ultimate goal, the relevant cognits may have to be reactivated after longer periods than those ordinarily bridged by working memory in normal behavior.

Clearly, to repeat, if action can originate anywhere in the cycle, there is no need in the brain for such an entity as the initiating "center of will" or the "central executive." An environmental event or the activation of the perceptual or executive sectors of cortex by any of their inputs will suffice to unleash a cycle or chain of cycles in the cortex. The critical input may come from within, in the form of an activated perceptual or executive cognit, a biological drive, or a sudden emotion.

The skeptic will say that we are not really free, for we are chained to the cycle and incapable of doing anything "by our own accord." I will reply with a question: who are "we" but our brain, covered by a mantle of knowledge and driven by countless motives, from the biological to the sublime? As such, our brain is free to choose and to act, naturally within the constraints of the nervous system itself and the world in which we live. Our choices and actions, whether conscious or not, are informed by much more knowledge than we consciously realize. In the absence of illness or compulsion, our cortex selects at every instant between myriad options. Mostly out of awareness, it estimates priorities and probabilities. I say "estimates" rather than "computes," for any computation in that context must be based on estimates of probability.

In any case, we cannot detach liberty from the consortium of the brain and its environment, including in that environment the internal milieu. We are free inasmuch as the PA cycle, which joins us to the environment, can lead us by choice between alternatives to high probabilities of success and low probabilities of failure. At every step of the cycle, in a continuous process of choice and evaluation, "a winner takes all," and this continues until the goal is reached, which may just be a small goal on the way to a larger one.

Here I wish to re-emphasize a general point on the neurobiology of liberty that is perhaps the most important point in this book. Liberty – that is, our freedom to choose, to think, to plan, to decide, to do, to undo, or not to do – rests exclusively on the engagement of our cerebral cortex in the PA cycle. Our exercise of freedom does not result from the agency of a conscious ego, however construed, or from a mysterious brain center of free will. Conscious awareness, such as that invariably accompanying deliberation, logical reasoning, and hard decision, is an epiphenomenon of highly activated cortex engaged in the PA cycle.

Treating consciousness and deliberate thinking as epiphenomena of cortical activity is hard to accept by anyone entertaining dualistic notions of the mind. It seems so much like putting the cart before the horse! Yet it is perfectly defensible if we identify the cortex with the mind and place it at the summit of the PA cycle. The cortex contains all the data, wisdom, and values that it needs to mediate successfully goal-directed behavior, language, and reasoning. All it needs for deliberate thinking before taking a decision is the internal cognitive environment, the "circumstance" of Ortega, updated if necessary by the senses.

There are, however, critical differences in the way the cerebral cortex deploys its cognitive resources, including thinking, depending on where and when the PA cycle is mobilized for a decision. If the cycle is mobilized by an external event, especially if unexpected, the cortex often engages in what Kahneman (2011) calls system-1 thinking, characterized by intuition, emotionality, and superficial reasoning. Obviously, in such cases, the dominant cognits with access to the cortical PA cycle come from the unconscious or the emotional cycle. Fear, prejudice, and hasty reasoning then easily take the upper hand. By contrast, system-2 thinking is characterized by orderly inductive and deductive logic. The neocortical cognits then intervene heavily in the PA cycle, and the executive functions of the lateral prefrontal cortex take the upper hand. That does not mean that this cortex is inaccessible to intuitive or emotional bias. In fact, this bias, more or less subtly, may lead to errors of judgment even under the cover of system 2. But in favorable conditions – that is, in the skilled, level-headed, and educated individual – system 2 prevails and system 1 is by and large under inhibitory control from the orbital prefrontal cortex.

In closing this section, I should like to reiterate its main points. Where is liberty in the PA cycle? The answer is, everywhere. Just as the cortical constituents of the cycle organize themselves in the circular interactions of the organism with its environment, the exercise of free action organizes itself within the cognits that constitute the cortical components of the cycle. Thus the "top-down" causation of the action (Juarrero, 1999; Murphy and Brown, 2007; Noë, 2004) will be complex, and will include executive networks (cognits) of the frontal lobe. But those networks are part of the cycle, and therefore under the influences of other cortical and subcortical sources.

Consequently, the "central executive," as well as the hypothetical centers of volition, free will, or conation, disappear into a distributed conglomerate of potential causes of action that includes the environment and practically any part of the brain. This does not make us less free, but more, inasmuch as it distributes the causes of action into myriad sources, including the imponderables of the environment, the peculiarities of our personal history, and the idiosyncrasies of our character. Many of those sources will offer choices to the cortex, but others will not.

THE REWARDS OF FREEDOM

The goal of each PA cycle is to attain reward. Here reward must be broadly understood to include the satisfaction of a biological need, pleasure, or the acquisition of something of value, in whatever manner measurable. Reward may also be the attainment of a minor goal on the way to a major goal; that is, a minor goal through a small cycle on a short time scale toward a major goal through a larger cycle on a longer time scale. Thus there are goals within goals, rewards within rewards, and cycles within cycles. In the cerebral cortex, the cycles can be processed in series, one cycle at a time, as well as in parallel, several cycles at a time through parallel neural circuits.

Liberty implies the ability of the organism to choose and carry out PA cycles to fruition. Almost all institutions that confer liberty, like public education, the protection of civil rights, public health, and free markets, are intended to promote peace, hope, and rewarding personal cycles. The experience of liberty is in itself rewarding, and also rewarding are the consequences of its exercise in both private and public life. Liberty enables the satisfaction of biological needs, successful child rearing, scientific and artistic accomplishment, commendable public service, excellence in sports, acquisition of wealth, philanthropy, practice of a liberal profession, and many other forms of rewarding activity. Their list is practically endless, especially if we take cultural variation into account.[16]

Is there a neuroscience of reward? There is indeed, though it is still beset by many unknowns. More than 50 years ago the psychologist James Olds discovered a curious phenomenon (Olds and Milner, 1954): When rats were free to stimulate certain locations of their own brain through implanted electrodes – by manually closing a switch – they did so for hours on end, to the point of exhaustion and even death. Apparently, the experience was extremely rewarding for the animals. A wide region sensitive to self-stimulation ("pleasure center") was thus identified at the base of the cerebrum, comprising parts of the hypothalamus, the brainstem, and the limbic system.

Subsequently, neuropharmacological studies led to the discovery that the pleasure center or region was exceptionally rich in certain chemicals of brainstem origin involved in modulating neurotransmission, notably dopamine (Siegel *et al.*, 1999). There are several types of dopamine transmitters and receptors. Those that are implicated in pleasure concentrate in cells, fibers, and connections that are distributed through parts of the upper

---

[16] Nonetheless, the psychologist Steven Reiss (2000), based on a study of more than 6,000 people, concludes that all human behavior is driven by 16 basic desires, with variable nuances and intensities between subjects: Acceptance, Curiosity, Eating, Family, Honor, Idealism, Independence, Order, Physical activity, Power, Romance, Saving, Social contact, Status, Tranquility, and Vengeance.

brainstem, limbic formations, and orbital prefrontal cortex. In the monkey, neurons within that system, especially in the orbital cortex, are markedly excited by the animal's access to food reward. Some of the neurons differentiate between foods and respond to them in proportion to the concentration or quantity in which they are available. On the whole, the system appears dedicated to the evaluation of external rewards – as well as aversive agents. The amygdala is part of that system. In primates, including the human, certain nuclei of that limbic structure are implicated in the emotional evaluation – appetitive or aversive – of external sensory stimuli.[17]

Within that reward system, there is a subsystem of centrally located brainstem structures that detect or signal reward or related aspects of it and are especially rich in dopamine terminals and receptors. Those regions form the *mesolimbic system*, which collects dopaminergic influences from the brainstem and elsewhere, and projects them forwards to the cortex (Berridge, 2007; Siegel, 1999). That mesolimbic system of dopamine neurons and connections funnels into the prefrontal cortex, and from there fans into widespread cortical regions, a wealth of nervous signals related to pleasure, evaluation of rewards, incentives, emotional significance of sensory stimuli, outcome of choices, and risk assessment; in sum, all signals related to reward in one way or another come into the medial and orbital prefrontal cortex. Because of the unifying anatomical convergence into it, that brain-core subsystem is appropriately named the "reward axis" (Figure 4.4). The system, as a whole, is an integral component of the emotional PA cycle.

The orbital prefrontal cortex clearly occupies a central position in the reward system. Its apparent role in the evaluation of reward is related to its functions in the control of emotion and instinctual impulses. To that end, inhibitory control from the orbitofrontal cortex falls upon limbic structures, the basal ganglia, and the hypothalamus (Ghashghaei and Barbas, 2002; Roberts *et al.*, 1992).

---

[17] For example, when a monkey or a human subject is presented with images of faces exhibiting emotions, neurons can be identified in the amygdala that respond to the faces in accord with the emotion they express (Gothard *et al.*, 2007; Rutishauser *et al.*, 2011).

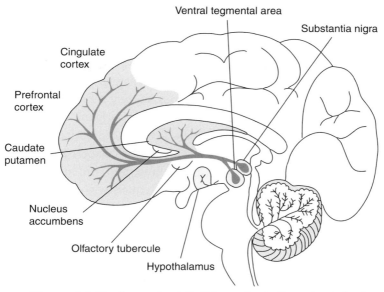

Figure 4.4 The "reward axis" of dopamine in the primate brain.

The cortical PA cycle collects through the orbital cortex a wealth of emotional and visceral inputs from the limbic brain and autonomic receptors (the "somatic markers" of Damasio, 1996). Those inputs steer the cycle to the pursuit of basic emotional goals in broad accord with homeostasis. Here we can include social goals, inasmuch as they protect a form of collective societal homeostasis or adaptation.

Accordingly, the pathology of the orbital prefrontal cortex leads to self-centered pleasure-seeking behavior and poor social adaptation, in fact often to the blatant flaunting of social norms (Chapter 7). The behavior of the patient with orbitofrontal pathology is commonly characterized by elevated mood, selfishness, impulsivity, and proneness to risk, sometimes leading to crime. By and large that behavior appears disinhibited, taking often the form of hyperactivity, eroticism, hyperphagia (excessive eating), and total absence of ethical judgment. At one time or another, these have been grounds for assuming that the orbital prefrontal cortex is the seat of moral sense. The evidence for this inference is inconclusive, however.

Because the orbitofrontal syndrome is often accompanied by disinhibition, hyperactivity, and disorders of attention, it has been suspected that some hyperactive children with attention disorders suffer from a laggard maturation of the orbital prefrontal cortex (Barkley, 1997; Fuster, 2008). This view is supported by the evidence that many such children, as they get older, outgrow their disorderly behavior. Presumably this happens as their prefrontal cortex matures, as it does, slowly, through adolescence and until the end of the third decade of life (Chapter 2).

To sum up, impulsivity, risk-taking, and difficulty in postponing gratification are features that frequently go hand in hand in the orbitofrontal syndrome and are common in individuals with psychopathic, and in some cases delinquent, behavior. Many such individuals are prone to gambling, which is a form of addiction to risk-taking for fast, easy reward. Others, in the field of finances, do nearly the same, alas often with somebody else's money.

Drug addiction is the clearest example of freedom mindlessly exercised to its own demise. For drug addiction is equivalent to adding a new drive to the organism, as compelling as any other, and more destructive than all. As dependency increases in the addict, the PA cycles guiding normal behavior drop out. At the same time the cycle of addiction to the drug restricts itself ever more tightly in drug-seeking behavior, to the exclusion of all others. That behavior becomes associated with concomitant sensory stimuli in the creation of new cognits, which include the drug in them. Thus by the mechanism of associative retrieval, those stimuli by themselves trigger irresistible drug-seeking behavior: a pathological PA cycle driven by positive feedback.

Today we know a host of brain structures whose activity is deranged by drug abuse (Everitt and Robbins, 2005). Those structures are practically identical to those that lead to self-stimulation; in other words, they are structures that are part of the presumptive "pleasure center" – that is, the "reward axis" and other structures connected with it. Almost invariably, they include the orbital prefrontal cortex. Almost invariably also, the addictive drug – whatever it is, from alcohol to cocaine – leads to increased concentration of dopamine in those structures, either directly or through the intermediate overproduction of other neurotransmitters that stimulate dopamine production. Further, temporary withdrawal from the drug leads to dopamine deficit, which in turn leads to uncontrollable craving to replenish it. That, in turn, in the presence of disinhibition from a sick orbital prefrontal cortex, leads frequently to crime in order to satisfy the urge. It is an all-consuming PA cycle that heavily restricts the freedom of the patient and, to some degree, restricts that of society around him. Without treatment, it is extraordinarily difficult to break that vicious PA cycle.

NEUROECONOMICS: MONEY

Reward and punishment, value, risk-taking, immediate versus delayed satisfaction: these are some of the critical variables of behavior that the modern science of neuroeconomics relates to brain function. Basically, this science attempts to treat those variables parametrically – that is, by methodical measurement and manipulation. A common objective is to compute their changes as a function of alterations in neural structures such as the orbital prefrontal cortex. Certain behavioral tests, such as the Iowa Gambling Task, have been devised to assess how a subject balances risk with prospective success.[18] Subjects with an injured or deficient orbital cortex, who are as a general rule disinhibited and prone to risk-taking, prefer a quick reward, at high risk of losing it, above a delayed, more probable, and larger reward. This tendency, reminiscent of the preference for investing in stocks over bonds, leads us to the discussion of a universally valued reward: money.

Money buys a measure of liberty, and liberty a measure of money. The value of money lies in its acquisitive power as a means of exchange. Therein too lies its potential for enhancing choice and security. In our active, productive life, many of the PA

---

[18] A typical test in a gambling task is performed by requesting the subject to make choices of cards from four decks. The drawing of a card from two of the decks implies potentially large gain, but also large loss, while the drawing from the other two decks implies the converse – small gain but also small loss (Bechara *et al.*, 2000).

cycles we engage in are geared to make money in addition to obtaining satisfaction from business or profession; money in the form of salary, compensation, or return on investment. Every cycle leading to expected monetary reward is informed by life experience, education, and consultation with experts and peers; in other words, it is informed by our cognitive and emotional background as well as those persons who have entered that background. It is also informed by public variables affecting the marketplace, such as inflation, taxation, and currency or commodity prices.

In the public domain of Western civilization there are two polar philosophies with regard to the money–liberty relationship. One is the libertarian philosophy, based on the idea that money and private property are connatural with individual liberty and are to be protected for the good of all, because private incentive is believed to be the best source of common good. Government and taxation ought to be minimal.

The other is the social-welfare philosophy, which stipulates that, whereas individual liberty may be the best source of economic prosperity, it cannot and should not be protected at the expense of the needs of society. If it is, the public interest usually suffers from the greed and neglect of a few. Taxation ought to be progressive, so as, at the very least, to provide freedom from want to the most.

Conflicts between those two philosophies, in essence between private and societal economic freedoms, are a common feature of the public debate in all democracies, and in America since the time of the disputes between Thomas Jefferson and Alexander Hamilton.[19] In modern America, there has gradually developed a mutual accommodation of the two economic philosophies. Still, it is interesting to note how the word "liberal" has come to have a radically different meaning for the followers of one philosophy as opposed to the other.

---

[19] The debate extended to the relative powers of the federal government versus that of the states, with Hamilton's federalists favoring the former and Jefferson's antifederalists favoring states' rights (*The Annals of America*, 1886–8 [*Encyclopaedia Britannica*, vol. III], ed. M. J. Adler, University of Chicago Press, 1968, pp. 53–213).

The intensity of the public debate on issues of public versus private money increases in times of economic crisis. Conflicts in this area become especially acute if they do not so much involve money from and for production of goods as money from and for financing the acquisition or possession of non-productive assets, such as real estate or gold. In that case, markets become shaky and overreactive, their collective PA cycles being driven by positive feedbacks from fear and anxiety. More fundamentally, in any economic crisis, the most pernicious casualty is not the possession of money for whatever purpose, but one of the most precious promoters of social progress – indeed the most important public commodity – trust. The issue is dealt with at length later, in Chapter 7, but because of its relevance to money, I wish to comment briefly on it here.

Trust is our reliance on somebody else to safeguard our interests. It begins with the infant's trust in the mother, which has unquestionable evolutionary roots. Trust is the pillar of responsibility, which is the unalienable complement of liberty. The success of any human association toward the pursuit of any collective reward relies heavily on mutual trust. This is true in any social group, from the family to the temple, to the sports team, to the business firm, to the scientific community, to our elected representatives. Trust binds common interests and expectations. Trust supports all common values, including the value of the currency. Without trust, no business runs smoothly and no rewarding human relation is sustainable. Most deleterious to the progress of a nation is politicians' violation of the public trust.

If public trust has been firmly established, both socio-economic philosophies – liberal capitalism and social-welfare democracy – become valuable in pursuit of the common good. But the two must be appropriately balanced for liberty and justice to prevail. The failure to achieve that balance leads to conflict between private and public liberties. The conflict becomes most apparent when there are asynchronies between PA cycles. Personal choices and decisions cannot be easily adjusted to the vicissitudes of economic cycles. Private long-term decisions, such as those concerning career, family, education, research projects, or business ventures, cannot be made against an unpredictable economic future. In a word, the personal PA cycle cannot be always adjusted to the economic cycle or to the governmental budget cycle – let alone the election cycle! Yet the liberty to plan one's future is a hallmark of human evolution, like language. Both rely on the predictive properties of the prefrontal cortex. We shall deal with them in the next two chapters.

Here, next, we deal with a human value that very much bears on our freedom and whose absence very much curtails that freedom: the ability to delay gratification. The opposite of that ability is the depreciation of a reward because we have to wait for it. The amount of that depreciation is called *delay discount*. Thus, delay discount is the loss in the value or utility of a reward if the latter is to take place in the future (Ainslie, 2001). As we will see in Chapter 7, the excessive delay discount of the value of expected monetary reward is ruinous to private as well as public economy, especially when that discount becomes part of the culture.

The animal pursues its prey, food, or mate by the most direct route in the shortest possible time. To be sure, there are detours and delays in the way for the marauding fox, the foraging ant, and the migrating bird, but those are imposed by physical obstacles or by forces of nature. To satisfy a basic drive, rarely will the animal choose other than the strategy that it has found most expedient. Even Sultan the ape, after learning how to reach a high-hanging banana, would not deviate from his problem-solving strategy, which was to stack wooden boxes and climb on them to reach the banana (Köhler, 1925).

Given alternatives, animals will choose the most rewarding, though the choice may be difficult and unpredictable when the objects to choose from have more than one rewarding attribute: quantity and quality, for example. To a monkey, one drop of grape juice may be more rewarding than two – but not four – of apple juice. The most rewarding combination of attributes confers on an object its highest value or utility, and with it its highest eligibility.

The young child, not unlike the animal, will choose the object with the highest *immediate* value, whatever the combination of attributes it may possess. Indeed, there is one attribute of a reward that clearly separates the choice of the human adult from that of the animal and the child: the time of occurrence of that reward. Neither the animal nor the child can easily wait for it. By contrast, the human adult is willing to wait if the future reward in one way or another is worth that wait.

In general, everybody expects timely gain from any decision. However, when risk and uncertainty are considered with regard to the future potential gains and losses from that decision, the so-called intertemporal choice becomes especially critical and subject to delay discount. At the time of decision, that value or utility is discounted in the measure of the length of time to elapse before the expected attainment of the reward.[20]

In most cases, however, the value of a given reward is subject to multiple imponderables that range widely, from physiological variables, such as blood-glucose level, to moral principles. In other words, the ultimate utility of an expected reward depends on factors so diverse and personal as to defy any algorithmic formulation. Nevertheless, whatever factors are at play in any decision on a future reward, delay discount is one of them, and it has an important influence on the PA cycle that leads to that reward.

Our life is a succession of interleaved PA cycles hierarchically and temporally organized in the pursuit of a hierarchy of goals. Low goals serve higher goals, whereas all of them are valued in proportion to their hierarchical level and the time to reach them. Accordingly, the value of each cycle rests on how well it suits the higher one it serves in the hierarchy. Because the higher and later goals carry the most delay discount, they demand from the agent greater patience and constancy than the lower and shorter ones. In general, it is reasonable to assume that the utility of a goal tends to counteract its delay discount. Thus, for example, the value of obtaining a professional license counteracts the delay discount of all the PA cycles leading to it. At a personal level, what makes the wait worth it is the value of the ultimate goal of the overarching cycle, whatever that is.

Conversely, the agent's lack of motivation to pursue a given subordinate goal will make its PA cycle succumb to a heavy delay

---

[20] That discount obeys a mathematical behavioral model based on the demonstrable fact that humans discount the value of a future reward by a factor that increases with the length of the time to get it and decreases with the value or utility of the expected reward.

discount, to the detriment of the higher cycle that one serves. For example, the repeated failure to show up for work on time will eventually jeopardize the higher cycle of one's job, which is geared to obtain financial compensation in the form of salary at the end of every month.

Because of its role in decision-making, planning, prioritizing executive objectives, and controlling impulsivity, it is reasonable to assume that the cortex of the frontal lobe plays a critical role in countering delay discount. The evidence in this respect, however, is still inconclusive. Two careful studies of frontal lesion failed to show unambiguous differences between patients and normal subjects in this respect (Fellows and Farah, 2005; Floden *et al.*, 2008). Both studies, however, highlight the "temporal myopia" and the impulsivity of the frontal patient.[21]

Delay discount is maximal in the PA cycles that are aimed at goals in the distant future, such as saving enough money for retirement, for covering the cost of future illness, or for bestowing an inheritance on one's children. Clearly, the reason why delay discount is so high in these cases is because they are related to events that are unwelcome or surrounded by uncertainty – old age, illness, and death. In modern society, saving in general has fallen victim to short-term planning, delay discount, and the incapacity to postpone gratification, whereby worthy long-term goals suffer. Those trends are promoted by the financial industry and the ever-higher reliance on government to satisfy our future needs and to replace our personal responsibilities (Chapter 7). Consumer society has regressed to financial immaturity and short-term decisions aided by the welfare state with its "entitlements." A culture of dependency on them has accelerated the universal appropriation of subsidies that were formerly designed to assist only the poor and the disabled, thus stretching to the limits – and surpassing – the ability of governments to cover their cost.[22] Consequently, the advertising

---

[21] The failure to show delay-discount differences between patients and normal subjects may have been due, in both studies, to the nature of the delay-discounting task utilized, which had a limited temporal scope and was based on limited potential choices.

[22] Chancellor Otto von Bismarck in Germany (1889) and President Franklin Delano Roosevelt in the United States (1930s) were the champions of the

and financial industries – together with the empty promises of politicians – have conspired to increase everybody's delay discount and temporal myopia.

In a very real sense, delay discount and short-term thinking rob the liberty of the modern citizen to plan for his future. The traditional value of saving for security is sabotaged by inflation and low interest rates, and it is replaced by questionable official assurances and insurances. All of that imposes a severe tax on choices for the future. By essentially "blinding" the prefrontal cortex, it impacts adversely on the freedom of the individual to choose an education, a career, and a stable future. In broader terms, it obliterates the "memory of the future," the subject of the next chapter, at the root of all wise decisions, reasonable plans, and valued creations.

CONCLUSIONS

The perception/action (PA) cycle is the circular flow of information that runs through the cerebral cortex and the environment in goal-directed behavior, reasoning, and language. It is essentially a cybernetic mechanism of self-control in all goal-

---

welfare state, which in both countries was originally intended to assist disabled workers in illness or old age. England and other European countries followed suit by adopting variants of the system. Everywhere, the middle classes eventually became dependent on it. Today, under demographic and political pressures, the system has become unmanageable in several countries. With the increase of aging and nonproductive populations, higher taxation and devaluation of the currency (the proverbial tools of governments in debt) are no longer sufficient to alleviate enormous state deficits. A prime example of how the financial industry, with the help of government, has abused the capacity to delay gratification by the emotionally immature and socioeconomically weak, is the emergence of hybrid (private-public) institutions such as Freddie Mac and Fanny Mae. These two institutions, officially intended to facilitate home ownership – with easy credit and low down payments – have perversely been operated by misguided policies that link private benefit to public debt. The expansion of their practices to the entire financial industry has had the effect of placing the entire economy of America at risk and perilously beyond the fix by governmental monetary policy. The easy and reckless credit, the capitalization of home equity, and the absence of regulation led to the inevitable result of an inflationary bubble of home prices, the dissociation of wages from equity, and the failure of politicians of all stripes who hide their impotence behind demagoguery and vacuous laments.

directed action sequences. This all-pervasive cycle is the ultimate and highest evolutionary development of the biological mechanisms, based in the brainstem, which adapt the organism to its environment.

In the human, the PA cycle is not only adaptive but also preadaptive, in that it allows the subject to prepare for future events and to shape such events in his physical and social environments. The preadaptation of the subject is largely achieved by the prefrontal cortex, whose executive functions at the summit of the PA cycle make that cycle not only predictive but also proactive. In order to achieve preadaptation, the prefrontal cortex receives influences from the external environment through the senses, from memory (perceptual and executive cognits in the cortex), and from the emotional structures of the brain (limbic system).

A major component of freedom, in neural terms, is the capacity of the cerebral cortex to make choices of perceptual and executive information and to feed those choices into the PA cycle. For this reason, the two cortical sectors of the PA cycle, perceptual and executive, can be legitimately construed as forming together the "hemicycle of liberty." The objective of a PA cycle is to obtain a reward, which may be simply the fulfillment of that cycle as a step to a larger and higher cycle. All PA cycles and rewards are subject to delay discount – that is, the depreciation of a future reward as a function of the length of time to obtain it. Rewards in the distant future, such as savings for retirement and future health, carry the largest discounts, thus imposing potential constraints on our freedom and on the public treasury.

5

Memory of the future

I dream my painting and then paint my dream.

Vincent van Gogh

Life can only be understood backwards, but it must be lived forwards.

Søren Kierkegaard

Once, the late David Ingvar sent me an article with the title of this chapter for an issue of *Human Neurobiology*, which I was editing; the article was to be devoted to the prefrontal cortex. The flanking quotation marks barely mollified the brashness of the oxymoron. It took me some time to accept the title – and the article (Ingvar, 1985). Now, after more than two decades, I appreciate the profound wisdom of that expression, for it characterizes the most essential feature of the functions of the human prefrontal cortex: their future dimension. At the same time the expression alludes to the fact that the product of those functions consists of past memory transformed by imagination and projected to the future. Ingvar was a pioneer of functional neuroimaging in the human brain, one of the first to discover the activation of the prefrontal cortex in the mental planning of movements and language. Indeed, what he was trying to convey with his peculiar expression was the evidence that the prefrontal cortex is activated by the internal representation of prospective action. Surely, since the action was yet to occur, that representation could hardly be called "memory." However, the insight of "future memory" becomes glaring when we consider that in our mind there is no planned or future action without the memory, by association, of similar actions in the past, by us or by others. Planning and decision-making consist in recreating old actions in new fashion.

Future action thus results from nothing other than the rearrangement of executive cognits, which pre-exist in the prefrontal cortex and which hold associations with perceptual memory in the posterior cortex. In essence, devising future actions is devising new PA cycles with old cognits. By doing this, the prefrontal cortex makes of the human brain a predictive organ, predictive of its own actions and of their consequences. Insofar as the ability to decide, to plan, and to create new PA cycles is at the core of choosing between alternative courses of action, the prefrontal cortex makes the human brain free to act. This is the topic of this chapter. In the next, we will consider how the liberty to decide, to plan, and to create applies to the organization of language, the most essentially human of the cognitive functions of the prefrontal cortex.

DECISION-MAKING

The freedom to make decisions is the most cherished and the most consequential of all liberties. By making up our mind to do something, we shape our future, and at times that of others. Like planning and creativity, of which it is an essential part, deciding to take action is projecting ourselves into that future. But taken at face value, this common-sense view of decision-making obscures the not so obvious truth that the future is made of the past, and that every decision, like every plan and every creative achievement, has a history behind it. Only by analyzing the antecedents of decision can we understand the genesis of executive action, as well as the role of the brain in it.

The verb "decide" comes from the Latin *decidere*, which means literally "to cut off." In this sense, to decide is to conclude, to terminate – a debate, for example – and to initiate an action, whatever that action may be. In every case, deciding is bringing closure to competing or compatible demands from the brain or from the internal or external environment. Regardless of the degree of intentionality behind it, each decision has a history and never comes completely "out of the blue." The decision may be triggered by a stimulus, a signal, a word, or a sudden event, but it is "informed" by experience, by memory of some sort, even if that memory is purely biological ("phyletic") in the form of a basic drive, such as hunger, sex, or the need to survive.

Biological drives are the most peremptory inputs to the PA cycle; thus they may weigh heavily on a decision. As we saw in the previous chapter, those inputs originate in the hypothalamus, the amygdala, and other parts of the limbic brain. They carry information about the internal milieu and the biological significance of external stimuli, entering the cortex mainly through the orbital prefrontal region, a region rich in dopamine terminals and receptors related to reward. Thus, through that region, information arrives in the cerebral cortex that encodes the sensory, emotional, and visceral experiences associated with each biological drive. Included in that information is the motivational valence of external events, especially their connotations of reward or punishment.

One exciting aspect of modern brain research is the discovery that the activity of many neurons of the prefrontal cortex is attuned to such value-related variables as the quantity, quality, or delay of an expected reward. In other words, judging from their level of firing, those cells appear to "predict" the amount and probability of a reward, such as a tasty food (Rolls *et al.*, 1996; Schultz, 1998; Watanabe and Sakagami, 2007). Neuroeconomics attempts to measure neural changes related to those variables, as well as their interactions with the length of time before the reward is expected to materialize (Glimcher, 2003).

From that research it is reasonable to conclude that the prefrontal cortex, especially its orbital region, contains or is part of neural networks attuned to at least three important attributes of reward: amount, probability, and delay. Especially critical because of its direct bearing on liberty is the ability to delay a reward – in other words, to postpone gratification. Patients with lesions of that cortex, like most children – and some investors – have difficulty in waiting for a reward, however small, even though the waiting might result in a bigger reward. As we have seen in Chapter 4, that phenomenon is the result of the delay discount of the value or valence of the reward. In the financial world, delay discount obviously separates the two most prevalent strategies of security investment – that is, investing for the short term or for the long term.[1]

The relationships between amount, probability, and delay of reward are of critical importance in financial decisions. Those relationships have been well substantiated experimentally by Rachlin *et al.* (1991). They show that those relations are so tight as to allow their expression in computational terms. Consequently, one variable can be quantitatively "titrated" with – that means, exchanged for – another in certain precise amounts, without altering a behavioral choice. In addition, risk-taking and delay of reward are also related to each other, in reciprocal fashion. At one extreme of that relationship, the gambler takes high risks for prompt reward. Gambling, however, is not the only human activity that thrives on expected prompt reward. Consumer credit depends to some extent on the difficulty that most individuals have in delaying gratification – even at the expense of future financial security.

The delay of gratification is closely related to the ability to inhibit internal impulses, whatever their biological origin; in other words, the ability to control impulsivity. That inhibitory ability is another function of the orbital prefrontal cortex, not coincidentally as we have seen, a region of prime importance for the evaluation of rewards. It is well known that both impulsivity and the incapacity to delay reward are common in early childhood. A persuasive case has been made for the proposition that ADHD (attention deficit hyperactivity disorder) in children of school age is attributable to laggard maturation of the orbital prefrontal cortex (Barkley, 1997; Fuster, 2008). Stimulants, such as Ritalin, may alleviate that condition by bolstering inhibitory, impulse-controlling neurotransmitters like GABA.[2]

A corollary to the concepts just outlined is that in human cases of orbitofrontal injury, such as those described by Damasio

---

[1] There is empirical evidence, however, that an individual may concomitantly aim for financial rewards with different degrees of deferment, even if they are in partial conflict with one another (Ainslie and Monterrosso, 2004).

[2] Gamma-aminobutyric acid, the main and most abundant inhibitory transmitter in the cortex.

and collaborators (1990), the patient is typically driven to socio-pathic behavior by uncontrollable emotional drive, impulsivity, and risk-taking. Arguably, the apparently "liberated" and carefree behavior of such individuals is paradoxically underpinned by severely limited liberty. These individuals are their own prison-ers, like drug addicts, who may share the same orbitofrontal pathology. Their decisions are far from free, in that there are few alternatives to their abnormal behavior.

Outside of neurology wards and the casinos of Las Vegas, however, the rewards that influence decisions in human beings vary infinitely more widely. Some such rewards clearly transcend the immediate gratification of biological drives ("biodrives"), whether directly or through money acquisition. Indeed, even the acquisition of money can be motivated by higher principles, such as philanthropy and providing for one's descendants. This is a place where the liberty to make money meets a commensurate responsibility.

Emerson's dictum that "the reward for a thing well done is to have done it" applies only to the human. There is no evidence that this kind of ethical reward guides the behavior of any animal, even accounting for the spontaneous playfulness of some pri-mates, dogs, cats, and dolphins, which is not motivated by any-thing resembling duty. Something similar can be said for the liberty to decide, which contains its own reward. This reward tops the list of a broad category of rewards that are not reducible to biological pleasure or avoidance of pain and that are largely limited to the human race. That does not mean that some of the loftiest rewards do not have biological roots. As I have noted, the rewards of being loved and trusted have profound evolutionary roots. Love and trust inform decisions much as other human motives do. In this respect, because of its importance in emotions, the limbic system intervenes most directly in decision-making.[3] One limbic structure, the amygdala, clearly intervenes in the

---

[3] By judicious use of functional imaging, McClure et al. (2004) determined that there are two distinct value systems in the brain: (a) one, limbic, associated with the midbrain dopamine system, which is activated by decisions eliciting immediate reward; and (b) the other encompassing prefrontal and parietal cortices, which is activated by decisions eliciting deferred reward.

attribution of value to cortical cognits associated with deep-seated sources of affective valence (Winston *et al.*, 2005).

Beyond basic instincts and affects, the massive cortical infrastructure of cognition plays a central role in the making of most free decisions. The rich distributed array of perceptual and executive cognits that the individual has developed in his cerebral cortex by experience, education, and the example of others influences every significant decision, especially if that decision requires a measure of deliberation on several alternatives. Some of the highest cortical cognits contain ethical principles and values based on the mores that humankind has found useful, even indispensable, for social harmony: charity, honor, and respect for others. They certainly play a role in shaping decisions, consciously or unconsciously.

Then, decision-making is also subject to constraints and influences from the rule of law.[4] In addition to institutional law, the rule of law applies to "natural law," which encompasses social rules embedded in phylogeny, such as compassion, trust, and affiliation. In summary, to one degree or another, legal and ethical principles intervene in the making of almost all decisions, even if they do it in the form of constraints on individual freedom. Such constraints on the self oftentimes protect the freedom of others.

Blended with social rules such as those are the values of possessions projected into the distant future, the value of rewards to be enjoyed in the long term by the individual or by his or her successors. Again, providing for the future of the progeny is not exclusive to the human. Natural ethology contains innumerable examples of it in animals: nest construction, gathering and hoarding food for offspring, defense of communal territory, and so on. In animals many of these activities are stereotypical and genetically programmed. In the human, however, the value of such activities and their consequences is less dependent on instinctual constraints than on the liberty to decide between multiple

---

[4] The rule of law is a principle formally established in the seventeenth century but traceable to antiquity. It says that all citizens must obey the law of the land, and no one, even with the highest authority, is above it (Dicey, 1889).

altruistic alternatives. In any case, the human generally values the liberty to be enjoyed by others beyond one's life.

Also unique to the human is language, the universal conveyer of meaning and expression. It is the ultimate carrier of semantic information between cortical networks of perception and action, as well as between brains. Language facilitates the access of cortical cognits to the PA cycle. It literally imparts the future tense to those cognits, thus projecting both past and present into the future. Therein lies the relation between language and prediction in prefrontal function that we will explore in the next chapter.

Language, in its own right, is a source of information that antecedes decision, not only in the form of internal language ("mentalese") but also as a support of all the other sources. Indeed, language serves to define, refine, synthesize, and reinforce all relevant knowledge for prospective choice. Language is a major mental tool of deliberation before decision. While we ponder consciously the consequences of our decision, language serves the underlying logic, which undoubtedly involves substantial portions of our cortex, the prefrontal in particular.

Hard decisions require intensive deliberation. Here we must resist the misleading inference of a conscious entity *directing* the deliberation from one antecedent of decision to another and from one expected outcome to another. In the deliberation within one self, there is no conscious ego other than the cortex itself activating its cognitive networks successively by association and, with the assistance of language, following the rules of logic. Consciousness is an obligatory byproduct of intense network activation, not its cause.

The liberty to decide is the liberty to choose between alternatives of information as well as alternatives of action based on that information. Therein lies the reason for viewing the present decision as a point of convergence of inputs from the past and divergence of outputs to the future. We can depict the situation graphically in the form of two cones touching each other at their apex in the present, one converging from the past and the other diverging to the future (Figure 5.1). Based on neurobiological evidence, we can include in the schema the most general

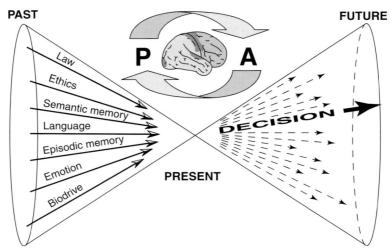

Figure 5.1 The two cones of decision-making, the perceptual (P) converging on the present, and the executive (A) diverging from it into the future. The converging influences originate in a multitude of cortical cognits representing all active forms of memory, in addition to the subcortical biological drives weighing on a decision. The decision is a resultant – chosen – executive vector of action among the many possible alternatives of action and "affordance."

categories of input sources from the past as well as the output of the prefrontal cortex at the time of decision.

An action can originate anywhere in the perception or action side of the PA cycle. This fact obviates much of the philosophizing about a "center of will" or of executive action in the brain without neglecting the enabling and orchestrating roles of the prefrontal cortex. Any one among the several sources of influence upon the decision process, categorized in Figure 5.1 and coming from one sector of the brain or another, can be the "deciding factor." But in reality most decisions result from the competition, synergy, and compromise between numerous sources of influence, internal as well as external, conscious as well as unconscious. Among the unconscious are a host of cognits and drives that can determine decisions under the rubric of "intuitive instinct" or "gut feeling." Some of them may not so much determine as simply bias or prime a decision.

Did My Neurons Make Me Do It? is the title of an insightful recent book.[5] In the light of what I have just said, my answer to that question should be, "Yes, but those neurons all together are very well informed." My point is that the choice of action is preceded by a choice or multiple choices of information. One decision – that is, one chosen action at a time – will emerge from the nervous system, but only after it has dealt with the present situation and its antecedents. These will be themselves subject to choice, even if this choice takes but a split second. In addition to the inputs in Figure 5.1, those antecedents encompass not only recent or current external stimulation but also its valence in the light of the entire experience of the organism – "phyletic" experience included.

Of course, the weight of each source of input onto the decision and onto the PA cycle can vary enormously from time to time, from individual to individual, and from situation to situation. In any event, various inputs will weigh differently on that decision, which may turn out to be a decision *not* to act at all, or to hold action in abeyance. Other inputs will lead to actions based on estimated probability of risk and reward. Some antecedents will be literally decisive, leading to a "winner-takes-all" outcome.

A relatively straightforward example will illustrate the complexity of antecedents leading to a free decision. Suppose you are considering an investment in the stock exchange. You have already considered several stocks, and examined the prospectus, history, and balance sheet of each of the issuing companies you are interested in. After careful scrutiny, you are inclined to choose shares of Chlotronic, a company (fictitious) in the energy sector. It is a vibrant, environmentally friendly ("green") company, led by young imaginative management. It has considerable potential for growth, and its stock pays dividends. On the minus side, you have heard that the Securities and Exchange Commission is eying the company for insufficient capitalization and excessive leverage. In

---

[5] The book is by the philosopher Nancey Murphy and the psychologist Warren Brown (2010).

any case, in the end, all that information – and your intuition – make you decide to buy one thousand shares of Chlotronic.

Your decision may have been "determined" by a mental estimate of risks and benefits after considering the most relevant sources of information (including opinions of broker, friends, and family). Chances are good, however, that other factors have led to your decision. Here, I venture, you have thought of your experience with previous stock investments, the social value of green energy, financial regulation, your long-term financial goals, a balanced portfolio, diversification, and so on. Many if not most factors are not quantifiable.

I have chosen the financial paradigm to emphasize that the antecedents and incentives of a human decision extend well beyond those that behavioral economics would take into consideration. Clearly, the expected financial reward, short- or long-term, must have played a crucial role in that decision. Some activation of your dopamine system at the base of the brain may have reflected the valence of that expected benefit as one of the precedents to the decision. But then also, to varying degrees, other precedents from knowledge and memory – abstract, semantic, episodic, and emotional – must have entered the decision. These are most assuredly based in pre-existing cognits in the cerebral cortex. Accordingly, whenever prediction, expectation, and working memory play a role in a decision, practically the entirety of the prefrontal cortex must be active to one degree or another.

What is the neural foundation of the freedom to make flexible decisions like that one that impact on our future? If we assume that freedom involves choice between expected values, the freedom to decide on an investment must be subject to the interplay of amounts, certainty, risk, and delay of reward, much as neuroeconomists postulate. Rewards, however, may be projected into the future, to be shared by others. It is difficult to construct models of neural organization and mechanisms, in computational terms, to account for long-term investment. Much of the problem lies in finding the appropriate neural metrics and independent measures of the relevant behavioral variables (for example, trust, greed, or altruism). Nonetheless, a body of data is emerging from brain-imaging literature that correlates such variables as financial trust and long-term value investment with prefrontal cortical activity.[6] As might be expected, the activity of the prefrontal cortex in these value attributions is in turn correlated with activity in posterior cortical areas, indicating the cooperation of the prefrontal cortex and these areas in higher-level valuation.

To sum up, a decision is the result of the evaluation of multiple inputs upon the cortex from a variety of active cognits, environmental stimuli, and internal drives. Each carries a different weight or degree of exigency, which depends on its relevance to an objective. That weight translates itself into the synaptic strength of input to the cortical substrates of action. The choice between alternatives, which is the essence of the freedom to decide, depends on the strength of the various competing or cooperative inputs arriving at a given time in a distributed action-network centered in the prefrontal cortex.

At rest, that executive network may be viewed as an "attractor network," made of multiple associations, and fluctuating between states around a state of relaxation or near-equilibrium.[7] When inputs from cortical or subcortical representations of values or incentives take an attractor network out of the relaxed state and into a state of excitation beyond a certain threshold, the network becomes an operant network, co-operant with other networks toward a decision and a goal.[8]

---

[6] For several reasons, this research is slow and incremental. Functional imaging measures minute changes in the blood flow of particular cortical areas. These changes are produced by changes in the underlying nervous activity – which consumes oxygen and glucose. But the biophysics of neurovascular coupling is not yet precisely understood, for which reason the brain-imaging of such variables as trust and long-term reward is difficult.

[7] The concept of "attractor network" derives from computational neuroscience (Amit, 1989). The state of one such network is defined and described in terms of patterns of neuron firing. Such patterns vary widely, from highly rhythmic firing to chaotic (disorderly) firing. They can be empirically encountered in the cells of cortical networks during working memory (Bodner *et al.*, 2005).

[8] Normally, at rest, cognits "silently" represent memories and knowledge by means of a relational spatial code in brain space – that is, cortical space. When a cognit is activated for behavior or language, that latent spatial code becomes a spatial-temporal code of firing neuronal assemblies sequentially organized in successive actions toward their goal. Then, the information contained in

Primate neuroscience has revealed that the coordination of a complex action involves the reciprocal activation of prefrontal and posterior – mainly temporal-lobe and parietal-lobe – areas as well as some of their subcortical relay stations (such as the thalamus, the basal ganglia, and the superior colliculus), all engaged in the PA cycle. Despite our ignorance of some of the mechanisms involved, it is disconcerting that some modern neuroscientists, ignoring the circularity and distribution of this process, still quarrel about the precise location of a highly questionable center of command, will, or decision.

The executive network receives not only excitatory inputs but also inhibitory ones. The latter may come from any source of neural information that is incompatible with the decision, its goal, or its timing. For instance, an ethical imperative to delay gratification will inhibit the prefrontal executive network, or one of its parts, which is in charge of implementing the decision. Inhibitory control is, in fact, one of the executive functions of the prefrontal cortex (Chapter 4). It is channeled through the orbitofrontal cortex upon subcortical motor structures (basal ganglia) and the limbic structures in charge of basic drives (hunger, sex, fight, and flight). Cognitive decisions may be instigated by these drives, but may also require their inhibition to prevent untimely or inappropriate interference with free goal-directed choice.

The decision to act in a certain way may be just an interim decision for an interim goal, which may be merely a component of a plan or structure of action with multiple decisions directed to an ultimate goal. For example, my decision to choose the subject of this paragraph is informed by previous paragraphs and the subject of the chapter. This calls for a degree of working memory. Working memory – that is, "online" active memory *for* pending action – is ubiquitous in decision-making: no sentence, no paragraph, no reasoned discourse, and no plan or temporally

multiple cognits dispersed throughout the cortex becomes orchestrated toward that goal. All of that occurs within the PA cycle, while the prefrontal cortex assumes the orchestrating role (Fuster, 2008). However, most of the action is self-organized, with only marginal need for the prefrontal cortex, like the performance of an orchestra that has repeatedly played the same symphony with the same conductor.

extended action can be conducted without it. Working memory is necessary whenever and wherever there are temporal gaps in the PA cycle.

Where is then the freedom of choice behind a decision that is in any event ultimately *determined* by many antecedents, drives, rules, chemicals, laws, and brain networks? My answer, however tentative, is as follows. True enough, behind each decision there is ultimately nothing but thermodynamic cause and effect somewhere in the brain at one time or another. There appears to be little room left, therefore, for individual choice. That room expands at the expense of determinism, however, if we take into account that most neural transactions, especially in the cerebral cortex are nonlinear and probabilistic, not strictly determined by the self, but by changes around us and by decisions of others. The room for free volition indeed expands if we take into account the enormous multiplicity of influences weighing on, if not determining, almost all our decisions. With experience, degrees of freedom literally multiply, and thus options multiply. Liberty for decision may remain *constrained* and *relative*, but at such high levels of latitude that the determinist argument becomes moot. In any event, every decision is "informed."

PLANNING

Evolution is all in the postdictable past, but has made of our brain the predictive maker of the future. This, together with the advent of language, is the most distinctive evolutionary advance of the human brain. The prefrontal cortex plays the pivotal role in both prediction and language, which are intimately intertwined. The planning and execution of new sequential actions such as those of speech require some of the same temporal organizing functions that only the prefrontal cortex can provide.

For a long time it has been known that the integrity of the frontal lobe is critical for effective planning. A deficit in planning is pathognomonic[9] of substantial malfunction of the prefrontal

---

[9] In medicine, the adjective "pathognomonic" is applied to a symptom that by itself is diagnostic of a disease.

cortex, especially if it affects the external, lateral convexity of the frontal lobe. Neurologists on both competing sides of World War I, especially Germans and Russians, were the first to describe the symptom systematically in soldiers with traumatic frontal injuries. The patient with frontal damage suffers from marked difficulties in formulating and executing plans of action, especially if they are long and elaborate. Bereft of initiative and driven only by routine, the patient is incapable of organizing new sequences of goal-directed acts. Arguably, a deficit in general drive, sometimes accompanied by general apathy, is the root cause of the frontal disorder, but the available evidence indicates that the disorder is mainly the result of a deep-seated deficit in the capacity to organize temporal gestalts of action, from conception to execution.[10]

A plan is a new temporal sequence of actions directed to a goal. Thus, by definition, a plan has a term, which is set by the goal itself, and a series of component actions to attain it. The route to a goal may vary greatly, as does, for example, the route from grade school to career, from date to marriage, from patent to industrial enterprise, from libretto to opera. Obviously, as the examples in this short list imply, small intermediate goals are necessary steps to big ultimate goals. Obviously also, many sequences of goal-directed actions to reach goals, big or small, do not qualify as plans. They may consist of old, more or less familiar routines that are nonetheless indispensable to the ultimate goal defining the plan.

Our plans may be part of larger plans devised in collaboration with others in society – for example, in our community, professional group, institution, industrial concern, governmental agency, sports club, or other. In such entities, several individuals share the efforts, rewards, and recognition for the attainment of common goals. The value of mutually achieved goals may be greater than the sum of the values of individual component actions. At the same time, because of the imponderables or

---

[10] Corroborating the clinical evidence, neuroimaging provides convincing evidence of the role of the prefrontal cortex, together with the posterior cortex, in the performance of a planning task (Rowe *et al.*, 2001).

uncertainties behind some individual estimates and actions, so-called "central planning" is often not commensurate with the cumulative value of all the individual contributions. Often, therefore, such planning leads to failure – to wit, some governmental budget expense plans, which are based on assumptions about unpredictable market forces.

There are two phases to a plan: conception and execution. Both need to some degree the prefrontal cortex and its cohort of connected brain structures, cortical as well as subcortical. The cerebral conception of the plan consists of several interlinked cognits at various hierarchical levels of abstraction. At the highest level, widely distributed in the associative frontal cortex, is the *scheme* of the plan with its objective, both part of prospective memory. It is a conceptual cognit, which is incompletely defined except for its essential elements – namely, the goal and the broad outline of the plan – together with broad representations of its timeline, costs, and risks. Nested under it, at lower levels of abstraction, are some of the ancillary goals and actors: the intermediary goals conducive to the overriding goal of the plan in addition to the persons that will assist the individual selves in the attainment of that goal. Note that the goal is at times highly conscious, meaning that we are fully aware of its particulars. But consciousness, though an obligated phenomenon of cortical activity in the formulation of the plan, is not in itself sufficient or necessary for it. What is sufficient and necessary is the elevated activity of a broadly distributed cortical network and its component networks.

Having been conceived, the scheme of the plan is represented in that broad cognitive network of the cerebral cortex, with nodes of heavy association in prefrontal cortex. "Represented" is a poor word here, which I use for lack of a better one. What is "re-presented" is a new self-organized rearrangement of cognits from the past, now with a future purpose. Before its implementation, the plan is mutable by reassociation within itself, and more or less ready to be enacted at the appropriate time and circumstances.

Perhaps the most difficult concept to comprehend here, worth repeating because it is essential to my argument, is that the organization of the plan does not need a unique entity, cerebral or mental, such as a deliberating "ego" or a "central executive." All that is needed is a wakeful cortex to organize itself, under the influences from itself and from the environment, and ready "and willing" for choice, decision, and orderly action toward a goal. It is true, however, that the prefrontal cortex will assume a role of organizer or orchestrator of the plan; but even that "executive" role is constrained by the functional availability of the rest of the cortex with which it closely cooperates. Further, any plan the prefrontal cortex enables and helps organize will be subject to continuous feedback from the environment and the rest of the cortex. All of it will occur largely autonomously by virtue of the self-organizing potential of the cortex.

Essentially, the implementation of the plan consists of the mobilization of the PA cycle(s) that will take it to its goal. The trigger for that mobilization can vary widely. It can be an external stimulus, such as a command, an internal urge such as a biological drive, or a set of circumstances that may include the calendar and the clock. It can be the request from someone in need, from the family, an institution, or some other sector of society.

Once started, the plan will temporally evolve under the control of the PA cycles appropriate to the ultimate objective and to each intermediate goal. The cycles will shift as the plan unfolds, but in any event they will involve receptor and effector structures of the brain, especially posterior and frontal cortices. Most intermediate goals will be governed by routine or automatic PA cycles (for example, walking) that do not contain novelties, uncertainties, or ambiguities, and thus will not encumber the prefrontal cortex. Some intermediate goals, especially obligatory for the final objective, will require discriminating choices, resolution of conflicts, error correction, circumvention of unexpected obstacles, and difficult decisions. Those PA cycles will course through the prefrontal cortex. The exercise of cortical freedom – that is, of choice in all those eventualities – will continue until the major goal or objective of the plan is reached.

The process, however, will not necessarily be continuous. The realization of a plan, as that of any PA cycle within it, demands above all the brain's ability to integrate percepts and actions in the course of time, even if there are temporal discontinuities in the process. To that end, among the most critical temporal integrative functions of the prefrontal cortex is the mediation of cross-temporal contingencies: (a) "If now this, then later that"; (b) "If earlier that, then now this." The first contingency "looks forward" in time, and the second "backward." We now know that the brain, especially the prefrontal cortex, has mechanisms to mediate both temporal aspects of contingency (Fuster, 2008). The discharge of some of its cells increases during the contingency-bridging intervals.[11] Their firing frequency ramps up toward an act, anticipating it. This phenomenon is unmistakable physiological evidence of prospective memory. The discharge of other cells, however, does the opposite; that is, it ramps down toward the act (retrospective memory). Those cellular phenomena are evidence of the memory of the recent past *for* the act – in other words, of working memory. In any case, prefrontal neurons are active with a future perspective: some retaining memory for the act, and others anticipating it. Both populations of neurons serve memory of the future by mediating cross-temporal contingencies. Both belong to prefrontal cognits working for a plan.

In the course of planned behavior, planned speech, or planned reasoning, the mediation of cross-temporal contingencies requires the bridging of time in variable amounts, as the contingencies are separated by variable intervals. Some intervals are short; then, there is little need for the two time-bridging functions of set and working memory. In complex cognitive operations, however, such as those that govern complex plans, intervals may be long, and both those functions are very much needed. I will resort to an "armchair plan" to make my point.

---

[11] Monkeys were trained to memorize color cues signifying different probabilities of one of two alternative actions necessary to obtain a reward (Quintana and Fuster, 1999). Cell discharge was recorded from the prefrontal cortex by means of microelectrodes. During the period of memorization, some frontal neurons, after a sharp increase, showed a steady decrease of firing – as if "looking back" to the cue color – presumably an expression of fading working memory. Others, conversely, accelerated their firing as the action grew near – as if preparing for that action, "looking forward" to it. Interestingly, the degree of accelerated firing increased in direct proportion to the predictability of the necessary action.

Reading a novel can hardly be called a plan with a goal, but the main character may well have one and we the readers may be called to share it. Thus, in surrogate fashion, we can become participants of that plan by following the events described and the reasoning of the protagonist. Consider Agatha Christie's 1934 classic, *Murder on the Orient Express* (Christie, 2011). Here the plan has for goal the finding of the perpetrator of a crime on board the famous train. In reading the book, we easily identify with the detective Poirot and feel compelled to follow his plan. By doing that, we engage in an absorbing series of cross-temporal contingencies between facts and findings, characters and actions, suspicions and coincidences, expectations and reality tests. Naturally, in the text the sequence of events is temporally fractionated and compressed with regard to the real time of the fictional plot. Nonetheless, as we proceed from chapter to chapter – each focusing on a different suspect – we are forced to use the same mental operations for reconciling the present with the past and with the hypothetical future. Our prefrontal cortex works, so to speak, in parallel with Poirot's and with Christie's. And with them we are obliged to mediate those contingencies with working and prospective memory. Further, with her inimitable psychological talent for describing characters and small details, the author makes us use plenty of intuition to skillfully guide our plan (sometimes equivocally, to fool us!).

Over and beyond our daily routines, many of us have several plans going on simultaneously. In fact, it is a measure of liberty that we are capable of taking on several tasks simultaneously. This can put a strain on our time and our neural resources. With respect to these resources, one particular prefrontal function is called to heavy duty in multitasking, whether with big or small tasks: inhibitory control.

In all our tasks, especially if they are complex, selective attention is required for the proper pursuit of the goal. Selective attention is a serial function; we can only attend to one thing at a time. Working memory is nothing but selective attention focused on one internal representation or cognit at a time. To protect selective attention, we need the complementary function of inhibitory control, which has a base in the prefrontal cortex, like working memory

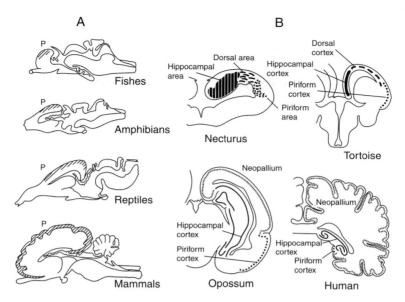

Figure 2.1 Evolutionary development of the cerebral cortex.
A: Lengthwise sections of the brains of four classes of vertebrates.
P, Pallium, generic name for cortex, both old and new
(phylogenetically). From Creutzfeldt (1993). *B:* Crosswise sections
of the brains of a primitive amphibian (*Necturus*), the box tortoise
(*Cistudo*), the opossum (*Didelphis*), and the human. From Herrick
(1956), modified.

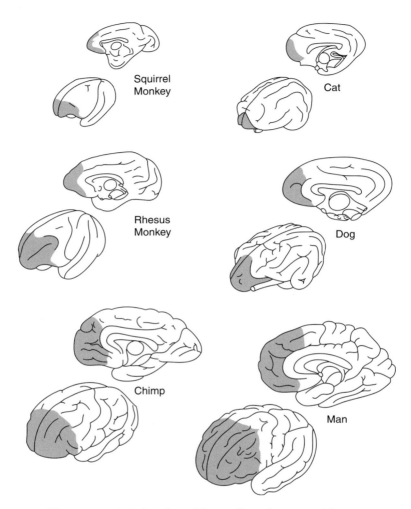

Figure 2.2 Relative size of the prefrontal cortex with respect to total cortex in six animal species (marked by *shading* of external and internal hemispheric surface). PTO, parieto-temporo-occipital association region (posterior association cortex).

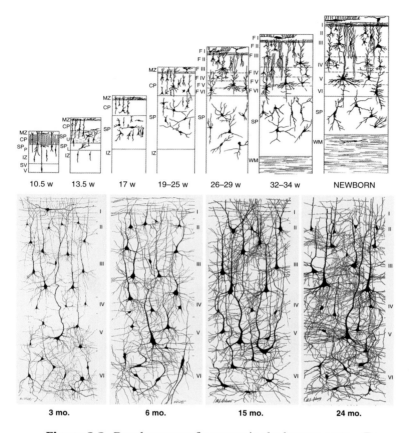

Figure 2.3 Development of neurons in the human cortex. *Top*: Prenatal period, from 10.5 weeks to birth. From Mrzljak *et al.* (1990), with permission. *Bottom*: Postnatal, at 3, 6, 15, and 24 months. From Conel (1963), with permission.

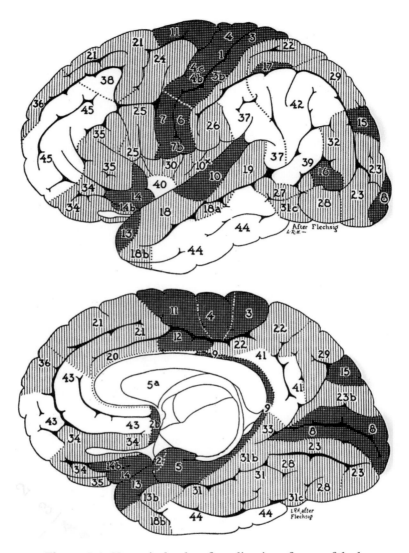

Figure 2.4 Numerical order of myelination of areas of the human cortex, according to Flechsig. Primary sensory and motor areas (low numbers, *in black*) myelinate first, association areas (high numbers *in white*) myelinate last. From Bonin (1950), modified.

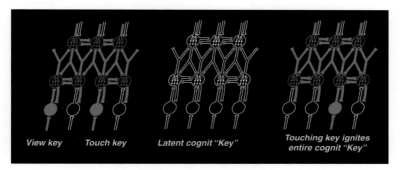

Figure 3.1 *Top:* Two basic principles of memory formation in cognitive networks (cognits). According to the first principle (*left*), when two cells in a chain (S1 and O) fire repeatedly together, the synaptic membrane of the output cell (O) will be modulated to transmit impulses more easily (+) from one cell to the other. According to the second principle (synchronous convergence, *right*), when the input impulses from two cells (S1 and S2) arrive at the same time in cell O, the membrane of the latter will be modulated to transmit more easily (+) inputs from either S1 or S2. *Bottom:* Formation and evocation of a cognit extending from the sensory up to the association cortex. The cartoon simplifies all the major modes of cortico-cortical connectivity (feed-forward, feedback, convergence, divergence, and lateral). *At left*, I experience the sight and touch, together, of my house key. *In the middle*, the cognit "key" consists of a network of cell assemblies linked together by facilitated synapses (*in red*). *At right*, the touch of the key in my pocket evokes the entire cognit, including the visual image of the key.

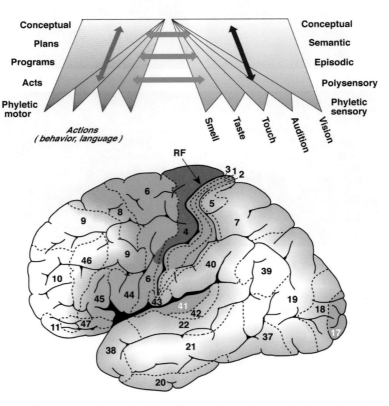

Figure 3.2 Organization of cortical cognits on the lateral surface of the left hemisphere (areas numbered as per Brodmann's cytoarchitectural map). The *lower* figure hints at the hierarchical organization of perceptual cognits, from primary sensory areas (*dark blue*) and motor areas (*dark red*) to posterior (PTO) and frontal association cortices (*white*), respectively. The upper figure, with the same color code, further schematizes the organization of areas, connectivity, and cognit categories. Abbreviation: *RF*, Rolandic fissure.

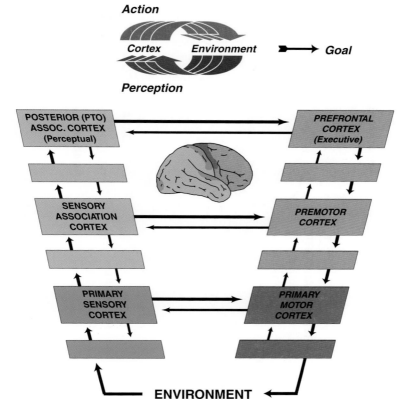

Figure 4.1 Dynamic flow of activation through the cortical hierarchical stages of the PA cycle in the pursuit of a goal. Unlabelled rectangles stand for intermediate areas or subareas of adjacent, labeled, areas. Large arrows – clockwise – indicate the main flow of the cycle. Small arrows – counterclockwise – indicate feedback flow.

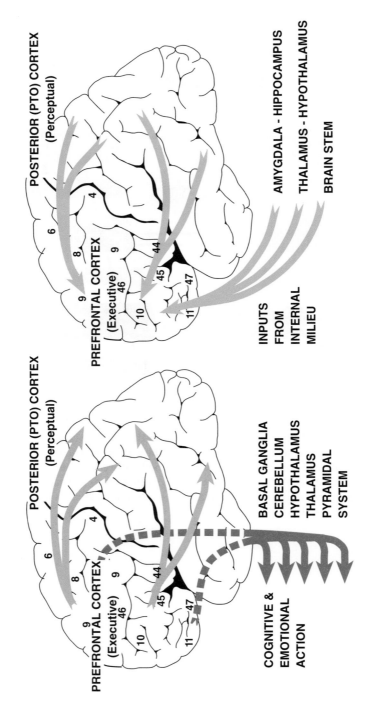

Figure 4.2 Inputs (*blue*) and outputs (*pink, red*) of the prefrontal cortex at the top of the PA cycle.

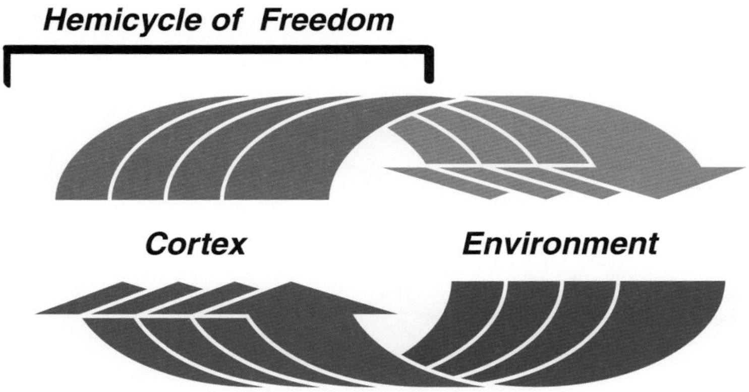

Figure 4.3 The hemicycle of freedom, Choices are made in the cortical compartment (bracketed) of the PA cycle. In the perceptual cortex (blue), the choices are between alternatives of experiential information (memory and knowledge). In the executive cortex (red), the choices are between alternatives of action.

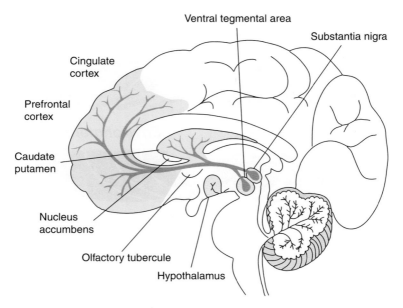

Figure 4.4 The "reward axis" of dopamine in the primate brain.

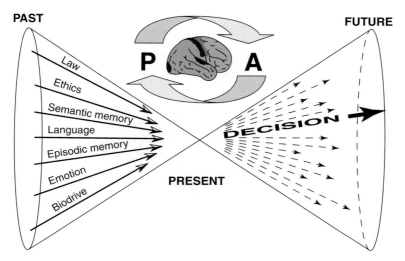

Figure 5.1 The two cones of decision-making, the perceptual (P) converging on the present, the executive (A) diverging from it into the future. The converging influences originate in a multitude of cortical cognits representing all active forms of memory, in addition to the subcortical biological drives weighing on a decision. The decision is a resultant – chosen – executive vector of action among the many possible alternatives of action and "affordance."

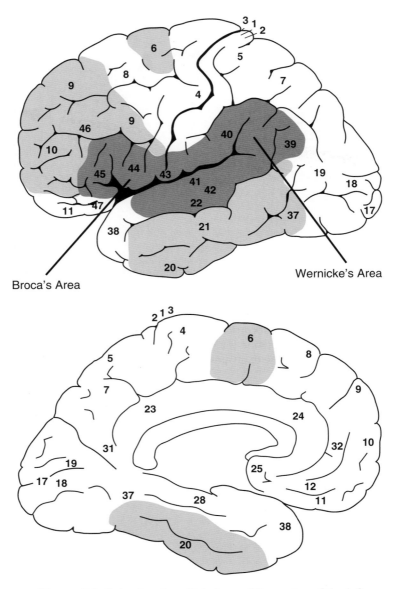

Figure 6.1 Lateral and medial views of the cortex of the left hemisphere (Brodmann's map) with areas marked whose lesions lead to speech disorders (aphasias). The most severe disorders result from damage in *red* areas, the less severe in *pink* areas.

and prospective memory (Munakata *et al.*, 2011). Without effective inhibitory control, extraneous cognits, distractions, and fragments of other plans interfere with the current plan and can lead it astray. In any case, some persons are better at multitasking than others. The best at it, we might say, can perform the most efficient "multiplexing"[12] of both excitation and inhibition without ever losing sight of any of several concomitantly pursued goals.

As we have seen, the process of implementing a plan of action is self-organized in the cerebral cortex. It is the cerebral cortex that "attends," "intends," and "decides." At any step of the plan, our consciousness of the process is literally a phenomenon, not its causal agent. Consciousness may be obligated, even inevitable, in almost any cognitive act toward reaching the goal, but is not indispensable *per se*. This does not detract from our freedom, for in any event our cortex retains the capacity to choose between alternatives, whether we are fully aware of the decision to choose any of them or not. The same is true for attention and intention, which are almost inherently conscious phenomena.

There is probably no cognitive function as well anchored in biology as attention. Attention, like evolution, is essentially selection; it is selective by definition. In the nervous system, attention is selective for two major reasons. One is the functional specialization of neural structures; the other is the limitation in the resources of any of them. Selective attention is a neural function that optimizes the function of any given structure with maximal use of its resources. Attention is thus efficient and economical. It is essential at every step in the execution of a plan.

Note that I speak about attention in nonsubjective, nonphenomenal, terms to emphasize its deep biological roots, as well as to make it continuous with its conscious manifestations, which we first encounter when we reach the cerebral cortex. Indeed, as any other level of neural function, the cerebral cortex accommodates the two fundamental aspects of attention: focus and exclusion. In the self-organizing process of a plan, the cortex allocates to every

---

[12] In engineering, multiplexing means combining several simultaneous signals into a single transmission line or channel, by rapid alternation of sampling from one signal to another.

percept and to every action in the PA cycle the cognits that will most adequately serve the plan. We are aware of those cognits in the focus of attention, though the awareness itself is not of the essence for the function. At the same time, cortical attention will suppress or inhibit all cognits that are in some respect germane to those in focus, but are inadequate to or incompatible with the plan. This is the exclusionary component of attention. Most probably, we will not be aware of it or of its contents.

Attention does not cease to work even during interruptions of the plan, such as those imposed by expected or unexpected delays. Consider a human or a monkey performing a working-memory task, which obliges the subject to retain words, numbers, shapes, faces, or colors during a delay. The task is in itself a "plan" imposed by the experimenter. During each delay, the subject is obliged not only to attend to the memorandum (the cue to be memorized), which is relevant, but also to inhibit, to "forget," those memoranda that may have been relevant during other trials of the task but are now irrelevant. Working memory is attention to an internal representation and "inattention" to all others.

Intention is attention to impending action. It involves the selective priming and preparation of motor structures for the action that the plan calls for. Intention precedes every action at every step in the PA cycle(s) of the plan leading to the goal. Here, to the perplexity of dualists who make of conscious intention a precedent to action, there is experimental evidence that the part of the cortex executing an action is activated about 200 milliseconds *before* the conscious intention to perform that action (Libet *et al.*, 1983). This is strong presumptive evidence[13] that the intention originates in the cortex, like all other cognitive functions, and the conscious experience of cortical activation is the consequence of that activation, not the cause.

Plans vary in term and duration depending on many factors, among them the urgency of the goal, the complexity of the plan, and the available resources. We may conduct several plans

---

[13] The evidence is solid and generally accepted, despite objections from dualists to the implication – not drawn by Libet anyway – of the nonexistence of conscious free will (e.g., Batthyany and Elitzur, 2009). Libet's research is discussed insightfully by Spence (2009).

simultaneously with different objectives, terms, and time scales, interleaving some of them with others. We can do this with the necessary shifts in attention, from one plan to another, and with appropriate alternation of inclusive as well as exclusionary (inhibitory) attention control. The failure to exclude extraneous influences by inhibition in the pursuit of any given plan can lead to interference, inefficiency, or both.

In broad terms, the exercise of liberty, as well as the subjective experience of it, augments with the number and term of simultaneous plans. Both are a function of the education, personality, intelligence, and resources of the planner. The good planner, in any case, maintains at all times flexibility to modify the course of a plan in accord with its progress or lack of it. At every step of the plan he will assess the feedback from the plan's PA cycle. Accordingly, he will adjust parameters and input data to steer the plan successfully to its goal. A break in the cycle from neglect of feedback signals will lead the plan to eventual failure and a missed goal. As a consequence, a fruitless exercise of liberty will come to an end.

When properly monitored and adjusted in their course, good plans devised by expert commissions have led to much social progress. This is a desired result of democratic liberty. Society owes much to the labor of committees and boards in universities, industrial firms, government, scientific societies, professional associations, philanthropic foundations, and so on. In theory and in practice, the plans made by such groups lead to results that usually amount to considerably more than the added contributions of their members. Their plans are usually effective if those in charge of their execution take care of collecting frequent and substantive feedback from the results of their implementation. Such feedback essentially plays in the communal plan the same role it plays in the PA cycle of the individual plan. Hence the value of reviews, progress reports, questionnaires, and other means of collecting feedback.[14]

---

[14] Conversely, the neglect of the proper feedback from a large and complex communal plan can lead to dismal failure. Consider, for example, a commission of elected political leaders, advised by economists, designing and implementing a large economic plan for the nation. Consider further that, as the plan gets underway, three cycles can get easily out of sync or in conflict with one another: the business cycle, the electoral cycle, and "the PA cycle" of the

CREATIVE INTELLIGENCE

Creativity is the mother of progress. The freedom to create, in a broad sense, is one of the most vital of all freedoms after the freedom from want and oppression. Creative intelligence is the ability to make the new and to remake the old for one's benefit or that of others. Benefit or value here can take myriad forms, from the pragmatic to the esthetic to the educational to the scientific to the humanitarian, in any order or combination.

From the viewpoint of cognitive science, the making by creative intelligence is largely reducible to remaking, because new knowledge is always reducible to old knowledge that has been expanded or recombined to yield a novel outcome. Therefore, a creation is largely the result of expanding or reassociating previously established cognits, perceptual as well as executive. The creative force of imagination impacts the cortex with a wave of activation that will recruit not only firm, old connections but also new ones with dormant or weak synapses in the penumbra of consciousness.

A "sweet" example will illustrate the recombination of prior knowledge into a new creative gestalt. I am sitting in front of the Periodic Table of Comfitures, made by an ingenious gourmet friend of mine, Georgina Regás, with the support of a private foundation.[15] She is an amateur confectioner who runs a small business-museum of fruit and vegetable preserves, where she exhibits and sells her numerous products. On the anniversary of the death of Dmitri Mendeleev, she, in collaboration with the chemist Pere Castells, came upon the idea of tabulating, as if

plan. To complicate matters, consider that no corrections are made for changes required by such imponderable or unpredictable variables as consumer confidence, demographics, employment, droughts, and commodity prices. Finally, add to that the fears, passions, and drives that affect all markets and defy all models. Under those conditions, the absence of self-regulation and timely feedback will inevitably lead to severe economic distress if not disaster. Indeed, the road to hell is paved with the good intentions of central government planners. In a nondemocratic society, that road may become the "Road to Serfdom" (Hayek, 1944), where the liberty and prosperity of all citizens will be casualties.

[15] Fundación Alicia, Manresa (Barcelona, Spain), dedicated to the promotion of healthy food.

they were chemical elements, all the different kinds of preserves, marmalades, and jellies she produces. Most of them are blends of fruit or vegetable ingredients. The table contains 89 "elements," each with its symbol and "atomic weight." Following the analogous historical precedent, her table is still awaiting completion.

However distant the analogies behind it, Gina's creation is unquestionably original. What makes it original is the large number of new cognitive associations with pre-existing knowledge that went into the making of the confections and their tabulation. At the sensory level, there are the associates of color, taste, and aroma; at the semantic level, the associates of fruit, vegetable, name, symbol, and so on; and at the personal level, Gina's memory experiences with it all, including her historical knowledge. In sum, all parts are old but the whole is utterly new.

There are as many examples of creation as there are conceivable variants of human activity within any field. That, of course, encompasses the arts, the sciences, medicine, technology, philanthropy, gastronomy, the law, and all kinds of businesses, plus personal and social welfare. Every creation necessitates planning and decision-making, the two already discussed quintessential supports of the liberty to "invent the future." Like them, creation necessitates internal drive to reach fruition.

Internal drive comes from the depths of the brain, notably the limbic system. From there, the aggregate of biological drive, reward expectation, and the neocortical associations of both of them are funneled through the orbital prefrontal cortex into the rest of the cerebral cortex to generate the new creation. That aggregate of neural influences comprises the inputs from the internal milieu into the cortical strata of the PA cycle with their immense reticular conglomerate of cognits.

The neural influences from the interior of the brain, the limbic system in particular, constitute the emotional energizer of creativity, the spark of genius, the source of the creative drive, which in its extreme form Marina (1993) has called the "creative fury." It is the all-consuming drive to achieve the invention or the discovery, the poem or the basilica, the symphony or the spaceship, the scientific treatise or the doctoral thesis. It is the drive that defies sleep, fatigue, and at times seemingly insurmountable obstacles. Without that creative drive, the truly original creative action never takes place.

The biophysical root of all creation is the strengthening and formation of synaptic connections in the cerebral cortex within and between cognits. The generative aggregate of those cognitive networks pre-exists in the cortex in various configurations before the creative process commences. In their neuronal and connective makeup, those networks, which we have called cognits, encode parts of the fund of knowledge and memory of the individual before that process begins – including the phyletic (genetic) sensory, and motor apparatus.

Consciousness is ordinarily present in the creative process, sometimes vividly as a consequence of cortical engagement, but is not the absolutely indispensable, let alone the sole, agent of creation. The thought process of the creative mind, however, is an extraordinarily valuable aid for us to glean the cortical dynamics of creation. The analysis of that process reveals its variegated origin. Creation rarely has an identifiable starting point, rarely a distinct epiphany. Especially rational creation, such as the outcome of complex inductive and deductive reasoning, is commonly initiated by context or circumstance. Unconscious processes play a role in the initiation and continuance of any form of creation.

Under creative drive, the process of creation begins with the activation of an ensemble of pre-existent, interconnected cognits. Those represent items of memory and knowledge that by virtue of prior experience have been associated with one another through synaptic connections of varying strength. The creative undertaking starts with their activation by internal or external stimuli, or both. Internal stimulation in the form of a mental image or schema of the final product originates in the cortex itself, either spontaneously or provoked by activation of reciprocal connectivity between associated cognits in areas of the cortex of association (Chapter 3).

Alternatively or at the same time, external stimulation enters the process through those areas of associative cortex via the sensorium. Sensory stimuli activate some of their cognits because of the relations of association between them and the arriving stimuli. Those stimuli may include the feedback from the effect of prior actions in the creative process. In sum, that process originates and progresses by the convergence of internal and external stimuli activating and modifying in succession a variety of established cognits. After being modified and converted into prospective memory, those cognits find expression through the executive frontal cortex.

Creative intelligence often follows uncertain routes. To the creative agent, the schema of the final product may at first appear ill-defined, as if "through a glass darkly." In the case of the rational pursuit, thoughts will succeed one another to their goal in the lineal direction of logical reasoning toward a more or less anticipated conclusion. In the case of an artistic pursuit, however, the creative force often impacts the cortex in several unpredictable directions at the same time, opening its way into the subconscious penumbra through many weak and seldom used synaptic paths.

Once initiated, the creative enterprise will adopt a largely autonomous character, guided by PA cycles toward the final product. As in any series of purposeful PA cycles, feedback will be of the essence for any successful creation. Thus the feedback from the outcome of any of those cycles will influence subsequent ones. At the same time, feedback at every step will be used to adjust every intermediate outcome to the original conception of the whole schema.

All creative actions follow paths of reason as well as esthetics, though the esthetics of a rational creation may not be evident until the product is completed. There is inherent beauty in the flawless work of reason. Indeed, there is art in reason and reason in art. The perfect creation, in whatever field, incorporates, in addition to the indispensable force of the inner drive to create, a harmonious blend of reason and esthetics. A musical example epitomizes this point.

Take the fourth movement (*Allegro energico e passionato*) of Brahms' Fourth Symphony. It begins with a simple solemn melody of eight harmonic chords. That theme is followed by thirty variations of that theme, all endowed with extraordinary coloration and scope, with sharp contrasts between them (Frisch, 2003). Their melody, tempo, and instrumentation vary widely. The main theme underlies them all, however, even though in some of them it is difficult to recognize. In fact, the ability of the composer to depart so much from that theme, and yet to maintain it throughout more or less hidden in the texture of every variation, is nothing short of astonishing. Everywhere, the "gestalt" of the theme is present in the relations between certain notes of each measure. None of this would have been possible without persistent feedback from the heard or imagined score of every variation. It is that feedback, together with the memory of the theme, that shapes every variation. Attesting to the ease with which the genius could muster passion (title of the movement) and inspiration for his creation is his comment to a friend that the entire composition had been a "pastime." Some pastime! It is difficult to find a more pristine blend of art and reason in the entire musical repertoire.

There is something else in Brahms' magnificent piece that illustrates the breadth of past memories that feed into the memory of the future – i.e., imagination – which any creation constitutes. It turns out that the composer fashioned his theme and variations in the form of the ancient chaconne, which Bach had extensively used in his compositions.[16] Brahms' symphony movement, therefore, as he himself noted, was a tribute to the old master and a historical expansion of the knowledge on which Brahms built his master-piece. Further, there is some evidence that the Fourth Symphony may have been partly inspired by Sophocles' tragedies, which Brahms was avidly reading at the time of its composition. As in any creative endeavor, the liberty to create is based on the liberty to choose the sources of inspiration.

In any case, what characterizes the true creation is its *origi-nality* – that is, the uniqueness and temporal priority of the associ-ations on both sides of the PA cycle behind the created work. Thus, in neural terms, creative intelligence is the ability to form unique new relations in perceptual memory and knowledge, as well as unique new relations in executive memory and knowledge. Originality of creation is a personal trait, highly individual. However, because it may be in some way useful or valuable to

---

[16] The chaconne is a variant of the passacaglia, for which reason the two are frequently designated with the latter name.

others, civilized society protects it and is willing to pay for it; hence, the copyright and patent laws.

In closing this chapter, let me focus briefly on how the free brain confers originality to creativity in two different fields of human endeavor, art and science. I will try to emphasize in terms of brain function the commonalities of achievement in both fields.

Just as we have seen the artist form in his brain new associations between established memories, the scientist does the same in his. Both do it under the creative drive instigated largely by the zest for originality. Both utilize their cortex to choose among items of memory of variable "vintage" to produce a new order in the world that corresponds to the new order they have formed in their brain. The final tangible expression of that order will be a new artistic gestalt that will be esthetically pleasing or a scientific paper that will advance our knowledge.

The new order from the artist or from the scientist will owe much to the prefrontal cortex of either. The reason is that this cortex is essential for the temporal organization of all novel actions, which in turn is attributable to its role in the bridging of cross-temporal contingencies. The mediation of such contingencies is at the core of creating a temporal structure, such as a new symphony, a new speech, a new algorithm, or a new scientific tract. Even the plastic arts require temporal structure, in the making as in the viewing. In the viewing, however, time is compressed because the viewer utilizes largely parallel processing while contemplating the artistic piece.[17]

---

[17] Indeed, the beholder will enjoy the piece in large part through the experience of harmony in the spatial structure of the painting or the sculpture that he perceives as a unified whole in a split second. There is some evidence that there may be differences in the degree to which the cortex of the two hemispheres participate in the holistic process of art creation and art appreciation. The evidence is still soft, but has been solidifying lately thanks to studies of patients with unilateral lesion and artistic abilities, as well as imaging studies of artists (Bogousslavsky, 2005; Huang *et al.*, 2012; Kowatari *et al.*, 2009; Schott, 2012; Shamay-Tsoory *et al.*, 2011). The aggregate of the evidence points to the following. Whereas art creation and appreciation necessitate both the left and the right prefrontal cortex, they mainly make use of the right (in contrast with language, where the left is dominant). Further, in patients with left-side cortical lesion, there seems to be a – disinhibitory – release of the right cortex for artistic activity, even in patients who lacked artistic ability before the lesion.

There is something else that the plastic arts, such as painting, reveal better perhaps than any other art category: the power of the unconscious in the creative process. And there is no better treatment of this subject, from the point of view of neuroscience, than Eric Kandel's learned and beautifully illustrated *The Age of Insight* (2012). The book is an in-depth exploration of the powerful influence of unconscious emotion on the production of the modernist painters of the early twentieth century in Vienna, notably Gustav Klimt, Oskar Kokoschka, and Egon Schiele. They were called expressionists, like others of the same period (e.g., Munch, Nolde), because they used art primarily as the medium to express emotion. Each of them had a markedly personal style, although they all used mannerisms (systematic distortions of reality) reminiscent of those of earlier artists (e.g., El Greco, Tintoretto). All used form and color to express, often by dramatic combinations of the two, a wide gamut of human emotions. Their pictorial expressions are highly subjective, defying verbal expression, but their emotional message is rich and powerful. As Kandel remarks, that message is the free expression of those unconscious and unavowed impulses that Sigmund Freud, through his psychoanalytic method, was exposing in his patients at about the same time in the same city.

To me what is most striking is that the artist uses his PA cycle to express himself, and that he obviously intends to engage the beholder of his art in the same cycle. Indeed, it is not difficult to see the artist immersed in two concentric cycles simultaneously, one cognitive and the other emotional (Chapter 4). The two cycles blend intermittently with each other in his prefrontal cortex, both communicating to and fro with an environment dominated by the work of art. It is not difficult to further imagine the artist and the beholder engaged in a silent emotional dialogue in which, through the masterpiece, they query and reply to each other about their most intimate feelings. That dialogue, an interpersonal PA cycle itself, takes place across decades in the context of what Ortega (1961) would call their respective existential "circumstance."

Although all art needs temporal organization, music relies on it more than any other artistic form, for its composition as well as appreciation. The obvious reason is that music essentially consists of temporal gestalts of sound. In that sense, music and language are closely related, and it is not coincidental that the prefrontal cortex is heavily involved in both. Indeed, both require syntax of sounds, both carry prosody, and both can express emotion.

Music, like any other form of creative activity, has a future perspective. Before it is written, it is in the composer's mind. The composer hears the melodies in his head before he plays them on an instrument or writes them down on paper. He writes them for his future enjoyment and that of his listeners. Anticipation is one of the most pleasant aspects of composing, indeed of any creation. The listener, like the composer, enjoys anticipation. After having heard a melody a few times, we relish the experience of anticipating it in our head. Immediately after a given movement of a symphony or sonata has come to an end, we can internally hear the beginning of the next. This too is memory of the future, only this one has been made for us by the composer.

The scientist will use his cerebral cortex to discover phenomena – that is, to create new relations between facts in the world. In science, as in art to some degree, there is a giant PA cycle at work that incorporates the PA cycles of scientists of all times. For generations, all scientists have been using their individual cortices within that collective PA cycle to discover unknown relationships between physical facts. Correlations between new cognits will be used to establish new principles of causality, which will inform the search for new correlations to establish new causalities.[18] This is essentially the circular process, a veritable scientific PA cycle, of discovery of new causal knowledge. In that cycle beats the heart of science with its systole and diastole of deductive and inductive reasoning.

---

[18] In science, it is always a problem to distinguish causal effects from spurious correlations. The problem is magnified in the study of the relations of causality between brain and mind, where only correlations are accessible for analysis. At best, only isomorphic relations can be empirically discerned between the two. However, when the correlations are temporal, the inference of causality from those correlations is greatly facilitated (Granger, 1988; Pearl and Verma, 1991).

Hayek has said, "Without a theory the facts are silent," which itself is an undeniable fact.[19] Yet theories are based on facts. Again, the circularity between the old and the new permeates creativity in science as in any other field of human activity. Inductive inquiry is necessary to classify the world into categories of facts, much as perception does. Analysis will lead to discrimination within those categories. That discrimination in turn will lead to new deductive inferences, which will lead to new hypotheses and new theories to be tested with more facts. And so on.

According to Popper (1980), no theory is worth its salt that cannot in principle be proven wrong ("falsified"). Creation in science thus progresses in circular fashion through a mass of falsifiable theories, verifying with facts those that can be verified. The process is circular – like any PA cycle – between fact and theory, but is not allowed to make any use of circular reasoning. Which means that in that process, there is supposed to be no *petitio principii* or tautology, either in induction or in deduction. All is empirically based in our experience or that of our colleagues and predecessors.

In sum, the liberty to create is a result of the immense plasticity with which evolution has endowed the human brain. That plasticity allows the brain to form and access an enormous wealth of information in memory, information that the brain can freely use to take a wealth of alternative actions. Creative intelligence is the ability of the cortex to utilize that memory and project it into the future in the form of original structures of action. Both the access to memory and the choice of actions are dependent on the strength of synaptic connections built on the plastic structure of the cortex. The synaptic strength of the evolving cognits representing the future creation will depend, in turn, on the firmness of their consolidation by re-entry within their networks. No less, however, it will depend on the power of the creative force that drives those cortical networks from the depths of the emotional brain.

---

[19] I have been unable to find the precise location of the quotation in Hayek's writings, though it is widely attributed to him in studies related to complex phenomena, including history (for example, J. Keegan, *A History of Warfare*, New York, Alfred A. Knopf, 1993).

CONCLUSIONS

At their origin, all human actions that result from free choice have a past and a future. The past consists of the precedents and precursors of the action and its alternatives; the future consists of the action itself and its expected consequences. When important decisions have to be taken and complex plans carried out, the prefrontal cortex comes critically into play as the mediator between past and future. At the top of the PA cycle, in the interface between the organism and its environment, this cortex has access to memory in the broadest sense and at the same time outputs to action also in the broadest sense.

For a decision on new action in the face of uncertainty, ambiguity, or ambivalence, a large variety of influences weigh on the prefrontal cortex, which is the enabling agent of the brain in those circumstances. Some of those influences are conscious, and others unconscious. They include biological drives, autobiographic and semantic memory, ethical and legal constraints, and all other manner of cognits of perception and action distributed over wide areas of association cortex.

The influences from the emotional brain (limbic system), such as those related to biological drives, are funneled to the prefrontal cortex through its orbitofrontal region; the rest, including cognitive memory – perceptual as well as executive – converge on that cortex through connections from other cortical areas. The same influences, through the same inputs, enter the prefrontal cortex in the formation and organization of plans with long PA cycles – that is, with temporally remote objectives.

The execution of a plan requires the complex coordination of several PA cycles directed to the attainment of the plan's ultimate goal. That coordination involves prefrontal executive functions, notably attention and working memory. Both these functions have a focus or nucleus of representation and an exclusionary (inhibitory) component – the latter to overcome interference or distraction. In any decision or plan of action, feedback is essential for verification or correction of goal-directed cycles.

Creative intelligence is the capacity to make new objects of value out of old material and established memory. The value of a created object can vary widely, from monetary to esthetic, from health-related to social, from moral to useful, from educational to cultural. Like planning, the creative process depends on the temporal organizing power of the prefrontal cortex. The next chapter deals with a characteristically human faculty of free will that is creative almost by definition: language.

6

Freedom in speech

Language is a process of free creation; its laws and principles are fixed, but the manner in which the principles of generation are used is free and infinitely varied. Even the interpretation and use of words involves a process of free creation.

Noam Chomsky

The subject of this chapter is the power of speech to protect and enhance our freedom. Thus the focus here is on verbal expression as the brain's tool and guarantor of freedom in human society. Speech is the most human of all human abilities, the ultimate achievement of the evolution of organisms in their long journeys of adaptation to their environment. By speech we demarcate our existence among our fellow humans. By speech *in the future tense* we expand that existence forwards in time and assert our liberty to do it.

Speech is the verbal expression of language, which is a core cognitive function in the neurobiological patrimony of our species. Language is so central to cognition that some have equated the two.[1] "Logos" (*Greek, word*) is at the essence not only of language but also of logical thinking, the two most distinctive constituents of the human mind. Their cognitive primacy, however, does not negate their primal origin. There are means of communication in lower

---

[1] This is a matter of considerable controversy. It is true that language is at the foundation of human cognition (Chomsky, 1985; Fodor, 1975). We now know that language shares with all cognitive functions the same cortical networks and the same neural dynamics. It is not true, however, that language and cognition are identical, for some aspects of cognition are irreducible to language.

species that qualify as precursors of language, though they are far from language itself. The cerebral evolution of language is accompanied by the evolution of the anatomical apparatus for talking.

There is hardly a part of the brain that is not involved in language in one way or another. Disorders of language, however subtle, can result from physical damage to any structure in the cerebrum or cerebellum, in the basal ganglia or limbic system, or in the cortex or subcortex. Nonetheless, language, like any other cognitive function, is most solidly and broadly based in the cerebral cortex. It is now well established that the cognitive aspects of language depend, above all, on the structural and functional integrity of that cortex. Certain areas in it are critical for semantics and speech production, although they participate in other cognitive functions as well, such as, most prominently, logical thinking.[2] Historically, the discovery of those language-related areas played a side role in the birth of phrenology, the long since discredited doctrine of the cerebral localization of mental faculties. However, that discovery also led eventually to the wide acceptance of hubs of heavy association and cognitive commitment in cortical networks.

The prefrontal cortex is heavily involved in language, as it is in any other temporally organized activity.[3] It is particularly

---

[2] The relation between language and logical thinking is unclear (Boroditsky, 2003). Some philosophers take the position that logical thought has a linguistic structure that precedes and gives rise to a natural language. Others take the opposite position: that language precedes thinking, which would borrow its structure from language. Neither position, however, appears more plausible than the other from the point of view of cortical neurobiology, which reconciles them tightly to each other.

[3] The high position of the prefrontal cortex as the temporal organizer and enabler of goal-directed actions defies a unitary neural process. Thus, most physiological studies of this cortex focus on one or another component of temporal organization (working memory, cognitive control, attentive set, corollary discharge, error correction, monitoring, etc.), which they ascribe to one or another of its component areas. However, in the frontal lobe double dissociations of areas and functions are rare and questionable. Indeed, the reductionist analysis of its areas and functions ignores the supraordinate role of the prefrontal cortex, where different areas cooperate closely with one another and with others in the posterior cortex. Besides, any inference of causality within the prefrontal cortex ignores the holistic character of its temporal organizing function and takes it out of the adaptive PA cycle, where there is no identifiable causal origin.

involved in the aspects of language that pertain to the future. Here in the prefrontal cortex is where the critical synergy takes place of decision-making, planning, and creativity on the one hand and language on the other. All four have a future perspective. All are instruments of liberty. All fall within the agenda of the prefrontal cortex, which consequently we are justified to name the "organ of liberty."

PREDICTION

To predict means, literally, to foretell. In general terms, it is synonymous with "to anticipate." It is only in the former sense, however, in the linguistic sense of *diction* or telling, that prediction applies to the human. It is in this sense that prediction bears most directly on freedom.

Animals can anticipate events, but they cannot foretell them because they cannot tell – they have no language – although they have symbolic means of communication (Lyn *et al.*, 2010). There is a great deal of research demonstrating that the nervous system of animals undergoes changes of activity in anticipation of expected events, especially if these involve biological reward or danger of some sort. Most remarkable in this respect is the evidence of anticipatory activity in the cortex of the frontal lobe of primates, the prefrontal cortex in particular.[4] Animal anticipation is the precursor of human prediction before language appears.

Only the human, however, can *tell* ahead of time; that is, humans can utilize language to symbolize future events by means of words – or thoughts – with reference to a time scale of clock and calendar. Even more specifically, human prediction has an

---

[4] Some of the first "anticipatory cells" were discovered among "memory cells" of the prefrontal cortex of monkeys performing delay tasks (Fuster *et al.*, 1982). These are working-memory tasks, in which the animal must retain a sensory cue for a prospective rewarded choice after a delay of a few seconds. The discharge of some cells ramps up in anticipation of that choice and consequent reward. In the human, the neural manifestation of anticipation is epitomized by the "expectancy wave." This is a large negative electrical potential that can be recorded from the surface of the frontal scalp in the interval between two events that are separate in time but mutually contingent upon each other (Brunia, 1985). The expectancy wave, therefore, appears in anticipation of the second stimulus.

existential dimension, in that it includes *self-prediction* – that is, the foretelling of events created by one's own actions and their consequences for the self and for others. It is by self-prediction that the subject can prepare for those actions – and their consequences – within the PA cycle. It is in this sense also that human liberty, with its inherent potential for choice, benefits from language. Language allows us to verbalize to ourselves and to others our predictions toward freedom of choice. This capacity allows us to abridge verbally the course of predicted free action and to form schemas of that course in our head.

A mental map of the future precedes, indeed, the execution of every plan of action to a goal.[5] That temporal map essentially consists of an executive cognit in the frontal cortex that defines schematically the sensory and motor events leading to that goal. As with any item in "future memory," that temporal map or schema is nothing other than a remapping of the past with a future perspective. Out of a mesh of executive memory, the prefrontal cortex "sculpts" in its executive networks that selective schema of future action. The sculpted schema is a network of more or less conscious, predicted representations with temporal order in it.[6]

The selectivity of that schema, however rough at first before execution, rests on the same weighing of priorities – determined by synaptic weights in its network – that we have seen goes into any decision (Chapter 5), only now with added linguistic structure.[7] The schema rests also on the ability we have to suppress

---

[5] The evidence for this is indirect; it derives from the evidence that patients with large prefrontal injury have much difficulty in imagining in any detail a plan of action (Shallice, 1982).

[6] We do not know precisely how time is mapped in the brain, although we are compelled by the evidence to assume that its neural representation is relative and self-referred, not absolute. Even biological "clocks" are "self-referred"; they are regulated by neuroautonomic functions and thus related to them. The diurnal and lunar cycles, in turn, may influence some biological cycles. In any case, our cognit paradigm (Chapter 3) accommodates rather well the Kantian relative and self-referred notion of the two major categories of knowledge, space and time (Guyer, 2004). Both would be relational frames of subjective reference embedded in the relational texture of every cortical cognit.

[7] The Russian neuropsychologist Alexander Luria was the first to remark on the importance of language in the temporal structuring function of the frontal lobe (Luria and Homskaya, 1964).

unsuitable or undesirable alternative actions that are also a product of the past. Selective verbalized planning, like any cognitive function, requires not only focus on a given course of action but also suppression of conflicting alternatives. Our prefrontal cortex does both as it predicts and plans our future. That selective interplay of enhancement and suppression is what I call the "Lebadea principle" of prefrontal function.

At Lebadea, in ancient Greece, there was the famous Oracle of Trophonios, consulted by many who wanted their future predicted (Habicht, 1985). Before being admitted to a sacred cave, where the priest would deliver his divination, the supplicant visitor had to drink the miraculous waters of two nearby springs. First, he drank the water from Lethe (Forgetfulness) in order to forget the cumbersome parts of his past, and then the water from Mnemosyne (Remembrance) in order to better remember what was about to be revealed to him. Similarly, while our prefrontal cortex makes a new plan out of our past, it must reject alternatives out of the same past that are incompatible with that plan.[8] Nothing of it needs to be conscious or verbalized, although some of it will be. Prefrontal activity of any intensity and duration is most likely to be conscious and internally verbalized. We set out to reach many of our goals unconsciously, however, prompted and guided by social context or subliminal cues.

Thus two prefrontal functions, focusing and inhibitory control, work in tandem to selectively predict one's goal-directed actions in the future and to prepare for them. These two functions are the same push–pull functions that will ensure the selectivity of attention to those actions once they get underway in the temporal organization of the planned behavior or language. Like all the cognitive functions that intervene in the temporal organization of actions toward a goal, those two functions have a

---

[8] It is confirmed evidence that the lateral prefrontal cortex – that is, the cortex of the outer convexity of the frontal lobe – is essential for the representation and execution of prospective actions, whereas the orbital (inferior) prefrontal cortex is equally essential for the inhibitory control of interference, distraction, memories conflicting with present plans (Fuster, 2008) – in addition to impulse control. There is also evidence that impulse control may be in large part exerted by direct inhibitory influences from the orbital prefrontal cortex upon subcortical structures, notably the basal ganglia (Aron *et al.*, 2004).

solid base in the prefrontal cortex. Therefore, they develop as the prefrontal cortex develops structurally and functionally in the course of one's life.

Any delay in those developments will result in a delay in the capacity of the individual to organize goal-directed action. In early life, nowhere is this more evident than in the child with ADHD (attention deficit hyperactivity disorder), a suspected consequence of a delay in the maturation of the orbital (inferior) prefrontal cortex (Barkley, 1997). ADHD children suffer from a severe difficulty in planning and conducting goal-directed behavior. In terms of the capacity to plan self-initiated behavior, their future scope is severely restricted. Their most striking disorder is in the area of attention. This disorder usually raises a challenging problem for parents and teachers, since these children are highly distractible, and unable to concentrate their attention.[9] This is because they lack the two prefrontal functions that support the two fundamental aspects of attention to lead behavior to its goal: the focus and the exclusionary inhibitory control, which are needed to avoid distraction. Both are essential requisites for successful schooling.

In the normal child, the predicted future expands gradually with the maturation of the prefrontal cortex. Especially the self-predicted future develops to accommodate the child's striving for independence and free choice. Hence, almost all scholastic programs are empirically adjusted to the capacity of the growing child to mentally expand learning gradually to a progressively more distant future. The ability to construct a self-predicted future grows with age into adolescence and young adulthood, together with – and as a consequence of – prefrontal maturation, which reaches completion at some time in the third decade of life (Chapter 2).

Around age 7, the child becomes powerfully possessed by interests in causality and teleology, the two temporal dimensions of change in the physical world (Piaget, 1952). At that age,

---

[9] No less a challenge for parents and teachers is the behavioral problem of hyperactivity, which is a direct manifestation of poor impulse control, another sign of orbitofrontal immaturity.

questions about the why, the how, and the what-for grow large in the child's mind. It is the time of intense occupation with mechanical and digital toys. It is also a time of social aperture beyond the family, with expansion of friendships and the range of emotional reactivity to other humans, as well as pet animals. The future consequences of study, play, sport, and relationship begin to take on for the child an importance they never had before.

Between ages 6 and 16, language expands enormously. Vocabulary grows by leaps and bounds, and so does the richness of sentence construction.[10] The use of the future tense increases rapidly, and so does the term of prospective action in both language and behavior. These trends are accompanied by an increase in creativity. This increase in creativity, which is clearly an expression of personal liberty, is especially evident in the teenager who discovers that he or she has an exceptional talent for music, art, sport, literature, mechanics, handicraft, or some other field. Understandably, this is the age when scientific careers begin to bud.

Two singular benefits have to be noted from the flourishing of liberty in young people. Whereas it is true that teenagers are capriciously volatile with their favorite activities, it is also true that, whatever one of those activities is at a given time, it usually seems to thrive on a fathomless reservoir of motivational energy. Unquestionably, this energy derives in large part from the discovery of the freedom and independence provided by the knowledge that one can do something exceptionally well, in school or out of it. The praise from others adds positive feedback to the enthusiasm and sense of accomplishment.

The other benefit from the teenager's explosive creativity is the crossover of abilities. Not unusually, the youth transfers to other activities, including schoolwork, the self-confidence and self-discipline that the cultivation of a special talent provides (for example, playing the piano). If multiple endeavors do not come to full fruition, it is generally because of incompatible

---

[10] The capacity for sentence construction increases exponentially together with the capacity to reason, especially in terms of the future. Hughlings Jackson (1915), the famous neurologist of London's Queen Square Hospital, was the first to write about the difficulty that the prefrontal patient had to "propositionise."

time commitments.[11] Along with creativity, mechanical or tech-
nical inventiveness surges, even in fields outside those of one's
talent or competence. Despite the impracticality of many of the
teenager's clever "inventions," there is no question but that his
mind is avidly creating what Gibson (1977) calls new *affordances*,
new possibilities of "doing": again, a sign of expanding freedom.

Whether a teenager has a special talent or not, and whatever
his or her scholastic status, it is clear that in adolescence the
individual is still cognitively and emotionally immature. The
young person does not yet possess the psychological wherewithal
to be a free member of society. That social immaturity derives in
large part from the absence of a full capacity to predict and self-
predict, which only comes with full maturation of the cerebral
cortex. It is especially the maturation of the prefrontal cortex that
confers on the individual the capacity for long-term planning that
goes with advanced prediction.

Evidently because of those developmental facts, society, for
the most part empirically and without the benefit of neurobiological knowledge, does not expect full use of an individual's liberty
until the third decade of the individual's life. To be sure, along with
the liberty at any age comes the responsibility. Although both
generally grow in age *pari passu* with prefrontal maturity, there
are considerable differences between individuals in chronological
age for assuming freedom as well as responsibility. On the way to
adulthood, there are two singular activities that carry both liberty
and responsibility: driving and voting. The age for the freedom to
drive precedes the age for the freedom to vote; and so does the age
for assuming their respective responsibilities.

THE CREATIVE NATURE OF LANGUAGE

Given the extraordinary development of language and of
the prefrontal cortex in the human, both take center stage in
the debate on the neurobiology of liberty. There is one

---

[11] For the sake of student performance, it is incumbent on school systems to
respect and foster special talents, in particular if these can be easily accommodated by appropriate changes in curriculum and without detriment to the
primary scholastic mission.

fundamental reason for it: the immense capacity to predict, and thus to plan and to create, that the prefrontal cortex confers on us. That capacity and its consequences are at the root of human choice. They reach their apogee in the use of language, which closely depends on the functions of that cortex. Language and the prefrontal cortex, together, constitute the ultimate crowning of brain evolution.[12]

More than anything, language – spoken, written, or mentally reasoned – is a creative function of the brain. All language is essentially new. Surely, the reactive, repetitive, instinct-driven, and expletive utterances of the infant or the adult are not novel, but they are not language either. Language is propositional by definition, consisting of sentences, which are concatenations of words linked by relationships of syntax and meaning. Logic and mathematics are forms of language dealing with relationships between propositions, symbols, or numbers. So is logical thinking, which is internal or mental language. Clearly, in whatever form, language, like the code of all cognition, is a relational code,[13] and precisely from this fact, and its recursive property (below), derive its novelty and its freedom. It is not only that language allows us to say new things, but also that it allows us to say many things, old and new, in many different ways.

The essence of a relational code is that it defines information about an object by sets of relations between the parts or

---

[12] *Ultimate* in the full meaning of the word, though in the biological sense no one can say that evolution is finished with us.

[13] Here, as throughout this book, I use the word "code" to characterize information, as transferred and processed by any system, such as the nervous system. The word *code* literally refers to the means of transforming a form of information into another while preserving the meaning of the information. Thus, for example, the Morse code allows the transformation of language into series of dots and dashes (encoding), and vice versa (decoding). In cognition, a relational code is one that defines objects and psychological entities (e.g., percepts, memories) exclusively by virtue of the relations between their attributes. Hence the futility of trying to understand language, or any other cognitive function (for example, perception or memory), by the conventional reductionism of the natural sciences. To understand cognitive causality by extending reductionism below the cognit – i.e., into the cell or the molecule – makes no sense. It is like trying to understand the written message by studying the chemistry of the ink with which it is written (analogy attributed to Roger Sperry).

properties of that object, and is irreducible to them. Thus, an automobile is defined by the structural and functional relations between its parts, and irreducible to them or to their sum. A carburetor, a set of tires, a steering wheel, a gas tank, an engine, a set of spark plugs, and so on are all necessary parts of the vehicle, but the sum total of them all does not define a car. What does define the car is the set of relationships between them. That is, without the relations between its parts, the automobile can neither be defined nor put together, least of all made to run. Any system, mechanical or biological, obeys a relational code of information transfer, processing, or storage, beginning with the genetic code.

Here I have been repeating things I have previously said about the cognit, the unit of memory or knowledge in the cerebral cortex (Chapter 3). I do it because they are central to the brain/liberty debate concerning language use and acquisition. A cognit in the cortex is defined by relations – that is, connections – between neurons, which are largely pre-existing in the cortex and are selected and reinforced, from early life on, by experience. Since cognits are the building blocks of cognition, it follows that all cognitive functions work with a relational code within and between cognits.

In the human, the supreme, most complex, most versatile, most adaptive cognitive function is language. The language code – that is, the syntax and meaning of language – derives from the relations between letters and words. In speech, the relations are between corresponding phonemes or sounds. The vocabulary of any language is generally quite large (a few thousands of words) but finite. However, the possible relations between those words are infinite, as is any combinatorial code of many elements. In this sense, language is no different from any other cognitive function.[14]

---

[14] Language, as much as any other cognitive function such as perception or memory, fits well the cognit paradigm of cognition described in Chapter 3. Like a percept or a memory, a unit of linguistic meaning consists of a network of interconnected neuron assemblies representing smaller units, such as morphemes or phonemes, which are shared by many other linguistic units. Connectionism does with language what gestalt psychology does with

In addition to combinatorial power, language feeds on another source of novelty: recursion. Recursion in language is the capacity to embed sentences within others, each sentence qualifying a part of the sentence in which it is embedded. It is also the related capacity to say or write something in many different ways. In the deep structure of language, each dependent or embedded clause *recurs* to its immediate "nesting clause." Thus, by language, one or several pyramids can be formed of sentences within sentences, each with recursion to a higher one. For example, consider the following statement: "*The tree that George planted when he was little, while still attending elementary school, at age 10, is now bearing fruit, oranges that is, which he is harvesting for his family, who are still living in the same farmhouse.*" Without detailed analysis or quibbling about order and level, this linguistic structure illustrates the principle of recursion. Each qualifying word or sentence in it is like a detour that returns to the main road. Obviously, with regard to the overall meaning of the statement, "oranges" and "age 10" are lowly qualifying elements of the entire sequence. "Tree," "George," "family," and "farmhouse" are at higher levels of the organization of the statement. The stacking of linguistic structures in the statement reflects the hierarchical organization of cognits that language adopts in the cortex and we use in everyday speech.

Recursion applies not only to sentences but also to wider structures of language: paragraphs, sections, chapters, documents, books, public speeches, etc. Clearly, as Chomsky (1957, 2007) has pointedly remarked, recursion is what makes language unlimited. Recursion, in addition, confers on language the same categorical and hierarchical properties that other cognitive functions, such as memory and perception, confer on their cognits. Take the percept or memory of a streetcar, for example. The perceptual or mnemonic cognit of this particular streetcar is nested within the cognit of electric vehicles, which is nested within the cognit of public transportation. Of course, the latter

perception. Both are based on a combinatorial, relational, code: the meaning of a sentence rests on the relations between words much as a geometric figure rests on the relations between points in space. Both language and perception can be reduced to cognits, but not any further, lest either loses its meaning.

category, broadly defined, includes also trains, airplanes, buses, and ocean liners.

There is a huge chasm between human language and the nonhierarchical animal communication. Clearly, it is a difference of several orders of magnitude in terms of the capacity for abstraction, complexity, and prediction. This is because animals simply do not have the cortical circuitry that is necessary to create, generalize, and conceptualize that we have. Nor can animals project their actions into the future by using symbolic representations of the time or order of their actions to a goal.

Without question, the critical difference between animal communication and language is the creative nature of the latter, which is largely attributable to recursion. Animals develop the means of "talking" to each other by imitation and by associating certain sounds with instinctual drives. Those sounds are "prewired" in their neural circuits and, as these circuits develop in the young animal, the sounds become signals for those drives (for example, to flee from danger, gather food, or find a mate). Even animals such as minah birds, finches, or squirrel monkeys, which have extensive "vocabularies," cannot create new combinations of sounds to signify new complex events in the present time, much less in the future.[15]

The human, by contrast, can generate an infinite number of new configurations of speech and meaning by relating in infinite different ways an extensive, though finite, vocabulary. From that derives much of the potential for self-prediction, which allows the human to formulate and carry out plans with reference to himself in them. Here language and thought become the most creative and powerful of all cognitive functions at the service of

[15] Arguably, dolphins and great apes are capable of some kind of very primitive "language," in that they can emit a great variety of sounds and learn to emit some special sounds to name certain individuals or objects. But they cannot use any combinatorial form of sounds to signify complex meaning as in real language, at least not one that humans can decipher. Nonetheless, it has been said that in the English Channel there are at least two species of dolphins, one inhabiting the French side and the other the English side of the Channel (Ansmann, 2005). The two species use different sequences of sounds. Perhaps, in addition to their elaborate system for echolocation, the two groups use their "Dolfrench" or "Dolenglish" for group cohesion and to defend their respective territories!

liberty, which includes the capacity to demarcate new paths of action.

The longer the temporal term of self-prediction and planning, the more important is the command of language. A fundamental reason for the relationship between prediction and language lies in the symbolic and abstract nature of thinking and the language that reflects it. The use of words allows the necessary logical transactions in reasoning and calculation that long-term prediction requires. Without words and syntax with a future perspective, it is impossible to conceive of, to verbalize, or to lay down on paper any plan of prospective action, especially if it is complex or involves elaborate contingencies. Therein lies the importance of the maturity of the prefrontal cortex for long-term planning. This cortex is critical for the temporal organization of willed actions of all kinds (Fuster, 2001) as well as for the language that will describe those actions ahead of time – that is, while they are still in the process of planning.

It is common knowledge that the articulate individual has more advantages in life than the inarticulate one. Being articulate means to be able to use language logically and convincingly, whether it is in speech or in writing, in intimate company or in the public forum. It is most important in all these contexts to use dependent clauses appropriately and the equally appropriate ranking of priorities. Socially, good linguistic ability opens many doors. Being articulate, in any field of human endeavor, enhances one's choices and chances to succeed. It is a must in education and academia, indispensable in business, and a valuable resource to any liberal profession.[16]

Therefore, it is not difficult to understand why better language leads to more freedom. For one thing, a better understanding and expression of our thoughts opens the range of our options. The key lies in the power of language to create new affordances, new possibilities of action for us and for those who in some way depend on us. Creative language expands alternatives, not only for choice of information but also for choice of

---

[16] Consequently, there is a great variety of training courses in public speaking, beginning with those pioneered and made famous by Dale Carnegie.

action that in one way or another is contingent on that information. In a linguistic frame, a well laid-out plan is one that, out of an assortment of well-evaluated data, serves the planner to generate a course of action that will lead to a valuable outcome. The feedback from any component action and its results is at the root of the success of a plan. This is applicable to any plan in the fields of science, business, architecture, engineering, medicine, or any other, including government.[17] It cannot be overstated that education in the use of proper language is the surest, most efficient, and most economical means to enhance and protect the liberty of the citizenry. The responsibility for this kind of education falls upon the private as well as the public sector of society.

NEUROBIOLOGY OF LANGUAGE

Neurolinguistics is a young science. It deals with the neural processes by which the brain develops and uses language. Until recently, neurolinguistics has been driven by much speculation and few solid facts. Nowhere else in cognitive neuroscience has there been such a gap between knowledge and conjecture. The gap is entirely attributable to the complexity of language, a uniquely human cognitive function without a real parallel in animals.

That situation is changing rapidly, however. There is now growing understanding and proof of three fundamental principles of the organization of speech in the brain. The first is that the cortical networks that represent language are widely distributed and largely coincide with the networks that represent the information for use by any other cognitive function. The second principle is that those same networks assist in the acquisition as well as the spoken expression of language. And the third is that speech depends on the good functioning of a PA cycle much as any other form of goal-directed behavior. All three principles have much to

---

[17] Sadly missing in many governmental plans, as already stated, is the self-monitoring feedback for midcourse correction. This is where self-perpetuating government bureaucracies almost invariably fail. No plan ever succeeds out of a public PA cycle if that cycle does not receive permanent feedback evaluation of the plan and its consequences. Without them, effective self-correction is impossible.

do with the liberty that speech gives us. In this section, I shall deal with the first two principles, and in the next section with the third.

Some neurolinguists treat language as a separate immaterial "substance," like consciousness or "the self," which somehow drives our brain to make us speak. This is a dualist position that cannot be reasonably defended. A more reasonable position is that there is a yet unspecified but specialized brain "module" for language. Among those who think this way are the so-called nativist linguists, who contend that language capacity is a genetic trait unique to man, hardwired in a brain module, which in due course – not later than puberty – becomes operational together with other genetic aspects of brain function. By contrast, empiricist behaviorists contend that the brain acquires language by experience in the same manner as any other cognitive ability, and that some parts of the brain, notably the left hemisphere, are better at it than others.

A major development in the early history of cognitive neuroscience was the identification of two cortical areas of association in the left hemisphere of the brain that seemed to specialize in the two principal components of linguistic ability: the understanding and the production of speech. The area for the second was found first. In 1861 the French neurologist Paul Broca described the peculiar case of a patient who, after a large lesion in the left frontal lobe, had a great deal of difficulty in spontaneously articulating speech (Broca, 1861). His speech was scanty and characterized by short, choppy, "telegraphic" sentences without articles and junction words. The cortical area affected was that of the third or inferior convolution of the left frontal lobe. With time and additional cases from similar lesions, that area became known as Broca's area, and the speech disorder resulting from its damage *Broca's aphasia*.

Some time later, Wernicke (1874) described the converse disorder – that is, *semantic aphasia* – which is characterized by difficulty in understanding the meaning of language; this type of aphasia is also called "fluid aphasia," because it consists of fluid, verbose, although nonsensical, speech. Such a disorder results from lesions of the left posterior cortex, around the so-called angular convolution. Eventually, the two cortical areas,

Broca's and Wernicke's, were universally recognized as the centers of major brain involvement in speech production and speech meaning, respectively. In due time, however, neurologists gradually found that lesions occurring around those centers also produced aphasias of essentially the same two kinds, although milder (Figure 6.1). Lesions of the fiber tracts between the two areas lead to mixed forms of aphasia, named *conduction aphasias*.

The clinical picture of an aphasia or disorder of speech is, we might say, the "photographic negative" of the function that the affected brain area normally performs in speech before the lesion. Modern functional imaging, by testing the speech functions of a normal subject in the scanner, is beginning to provide the "positive picture" of the involvement of the brain in speech *and related cognitive functions*.[18]

It has long been known that brain lesions causing aphasias also cause disorders in other cognitive functions, such as perception and memory, which are intimately related to speech. For example, lesions of posterior association cortex commonly result not only in semantic aphasias but also in nonverbal semantic memory deficits, and agnosias.[19] Conversely, frontal lesions produce deficits in the ideation of plans of action in addition to varying degrees of speech production aphasias. Norman Geschwind, a Harvard neurologist, in seminal publications (Geschwind, 1965a, 1965b), was the first to recognize the role of connections between cortical neuron assemblies far apart from one another in a number of cognitive disorders from cortical lesions. His study instigated a profusion of anatomical studies of

---

[18] Remarkably, several studies (see reviews by Bookheimer, 2002; Price, 2010) show paradoxical activation of the frontal cortex (i.e., Broca's area) during semantic processing of meaning. This highlights two problems: one is the difficulty that functional imaging has in dissociating meaning from speech production; the other is the inescapable reality that, also in the dynamics of speech, we cannot dissociate the two functions, in any case not any better than we can experimentally split the PA cycle. A recent imaging study highlights the joint activation of the left posterior and the frontal cortex in the syntax of language (Griffiths *et al.*, 2012).

[19] The word "agnosia" was invented by Sigmund Freud (1891) to refer to the difficulty in recognizing the names of common objects. Semantic agnosia, a special case of both anomia (name loss) and amnesia, is the difficulty to recall words or names.

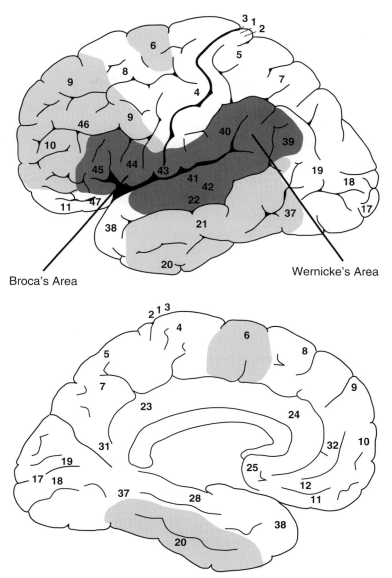

Broca's Area

Wernicke's Area

Figure 6.1 Lateral and medial views of the cortex of the left hemisphere (Brodmann's map) with areas marked whose lesions lead to speech disorders (aphasias). The most severe disorders result from damage in the *red* areas, and the less severe in the *pink* areas.

cortical connectivity, which eventually did much to generate my concept of cognitive network or cognit (Chapter 3).

Lesions of the prefrontal cortex are instructive, as they produce disorders of language that, despite being relatively subtle, can severely undermine the flexibility and freedom of speech. Alexander Luria, the eminent Russian psychologist, called the prefrontal language disorder *frontal dynamic aphasia*. Indeed, the prefrontal patient is deprived not only of planning ability but also of the propositional properties of language.[20] The patient's speech is generally impoverished and lacks spontaneity, fluidity, and future perspective. The most typical though subtle abnormality is the almost complete absence of recursion, which means a dearth of dependent, embedded sentences in the patient's speech. The abnormality is surely the "negative" of rich, elaborate, and creative speech. It is the contrary of the unfettered linguistic flexibility and freedom that grace the speech of the creative speaker.

No one can seriously contest that the neural infrastructure of language is an inherited product of evolution, as complex and adaptive as any other, and, at the same time, open to experience and innovation like none other. Yet, concerning language, there is a perpetual, never quite resolved, nature/nurture debate. Because complex propositional language is uniquely human,[21] the debate is often fiercely anthropocentric. The nature of universal grammar (UG) is a prime focus of that debate. Noam Chomsky (1965), in reaction to the excesses of behaviorism, and based on the prodigious ability of children to create proper syntax, proposed UG as an innate, inherited, ability or faculty that invariably appears in every normal child as he or she develops.

Many brain scientists are skeptical of innate grammar. There are two principal reasons for that. One is the difficulty

---

[20] We have known since Jackson (note 10), for example, that the first casualty of frontal damage is the ability to "propositionise," another word for recursion or its derivatives in the construction of language, especially with reference to future action (Jackson, 1915).

[21] To be sure, animal communication can be considered a precursor of human language, and there are examples of "proto-languages" in certain primates, like chimps and vervet monkeys. But neither recursion nor syntax, two essential characteristics of language, has been conclusively demonstrated in animal "language."

that biologists have in accepting the inheritability – versus the learning – of any kind of "rules" of behavior. The other reason is the simplistic position of many neuroscientists with regard to learning and memory in general. With respect to language, their position is almost exclusively based on the duality of the two described cortical areas of the left hemisphere: one for the understanding and the other for the expression of language. They fail to see the global aspects of language and the participation of other cortical areas in it.

The language/brain controversy has been muddied further by the misuse of computer analogies. There are computer "languages" and computer synthesizers of language, and there is symbolic language (for example, algorithms) for mathematical computation. But the neuro-computational aspects of language are beyond our reach and will remain so. The reason is simple: a lexical entity such as a word derives meaning exclusively from its relations to many others in the same or different context. Here again reductionism – that is, reducing everything to its minimal parts – is self-defeating. No computer can ever simulate the zillion chemical reactions and cell action potentials that sustain the huge combinatorial code of the cerebral cortex engaged in language. Both the epistemology and the methodology of neurolinguistics need a "floor" such as the cognitive network or cognit, which is the unit of memory and knowledge. Below that floor, language loses its meaning, literally.

Language nativists are correct when they claim that we are born with a unique piece of "hardware" in our brain that with the proper "software" – from culture and learning – will produce language and speech. What gives that hardware–software brain duality its power to represent and handle language is not the volume or even the number of neurons in it, but the *connectivity* between them, with which we are born. Connectivity provides our brain with infinite combinatorial power for *syntax*, not only in language but also in all other manner of coordinated action.[22] The

[22] Karl Lashley spoke of the "syntax of the action," extending the concept beyond linguistic syntax to goal-directed actions in general (Lashley, 1951), a concept also espoused by the developmental psychologist Greenfield (1991). They did not, however, single out the cortex of the frontal lobe as the

combinatorial information present and potential in the cortex exceeds by much that of the genome. From that potential stems the creativity of language. This is the real root of our liberty to choose language and to use it freely. In any event, the more free and novel our choice of words is, the more assertive and resilient our freedom will be among those who listen to us.

Now, what about the uniqueness of human language? Many evolutionary biologists point to the enormous, indeed exponential, increase in the size of the cortex as evolution progresses to primates and *Homo sapiens* (Chapter 2). A less known fact is that the increase in white matter – that is, in cortical connections – is even sharper than the increase in cortex size (Frahm *et al.*, 1982). Cortical connectivity, more than volume and cell numbers, is the decisive evolutionary expander of the cognitive code, and thus of the linguistic code. With expansion of connectivity, the potential for relational information expands and, because that expansion is exponential, the potential for language increases sharply in the human.

With these facts in mind, the question of continuity versus discontinuity in the evolution of cognition, language in particular, becomes meaningless. Indeed, a very steep exponential increase in the curve of cortical connectivity as a function of evolution – say, between a great ape and man – is bound to appear as a step function. For all practical purposes, it is. In other words, the newness and uniqueness of human language may be simply products of a drastic increase in cortical connective complexity, as especially evident in the absence of intermediate species for comparison, whether they were apes or hominids.[23]

Does any of that negate Chomsky's contention that we inherit the rules of grammar from our predecessors? I do not believe it does, if we properly qualify the origin of those rules.

---

temporal integrator of action, as I have proposed on the basis of extensive evidence from many studies (Fuster, 2008).

[23] Here a fact of the upmost importance is that, in the evolution up to the human, the white matter of the prefrontal cortex – its fast-conducting myelinated connectivity – is the one that increases the most among those of all brain structures (Schoenemann *et al.*, 2005). Therefore, it is correct to conclude that the connectivity of the prefrontal cortex, the foundation of free language, sets us humans apart from all other animals.

In fact, a careful analysis of the evolution of language and of its cognitive and cerebral foundations lends some credence to that notion. Here I am compelled to provide a qualified defense of it because in my view the use of grammar has much to do with the liberation of man from the here-and-now and with his aperture to the future.

I will base my qualifying argument on three premises. The first is that the human brain is endowed with the connective hardware to *categorize* both objects and actions. By categorizing I mean classifying. Perception is the classification of objects by relations within themselves and with other objects (Hayek, 1952). In the same manner, we also categorize actions by associations within and between themselves and with reward, purpose, and goal. Many of those associations are innate, phyletic, and genetic. Just as there are, in the brain, primitive perceptual cognits like faces,[24] there must also be primitive cognits of action in terms of certain spatial-temporal attributes of action in general: temporality (when actions occur, and for how long), probability (how likely they will occur), causality (how are they produced, and by what or whom), conditionality (on what events or other actions, past or future, they depend), and numerosity.[25] The rules of grammar would be essentially based on those attributes of action, especially if they have a substantial temporal dimension.

The second premise is that, in the cerebral cortex, the cognits of action as well as those of perception, are *hierarchically* organized (Chapter 3). Perceptual cognits are organized in the

---

[24] Because of their intense associative nature, network nodes of the visual representation of faces can be found all over the cortex. However, functional neuroimaging has identified a cortical area in the lower part of the brain where all faces are most consistently represented: the fusiform gyrus (McCarthy *et al.*, 1997). That cortical area is near the primary visual cortex, and thus is very early and hierarchically low in the chain of areas engaged in the processing of visual information. It could be the seat of an inherited (phyletic) cognit for the basic characteristics of a face (eyes, nose, lips, etc.) linked by relationships that are constant, prototypical, in every face. Higher in the hierarchy, each individual face in the world around us, beginning with that of our mother, would acquire associations with age, gender, name, and so on, to become the "face cognits" of our individual memories.

[25] Numerosity is the conceptual and developmental basis of numbers and mathematics (Dehaene, 1997). In this case it refers to the number of agents, actions, and their antecedent or consequent events and contingencies.

posterior cortex by order of complexity, with the most concrete cognits at the bottom near the sensory cortex and the most abstract in the higher association cortex. Similarly, in the frontal cortex, cognits of action are hierarchically organized, with concrete (phyletic) actions in the motor cortex and the most complex in the prefrontal cortex. Similarly, one of the fundamental concepts of modern linguistics is that language is also hierarchically organized. Accordingly, there is in the posterior cortex a hierarchy for the semantic, perceptual, cognits of language, and another in the frontal cortex for its syntactic, executive, cognits. Linguistic sentences, especially if they are elaborate and rich in dependent clauses, contain a range of overlying and embedded cognits – that is, of constructs of perception and of action that are dynamically interlinked by grammar in the PA cycle of speech.

The third premise is that the prefrontal cortex not only contains the cognitive representation of the most complex sequences of goal-directed action but also participates in their *expression*. Transposing to language that principle, the prefrontal cortex emerges as the highest organizer of language and its grammar. It is no coincidence, but a manifestation of biological causality, that with the development and maturation of the prefrontal cortex, language becomes progressively richer and grammar becomes open to the future and to the infinite possibilities of expression that language offers.[26] At the same time, neurobiology provides clear indications that linguistic syntax is a special case of Lashley's (1951) syntax of action and that the two share the same cortical infrastructure. Another revealing fact in terms of the neurobiological relation between language and general action is that the evolution of Broca's area, a subdivision of the prefrontal cortex, correlates with the evolutionary development of tool usage (Greenfield, 1991).

---

[26] Future action is categorized differently in different languages. In languages derived from Latin, it is categorized by an inflection of the verb. In English, future action is categorized by preceding the infinitive of action with the verb *will*, and in German with a conjugated form of the verb *werden* (to become). Interestingly, both Germanic auxiliary verbs imply temporal change into the future, a change that is "voluntarily" (transitive) induced in the case of English – even if it is by an inanimate force.

It is an error to separate language from the other cognitive functions. This artificial separation ignores the obvious fact that language in all its forms depends on all other cognitive functions. These are essential to guide speech, to store it in memory, to acquire semantic knowledge, to retrieve such knowledge, to perform any task requiring verbal intelligence, and to make decisions on choice of language. Therefore, we must inescapably assume that language and speech use the same cortical networks, the same cognits, that other cognitive functions use. Cognitive neuroscience amply supports this assumption.[27] Essentially, linguistic cognits largely overlap, if they do not coincide with, the cognits representing the subjects and objects of speech, and the recognition and use of those subjects and objects activate the same cortical areas that are activated in their spoken expression. The damage to these areas degrades the expression of language.

To sum up, linguistic cognits are hierarchically organized like perceptual and executive cognits. Simple lexical expressions with concrete meaning lie in networks of the sensory and the motor association cortex, whereas complex expressions lie in more widely distributed networks of the higher posterior or the frontal cortex. In either case, expressions with concrete meaning are nested within wider, more abstract, expressions.[28] In memory recall, words with sensory connotations tend to activate cognits predominantly, but not exclusively, in the posterior cortex, whereas words connoting action – such as active verbs – activate frontal cognits (Cappelletti *et al.*, 2008; Caramazza and Hillis, 1991;

---

[27] Here I could refer to the work of many researchers, which I have covered in some detail in two other publications (Fuster, 2003, 2009). In summary, the evidence comes basically from two major fields of neuroscience: neuropsychology – that is, the study of the clinical and psychological effects of cortical lesions – and functional neuroimaging by positron emission tomography (PET) or functional magnetic resonance imaging (fMRI).

[28] *Nesting* in this context means that small cortical units of meaning and syntax are embedded within larger ones, just as in the formal structure of language. The meaning of "cocker spaniel" is embedded in the network category of "dogs," and that one into "domestic animals," and that into "mammals," and so on. The color "yellow" is embedded into many categories of objects, such as "canaries," "yellow roses," and "bananas." Any of these words can be part of many dependent clauses embedded in larger sentences, and these into yet larger ones. Many linguistic cognits are "heterarchical," in that they are associated with others at different levels of a hierarchy.

Tyler *et al.*, 2008). It appears generally true that two linguistic hierarchies, one in the posterior cortex for the meaning of words and sentences, and the other in the frontal cortex for their expression, closely overlap, if they do not coincide with, the two corresponding hierarchies for perception and action, respectively.

Now, with the premises and evidence summarized, we can attempt to substantiate the relationship between neurobiology and an "innate" UG. To begin with, we must provide UG with an inheritable base in the brain. The only plausible way to do it is to immerse language in the anatomical substrate of the other cognitive functions, which language obviously needs for its development: attention, perception, memory, and intelligence, the last one deeply anchored in language as well as in the other three. This implies that if language has a genetic base, this base must be in the cerebral cortex.

The hierarchical cortical substrate that supports the dynamic aspects of linguistic syntax is made of all the cortical areas, and their resident cognits – perceptual and executive – that support the PA cycle in language. At the base of that substrate are the primary sensory and motor cortices, the hardcore of the evolutionary, indisputably genetic, parts of the cortex that I call *phyletic* memory. Those cortices, undeveloped as they are at birth, are clearly insufficient to produce syntax at any level, innate or acquired, but are indispensable for the genetic expression and acquisition of language. Above that base, in the hierarchical organization of cognition, as well as language, are the associative areas of the posterior cortex and of the frontal – i.e., prefrontal – cortex. Any kind of syntax will require the function of these areas. Thus, with these areas, sensory, motor and associative, we have identified the cortical "hardware" for linguistic syntax that the proponents of a UG assume.

But then, to follow their logic, we also have to postulate "software" for the elementary syntax of coordinated action as well as of speech. That software, I propose, consists of the dynamics of the PA cycle, which engages those cortices in the temporal and hierarchical integration of goal-directed actions, including speech. Thus, a basic linguistic syntax would share those cortices with the "syntax of action" postulated by Lashley (1951). That syntax, linguistic or executive, would involve practically all areas of the posterior and the prefrontal association cortex, in particular Wernicke's area and Broca's area.[29]

From these considerations it is reasonable to conclude, as I attempt to do, that a UG is a special case of the cortical dynamics of the syntax of coordinated action in the PA cycle. Both forms of syntax would strengthen each other in the dynamics of the PA cycle. At low hierarchical levels, concrete sensorimotor action would support concrete, low-level lexical syntax; conversely, high-level cognitive action would support general PA rules. Thus, the PA cycle, working at various levels of temporal integration of perception with action, would yield and use the rules of a grammar at different levels of complexity – that is, at different levels of a linguistic hierarchy.

Thus, the rules of grammar would co-emerge in the mind of the child with the rules of goal-directed action. That explains why children develops the rules of speech at the same time that they develop the concepts and cognitive functions for the temporal organization of actions: working memory (Gathercole *et al.*, 2004), time (Berndt and Wood, 1974), the future (Hudson, 2006), conditional reasoning (Markovits and Barrouillet, 2002), causality (Kuhn and Phelps, 1976), temporal contingency (Keller *et al.*, 1999), temporal order (Bullock and Gelman, 1979), gender (Emmerich *et al.*, 1977), and numerosity (Butterworth, 2005). The general rules of grammar, including the use of function words and inflexions, would derive in the mind of the child from these concepts and operations.

In my view, therefore, a "universal syntax" emerges in the evolving cortex to organize goal-directed action, including speech, in the temporal axis. Language expands that syntax

---

[29] The widespread base of the lexicon in the cerebral cortex explains why Ojemann and his colleagues, by electrical stimuli applied directly to the human brain (a form of brief reversible lesion), were able to block the expression of assorted words and the naming of objects from so many and so widespread points of the cortical surface (Corina *et al.*, 2010; Lucas *et al.*, 2004; Ojemann *et al.*, 2008). Most such points, however, were found in the dominant hemisphere (left in most people). Further, some differences – in effective locus of blockage – were observed in bilingual subjects between the first and the second language.

backwards and forwards in time, by giving actions an active and a passive voice, a past and a future, and by mediating the contingencies between the last two. The child will implement that natural syntax with the innate faculty to use function words, inflexions, and, above all, the future tense. With it, in the adult, ultimate goals will become mottos, and intermediate goals will become verbal guidelines or dependent clauses. Thus, a genetic UG would derive from, or rather be connatural with, the genetics of the brain (Christiansen and Chater, 2008).

In summary, speech results from the coordinated and timely activation of cognits of perceptual memory in the posterior cortex and cognits of action (executive) memory in the frontal cortex. To understand how those cortices cooperate in the production of speech requires some discussion of how they engage in the PA cycle, which underlies the dynamics of creative freedom in language as in any other cognitive function.

SPEECH IN THE PA CYCLE: THE VOICE OF LIBERTY

The two language regions of the cortex, one in the back for meaning and the other in the front for articulation, constitute the two dynamically interlinked cerebral poles of the PA cycle for speech. As we speak, we assemble meaning in the posterior cortex, which informs our expression in the frontal cortex. This in turn is monitored by the posterior cortex for meaning and external impact, leading to further expression, and so on. All of this happens mainly but not exclusively in the left or dominant hemisphere. The cycle goes on until our speech reaches its objective of giving full meaning to what we say and of having its expected effects on our listener(s). Less evident, though essential to understand the neurobiology of the spoken language, is the fact that in the verbal dialogue between two speakers, their PA cycles are nested within the wider PA cycle that runs through their brains and their environment. For each speaker, the interlocutor is at that time the most relevant changing part of that environment.

As we speak we also engage in thinking, which is internal language, where the interlocutor is oneself. Cognitive reasoning becomes part of that internal language which bridges meaning and syntax in the cycle of a speaker. The relations of meaning and syntax that go into speaking include a wealth of associations – more or less free and more or less conscious – with the knowledge and memory that pre-exist in the cerebral cortex of the speaker. That wealth of associations is going to inform and bias his speech, even though much of that associative baggage may be unconscious or intuitive. An essential component of that baggage is emotional memory and what Kahneman (2011) calls system-1 thinking.

Indeed, to one degree or another, associations with items of emotional memory color our conversation. In some instances the emotional bias is obscured by protocol and formality; in others, it is patently obvious and accompanied by the nonverbal language of emotion. Aside from the color that emotion gives to our speech prosody, our body language can be sometimes as nuanced as – and often even more explicit than – our words. Especially when we talk about liberty, we can rarely do it without a tinge of pathos or enthusiasm in our voice. In fact, where our liberty is in danger, there is usually more than a tinge. "Give me liberty or give me death!" Patrick Henry cried in arguably the most impassioned assertion of liberty in American history.[30]

With emotion in the PA cycle for language, our discussion in this chapter comes literally full circle – no pun intended. The reason is because, in the history of the individual as that of the species, the PA cycle (Chapter 4) begins with the fulfillment of the most basic needs of the organism, and that fulfillment is often brought about by verbal expression. The cry of the newborn, together with the palpating search of the mother's breast, are the most elementary inborn actions of the nascent PA cycle. At that time the cycle is pure biology, as perception is yet to be born and action to be refined. But that sensory-motor cycle, consisting of little more than natural reflexes, will eventually evolve into the adult PA cycle. The individual development of the PA cycle is a long process that, like the evolution of the brain, culminates with the appearance and maturation of the prefrontal cortex.

---

[30] In a speech he made to the Virginia Convention, on March 23, 1775, in the presence of Thomas Jefferson and George Washington.

The maturation of the cerebral cortex brings cognition, which is made of memory and knowledge. And with cognition comes language. The cries of the infant will become babble, and in due time the spoken language with its naming, indicating, and imitating (Karmiloff and Karmiloff-Smith, 2001; Mehler and Dupoux, 1994). Elementary sensations will agglutinate into perceptions, and these, with their history in the form of cognits or cognitive networks, will begin to populate the posterior cortex of association. Part of that history will be contained in nervous associations with the sounds of words, along with their written symbols and their meaning. That meaning will include connotations of need and reward, and along with them the affective states and emotions they evoke. All of those inputs of neural information will enter the PA cycle of behavior and, together with it, speech.

In Chapter 4, I have argued for an emotional PA cycle paralleling the cognitive PA cycle, and at the same time feeding limbic (emotional) influences into it. Here, in the context of language, I have to expand the discussion by arguing for the biological primacy of the first cycle and for the functional unity of the two cycles. There is no question but that the cognitive language of the child, together with reasoning capacity, evolves from the rudimentary expressions associated with the biodrives. It is on that biological foundation that the ability to communicate logically with others arises. Gradually, propositional language enters the picture. The young subject begins to put sentences together in logical fashion, to stack them hierarchically by level of abstraction, thus using recursion in the structure of language. In terms of evolutionary biology, the latter faculty, with its inherent capacity for linguistic innovation and creativity, is the most distinctly human of all the properties of early language.

By virtue of the biological origin of language and the role of emotion in it at all ages, the PA cycle for speech retains the interplay of cognition and emotion throughout our life. In previous chapters I have pointed out the importance of the prefrontal cortex, at the summit of the cycle, to guide planning, decision-making, and creativity. Here I have to do the same with regard to language, where the prefrontal cortex of the human assumes the same high position in the linguistic cycle as it does in goal-directed behavior.[31]

The choice of speech, like that of any other structured action of the organism, is driven by cognitive and emotional influences. That choice, thus our liberty to chose between verbal alternatives, will fall on the prefrontal cortex, which will weigh all those influences – in or out of consciousness – to guide the entire cortex engaged in the verbal PA cycle toward the goal of the language chosen. Except in emergencies, there is no single "determinant" of our choice of speech. That choice is commonly the exit path of innumerable avenues of neural information entering the cerebral cortex for evaluation and for the weighing of risks and benefits, now and in the future. The choice is determined by the consequences of past choices of information, cognitive or emotional, internal or external, conscious or unconscious. Thus, the possible "determinants" of choice are so many and from so many sources (Figure 5.1), their weight and probability so variable, and their mutual compatibility so uncertain, as to make the determinism of the chosen speech a useless concept. *Within constraints*, our brain is indeed free to choose what to say and when and how to say it.

Again, as with every other kind of action, the choosing agency for speech is the cerebral cortex, which, with its perceptual and executive halves, constitutes the interface between the sensing and acting self and the internal and external worlds. The choosing agency here is the cortical ensemble of the semantic and executive cortices for language, with Wernicke's area and Broca's area at their centers, engaged in the verbal PA cycle. It is that cortical unitary system in the brain side of the cycle that in

---

[31] The anatomy of that confluence of cognitive and emotional influences on the PA cycle is well established. Cognitive inputs come to the prefrontal cortex from the entirety of the neocortex, including the primary sensory cortices, which convey to the dorsolateral prefrontal cortex (the cortex of the outer frontal convexity) signals from the environment. In parallel, emotional inputs come also from the environment, through sensory analyzers, and in addition from the limbic brain – notably, the hypothalamus, the amygdala, the hippocampus, and the cingulated cortex. These emotional inputs enter the prefrontal cortex mainly through its inferior or orbital region, and from there they flow into the prefrontal dorsolateral region, where they join cognitive inputs and thus complete the emotional PA cycle.

Chapter 4 I have named the "hemicycle of liberty." That system is essentially, in itself, our free choosing and deciding I.

Now that I have placed my *I* squarely in my cortex, I can do here a cursory self-analysis of the multiplicity of factors that on a certain occasion – referred to in the preface – acted on my cortex to "determine" my decision to speak to some people in a certain manner. The Ipsen Foundation had given me an award[32] and invited me to Paris to receive it in the Charcot Auditorium of the university medical school. After being presented with the award and expressing my gratitude, I gave a short speech to an audience composed mainly of neurologists and neuroscientists. Its title, of my own choosing, was "Liberty and the executive of the brain." My experience then, as now, was and is that my choices of title and content for that speech were entirely free, certainly picked out of many alternatives for choice. Surely, however, those choices were in large part a direct consequence of my education, scientific background, and humanistic interests. The frontal lobes, which Karl Pribram (1973) had once called "the executive of the brain," were at the center of my research, and I had recently completed the third edition of my book on them. That research and related studies had convinced me that no truly biological explanation of human liberty was possible without taking the prefrontal cortex into account. That was the essence of my little speech.

It is clear in retrospect, however, that, on that occasion, my choices of language and content were to a large extent biased if not determined by some circumstances of the moment and some unconscious motives of my own. Charcot, after whom the auditorium was named, was a famous neurologist at the Salpêtrière Hospital, where I was speaking. He was the undisputed pioneer in the study of hysteria. Charcot and Freud (De Marneffe, 1991), who were very close friends, had extensively debated the psychological determinism of the conversion symptoms of the illness ("psychogenic" fits, fainting, paralysis, mutism, pain, and so on),

---

[32] The award was the Jean-Louis Signoret Prize for the year 2000. Professor Signoret was a famous neurologist at the Salpêtrière and one of the most illustrious investigators of the neuropsychology of language.

those robbers of personal freedom from the depths of the unconscious. Having had psychoanalytic training earlier in my career, my speech may have contained some subtle attempt to liberate my cortical liberty from the constraints of the limbic system, "the seat of the id." Then there was my choice of giving the speech in French, which I spoke much less than proficiently. Surely that choice must have been a gesture of courtesy toward my hosts. But with it I was obviously running the risk of offending the Parisian French, who are exceedingly proud of their language and whose tolerance for its transgressors is near zero. Was I emboldened to do it because my native Catalan resembles French? Did the fact that I had had a French nanny in my infancy play a role of some kind? An even greater risk than my choice of French was the pretense, which some may have interpreted as intellectual hubris, of attempting to explain in a few minutes, to specialists of the nervous system, the complex matter which is now the subject of this book.

If I have gone into so much detail about my speaking experience it has been simply to illustrate the variety of "determinants" that go into many of our private decisions to choose our words. To speculate about the determinism of our free speech at the biophysical level may be philosophically reasonable but is completely irrelevant to the neurobiology of liberty, which obeys principles of neural dynamics at a much higher level of causality, where the word governs the behavior of brain cells, not the other way around. This in no way denies the physical constraints on free speech, which are exacerbated by disability and oppression. In any event, whether free will exists or not, I am sure I would have said in Paris the same things that I did say. And so would have done Patrick Henry in Richmond in 1775.

The speech of a slavery foe in early America brings me to the present public discourse on liberty and its relation to neurobiology. Hardly anyone will argue against the fact that private liberty and public liberty are mutually and tightly interrelated. On evolutionary as well as neuroethological grounds, there is supposed to be harmony, even synergy, between the two. Evolution is a process of adaptation of the population to the milieu; therefore, evolution has made the individual members of present and future populations more adaptable to that milieu. The liberty of choice gained today by many will benefit the individual of tomorrow. Conversely, today's individual liberty benefits from prior liberty of the population. The same process takes place in the history of humankind. Human institutions codify in writing the benefits to both private and public liberty, and they legislate the ways to preserve them and protect them.

Conflict often occurs, however, between private and public liberties. In a democracy, our representatives in government make laws to resolve that conflict, and their speeches in governmental chambers and in the media portray their attempts to do it justly. Typical conflicts develop around taxation, for example, which commonly lead to the fiery rhetoric of politicians in defense of the public interest. That interest is bound to infringe to some degree on private property, which is one of the alleged pillars of individual liberty. The radical libertarian will advocate minimal taxation, only to cover the elementary needs of the nation – whereby other private and public needs may remain unmet. The radical socialist will advocate maximal taxation, especially of the rich. So, barring both extremes, the question is always, how much to tax and to whom. The question becomes the more pressing in bad economic times. Here the politician is often caught between the public cry and commonly unreliable statistics.[33]

No wonder that in times of uncertainty, public opinion and the rhetoric of politicians become so voluble. Under the circumstances, the role of the political leader in the defense of liberty consists in entering with persuasive reasoning a giant PA cycle between him and the collective cortex of his constituents.[34] That cycle, of course, runs through the ballot box.

---

[33] The best governmental statistics and the supposedly most solid algorithms are fraught with imponderable future variables (wars, cost of commodities, natural disasters, employment, etc.). Some of those variables are driven by the unpredictable cognitive and emotional choices of people exercising the very liberties everybody is trying to protect.

[34] The demagogue will enter the cycle through a "collective limbic system," the aggregate of neural substrates for the emotions of the popular masses, which he will attempt to mobilize to support his more or less rational discourse.

CONCLUSIONS

The power of speech to support our freedom stems mainly from the predictive and executive functions of the prefrontal cortex at the summit of the PA cycle. These functions facilitate the exchange of information between the prefrontal cortex and the brain structures that store memory and are involved in the expression of language. Thus, through that cortex, the inputs arising from cortical networks (cognits) and limbic circuits feed into the PA cycle the semantic and emotional influences that create sequences of speech.

As in other forms of goal-directed sequences of actions, the concatenation of speech takes place under continuous feedback from sensory and motor cortices upon the frontal cortex. That feedback will steer the PA cycle to its goal, protecting it from interference by distraction or uncontrolled impulses. The creative nature of language rests almost entirely on its relational code – that is, on its capacity to produce an infinite variety of verbal utterances by combination of words.

Fundamentally aiding the novelty of speech is its recursive capacity – namely, its ability to diverge into potentially infinite qualifications of meaning and return to the main statement. Recursion also promotes the hierarchical structure that language shares with other forms of goal-directed sequential behavior. By temporal organization and recursion, the prefrontal cortex supports the dynamics of the highest, most abstract expressions of language as well as their dependent clauses.

I argue that linguistic syntax is a special case of the syntax of action. What makes linguistic syntax specifically human and the expression of a putative UG is the capacity of the human mind innately to categorize and enact attributes of sequential goal-directed action, such as dependence, causality, conditionality, numerosity, order, and temporality; the latter attribute confers on language its *future tense*, and with it the capacity to express, shape, and plan future actions as only the human can.

For their implementation in the form of spoken language, those *phyletic* qualities of sequential action require the rule-based use of function words and inflexions peculiar to each language, which the child acquires from others. Language develops concomitantly with all other cognitive functions and their neural substrate. Of special importance for the capacity of the individual to choose and plan his or her future is the exceptionally long process of functional maturation of the prefrontal cortex. That maturation underlies the development of the capacity of the human being to put speech at the service of independence, creativity, and free choice.

7

Liberty, responsibility, and social order

Love and do what you want.

St. Augustine

Where there is no law, there is no freedom.

John Locke

Our liberty, our ability to choose one course of action or another, emerges from the relationship of our cerebral cortex with our environment. As we have seen in previous chapters, any willed act results from the interactions between the perceptual and executive networks of the cortex, which are at the interface of our organism with the environment. In the free pursuit of our goals, that interface is continuously crossed in both directions by the PA cycle. We have also seen that, internalized in our cortex, we carry much of the outside world in a big bundle that includes our history, our culture, our mores, our traditions, our knowledge, and all the rest of our experience, which in the aggregate defines our persona[1] and which Ortega (1961) calls *circumstance* ("I am myself and my circumstance") and Dennett (2003) *culture*.

By now I trust I have succeeded in helping my reader reach the correct conclusion that the argument about the existence or nonexistence of *free will*, as an absolute all-or-none, is moot and

---

[1] From Latin, originally probably from Etruscan "phersu," signifying an actor's mask, whereby in several languages it refers to our personal role in society.

not relevant to neuroscience. Freedom is graded, like most nervous functions, and so is responsibility, which is inextricable
from it. We are indeed free, inasmuch as our brain, more specifically our cerebral cortex, has the option to take one action or
another. But we are not completely free, inasmuch as its options
are limited, and thus inasmuch as the brain has limits, and
inasmuch as the society in which we live imposes on us limits
of its own.

It is a truism that the brain and the body, as the physical
structures that they are, have physical constraints. These constraints, however, are not the issue here. This chapter concerns
those other constraints that derive from the fact that we are
social beings, and as such we have responsibilities not only
toward ourselves but also toward others. Thus, in this chapter
we face the inescapable reality that freedom and responsibility
are inseparable on social, ethical, political, and economic
grounds (Hayek, 1960). Society demands responsibility in return
for the protection of personal liberty. In fact, there is no liberty
worthy of protection without responsibility. Nor can liberty be
defended without trust, for trustworthiness is one of the essential traits of responsibility.

TRUST

Philosophers and statesmen have put liberty and happiness
next to each other as desirable coequal goals, but the two are also
linked by relations of mutual causality. This means that when you
are happy not only do you feel free, but you also *are* free. Optimism
opens options. Conversely, the exercise of freedom lifts your spirits
and, in addition, it makes you protect the freedom of those who are
close to you and have deposited their trust in you.

At first blush it seems strange that by defending my freedom
I am helping others defend theirs. It also seems strange that by
satisfying my desires I am helping others satisfy theirs. Both statements are essentially correct, but need some explanation. For one
thing it is obvious that if my liberty and desires are geared only to
my seeking my physical pleasure, no one else will benefit from
them, and probably someone will pay the cost. It is easy to argue,

therefore, that crass hedonic pursuit is irresponsible and does not bring real happiness, but at best only momentary pleasure.[2]

On the other hand, the pursuit of happiness that goes beyond physical pleasure into the social nature of humanity is unquestionably responsible and desirable on both personal and social grounds.[3] To reach this conclusion, we do not have to invoke cultural reasons, such as the "common good" of Adam Smith (1759), which supposedly comes from the "invisible hand" of the free market, or the utilitarian argument that happiness is good *per se* as the ultimate ethical principle of conduct, as John Stuart Mill (1859) advocated 100 years after Smith. Rather, the reason is much more deeply rooted in human existence, indeed in evolution itself: that reason is *trust*.

Trust is the reliance on the integrity, strength, ability, and surety of a person. It is an ethical value, and as such should be discussed in the next section, but here I deal with it separately in advance, as it plays an enormous role in any social system and in our liberty within it. As Barbara Misztal (1996) says, trust makes social life predictable, creates a sense of community, and makes it easier for people to work together. Here, I add, is where our happiness and freedom join in a common goal with those of others, and where selfishness turns into selflessness and the common good into the individual good.[4] Trust is the basis of it all, and there is a long history to prove it across cultures, which has been brilliantly presented by Fukuyama (1995).

Trust is not only an ethical principle. In its most elementary form, it is also a condition for the preservation of life. The neonate of any mammalian species relies on its parent to be taken care of. Without the mother, or someone to take her place, the neonate

---

[2] It can also be argued, however, that physical pleasure contributes to happiness when it is immersed together with that of another person in a "climate" of romantic love (Maurois, 1986) or in other cultural elaborations of basic drives, such as gastronomy or competitive sport – to use examples in which happiness results from the sublimation of a biodrive.

[3] It was in this, the Lockian sense, that the expression "pursuit of happiness" was introduced as an inalienable right in the American Declaration of Independence (Wills, 1978).

[4] President Theodore Roosevelt said, "The welfare of each of us is dependent fundamentally upon the welfare of all of us" (New York State Fair, September 1903).

starves to death. This is the first taste of trust for a little human being.

Countless times it has been correctly said that evolution only works and makes sense at the level of the population, not of the individual. Natural selection, however, will play a major role in the ways the individual organism handles the environment – including the internal milieu (Dennett, 2003). Trust is the very first such way. In the *biological* sense, the neonate is the first trustor and the mother the first trustee.[5]

In recent years, a particular hormone, the polypeptide oxytocin, has been associated with trust. It has been observed that the administration of oxytocin to adult human subjects increases their trust in others (Baumgartner *et al.*, 2008). Moreover, they do not feel threatened when told that their trust has been betrayed. It is partly on the basis of such evidence that Patricia Churchland (2011) reasons that the circulating amount of oxytocin in the blood marks the degree to which the subject relies on, and tolerates, others.

In any event, oxytocin is intimately involved in child care and reaches high levels in the blood of mothers during and after childbirth. It works as a neurotransmitter, through which the brain facilitates physiological processes, such as lactation, that are conducive to successful child rearing. There seems to be somewhat of a contradiction here, however, for the trusting individual is the child, whereas it is the trusted individual, the mother, who has the higher oxytocin concentration in her blood. The apparent contradiction disappears, however, if the dyad of mother and child is considered the essential constituent of the "nourishment loop," where there is no true origin but continuous feed-forward and feedback between mother and child. Indeed, the cycle of trust that ties the mother to the child may be the continuation of the "nourishment" PA cycle of the baby right after birth or, more precisely, after his having found by palpation the feeding breast (Chapter 2).

---

[5] In the eyes of many, parental care is the most fundamental trust to derive from evolution, with the "purpose" of ensuring the preservation of the species (Churchland, 2011). Beyond the offspring, the parental self enlarges the caring and trusting circle to encompass the mate, the kin, and others.

From childhood through adulthood and beyond, trust will take many forms while expanding its social role. Beginning with family relations, it will enter all aspects of cooperativity between individuals. It will become essential in all forms of human sociality. It will penetrate all liberal professions, from science to healthcare, to law, to economics, to engineering. In fact, trust will become the universal currency of all human relations, the mediator of all business transactions, and the foundation of all human institutions. It is impossible to exaggerate the monumental importance of trust for a free and happy society.

The importance of trust becomes acutely evident in the consequences of its failure. Failing trust can be found in all marital discord, in most dysfunctional families, in disputes between educators, in all legal conflicts, in many scientific disputes, in ethnic or religious discrimination, in territorial conflicts between nations (and between neighbors!), in generational conflicts, and, of course, in politics, where mistrust seems sometimes to be the norm. In economic crises, mistrust permeates all sectors of society, like an uncontrolled epidemic.[6] In my view, at least 90 percent of the recent economic recession is attributable to mistrust. Much of that mistrust has its root in the failure of politicians to deliver on their promises. Even more injurious to our trust and to our liberty is the corrupt behavior of some of them. Trust is the foundation of thriving free trade, between individuals as well as between nations.

A major deterrent to prosperity, in the absence of trust, is the lack of predictability. Indeed, trust, whether based on competence or benevolence, makes life – and, of course, business – predictable. In psychological terms, my trust in a person is the belief and the expectation that that person *will* take care of my interests and *will* act to satisfy them. In other words, trust brings predictability to our plans inasmuch as they rely on the actions of

---

[6] In that predicament, legislators mistrust their constituents, and vice versa; creditors their debtors, and vice versa; employers their employees, and vice versa; union leaders their rank and file, and vice versa. There seems to be a pervasive atmosphere of mistrust that makes most everybody unhappy, though most of the time that social illness is by and large covered by a veneer of civility.

those we trust. Further, failures of trust require correction. These two facts tie trust directly to the frontal lobe, which makes our brain predictive as well as executive (Chapter 5). Here it seems appropriate, therefore, to briefly summarize the role of the frontal cortex when we make our plans and decisions, as well as the role of other people in both.

There are basically two sources of internal influences on planning and decision-making in the cerebral cortex. One is the cortex itself, which contains a massive array of interwoven networks (cognits) representing knowledge and memory, perceptual as well as executive. We may call that cortical "archive" the cerebral book of our personal history or autobiography, which encompasses all the knowledge we have acquired in the course of our life. In sum, it is the internalized culture, which we will meet again later.

The other source is the "internal milieu," also generating a massive conglomerate of inputs from the internal organs channeled into the cortex through the limbic system and the orbitofrontal cortex.[7] That is the neural conveyor of affect, value, reward, punishment, and like, as well as dislike. It is what colors cortical memory with emotion, and thus it is the foundation of so-called emotional memory – and emotional intelligence (Goleman, 1995).

The external influences on planning and decision-making come from the surrounding environment, in the form of stimulation of our senses. The cortex converts that stimulation into perception, as there, in the cortex, it will be interpreted, filtered, analyzed, and categorized through the cognitive archive of our personal history. A large part of those external influences, however, will come from other persons around us sustained by trust. A large share of those external influences will come from our witnessing others behave in certain ways.

In the last decade of the past century, Rizzolatti and his colleagues (Di Pellegrino et al., 1992; Rizzolatti et al., 1990), while exploring with microelectrodes the frontal lobe of monkeys, discovered a highly peculiar kind of cell in the part of the frontal lobe called the premotor cortex. Those cells were activated not only

---

[7] The amygdala, which acts as an evaluator of the motivational significance of sensory stimuli, is an integral component of that system (Le Doux, 1992).

when the animal performed certain actions but also, most remarkably, when the animal saw another subject, such as, for example, the experimenter, perform the same actions. Because of the latter feature, those cells were dubbed "mirror neurons."

Much has been said and written about those neurons, such as that they have to do with "empathy." Interpretations of this kind are obviously quite speculative. To me, a probably better interpretation of mirror neurons is that they are part of large cognitive networks – cognits – that represent skeletal movements with intent. The evidence that they are active in the perception as well as the performance of a movement is clearly a manifestation of the involvement of the network to which the cells belong in the PA cycle for that visual-motor action.[8]

In any case, mirror cells are an indication of two important hypothetical principles. One was enunciated by John Hughlings Jackson, long ago, when he said that in the "higher motor centres" (premotor and prefrontal), as in the primary motor cortex, the same areas probably represent an action that takes part in the coordination of that action (Jackson, 1882). The other is that an action, even by others, is represented in our frontal cortex, and thus presumably is available for us not only to expect it but also to make it part of our plans. Thus it is reasonable to infer that trusted action by others enters the neural substrate of our PA cycle in the pursuit of our goals.

Like trust, those internal and external influences, which constitute the determinants and biases of decisions and plans, may be either innate or conditioned and acquired. They may also be conscious or unconscious depending on the intensity of the cortical activation they evoke in the processes of attention, intention, deliberation, and working memory before and during our actions. The actions themselves will not be elicited by consciousness, but the other way around. The agent will be the cortex, and consciousness will be a byproduct of the action. Imperative action, however, will be conscious by necessity, because it will be driven by intense cortical activity under the influence of

---

[8] As Rizzolatti and I agreed in a public discussion (International Conference on the Frontal Lobes, Toronto, 2010).

selective attention and powerful motives. But many of our actions will be driven by subtle motives, perhaps peremptory yet unconscious, that can be attributed to "gut feeling" or intuition – in other words, to unconscious reasons and reasoning. In the same manner, the trust granted to someone may be intuited, perhaps on the basis of unconsciously interpreted body language.

Each individual has been endowed by evolution with the benefits of trust and social adaptation enjoyed by the human population as a whole. Language is undoubtedly one of those benefits, arguably at the very root of our inherited social self. Language, as we have seen in the previous chapter, confers on the individual a wide horizon of liberty, and thus of social adaptation. Note, however, that language, as well as the rest of our phyletic endowment, is an evolutionary benefit from and through the population to ourselves, and as such it must naturally revert to the population in the form of personally responsible actions. I say naturally but not ethically, though in a civilized society it is supposed to be both. By the same token, the liberty that we as individuals enjoy is a benefit to society, and as such it is justifiably protected by society. This is essential to democracy, at the very least on utilitarian grounds. It is also one of the foundations of free speech in any self-governed society.[9]

VALUES

All our choices in life are informed by value judgments of past, present, and future experience. We move about in the world by constant judgment, conscious or unconscious, of what is good or bad, better or worse, in the precedents of each choice, as well as in the choice itself and its consequences. That judgment is made on many scales of goodness or badness, which means with many

---

[9] American society has done a splendid job of institutionalizing freedom, but we cannot say the same thing about its twin, responsibility. It is said that Viktor Frankl, the famous Austrian psychiatrist, founder of logotherapy and a Holocaust survivor, once proposed that in addition to the Statue of Liberty the United States should erect a Statue of Responsibility. Indeed, sadly, under the protection of free speech, untold harm is inflicted on people in the form of libel and defamation. Although there are legal defenses against them, these are usually clumsy and late to restore the public reputation of the victim.

criteria of value, from the physical and mundane to the ethical and sublime. Here I attempt to categorize some of the values that move us in life and to specify their brain base if it is known or else to reasonably speculate on it.

We attribute value to objects, persons, ideas, motives, intentions, plans, goals, natural urges, and all manner of human actions. In general terms, value theory distinguishes between moral goods, which apply to the behavior of persons, and natural goods, which apply to the goods in and of objects. Moral goods fall in the field of ethics, whereas objective goods fall in the field of economics. All are of interest to psychology, philosophy, and sociology.

Some moral values, like trust and affiliation, and natural goods, like food, have inherent and inherited value, with a clear evolutionary origin. Others, like professionalism and money, have a more complex and socially derivative value, the first as a social need or service and the second as the universal means of exchange. In reality, however, most values have a mixed origin and degree of goodness within themselves. Some objects have contradictory values depending on measure or circumstances. Take a substance like alcohol. Wine, in moderate amounts, not only is pleasurable, but also has positive value as a promoter of social exchange and even, purportedly, cardiovascular health. In larger amounts, and especially when it becomes addictive, however, wine has deleterious, sometimes calamitous, consequences on one's health and on society. Here then we have an object, wine, whose value, depending on several factors or circumstances, can be good or bad.

Pleasure itself, as well as being the reward for good action, can have many origins, from the morally commendable to the hedonically exquisite. Yet, all is subsumed under the general rubric of *reward*. In principle it is not justified to assume *a priori* a uniform brain foundation for rewards of so many sources. Indeed, that foundation might be vastly different whether the reward comes from, say, winning a chess game, having sex, curing a patient, winning the lottery, or teaching a class to good students. However, but for a few differences of detail, modern neuroscience shows a remarkably similar neural substrate for a large variety of rewards. The center of that neural substrate is what I have called the "reward axis" (Chapter 4).

In the "sensory" input side of the reward axis and the emotional PA cycle, recent functional studies[10] demonstrate the activation of limbic structures, such as the amygdala, by emotional stimuli such as human faces with obvious emotional expressions – in other words, stimuli with emotional valence (Atkinson and Adolphs, 2011; Rutishauser *et al.*, 2011). Conversely, in the action side of the emotional PA cycle, other brain regions are activated by the value connotations of action. Thus, the medial and anterior cingulate prefrontal cortex is activated by choice selection in uncertainty (Rushworth and Behrens, 2008; Seo *et al.*, 2012). A most remarkable finding is that those cortical areas are activated in the evaluation of social-value choices as well as monetary-value choices (Lin *et al.*, 2012; Seo *et al.*, 2012). This is a clear indication that these areas intervene in the selection of wide-ranging and heterogeneous values.

In connection with the mentioned emotional value of facial expressions, we cannot avoid dealing with the controversial issue of the "theory-of-mind." Theory-of-mind is the capacity to infer in another individual his or her state of mind, intentions, and other mental attributes. Although originally postulated in apes (Premack and Woodruff, 1979), the concept has entered the debates of philosophers, neurobiologists, and psychologists (Tomasello, 2000). Its substrate in neuroscience is still unresolved, but has instigated a large number of studies, especially with neuroimaging methods. Practically the only thing on which there is some agreement from these studies[11] is the evidence that

[10] Many such studies are based on neuroimaging, a method now already well time-tested. However, the studies are subject to certain limitations of that method, still unresolved, such as its poor temporal resolution and the prevailing uncertainties surrounding the neurovascular coupling (the translation of neural signals into vascular signals, which is what the method measures). Nonetheless, studies from well-recognized laboratories with proven self-critique of methodology and judicious use of statistics command respect and offer reliable data.

[11] Imaging studies for this purpose have a serious methodological difficulty. That difficulty is the absence of an independent measure of such an elusive and multifaceted variable as theory-of-mind: that is, a measure, independent of the brain signals that are supposed to measure theory-of-mind. Failure to use that independent measure not only courts tautology but also leads almost inevitably to the fallacy of "reverse inference" (Poldrack, 2006). Functional neuroimaging is beginning to be used in the study of human interactions (Montague, 2007). For reasons stated above, however, inferences from such studies are still rather crude.

the exercise of theory-of-mind activates the anterior medial prefrontal cortex – that is, the anterior cingulate area (Carrington and Bailey, 2009; Fumagalli and Priori, 2012).

A most important issue here, in the discussion of values with regard to liberty, is that of *expected value*, again a value that guides behavior with a future perspective, which almost by necessity must involve prefrontal physiology. The prefrontal cortex, as we know, is involved in temporal integration and, accordingly, in all future aspects of the temporal organization of behavior, language, and reasoning. Expected value, therefore, very much falls within the prefrontal purview. In theory, expected value – that is, the value of a prospective reward – is a function of the average probability of the success of a forthcoming decision – to invest money, for example.

However, the behavioral economists Kahneman and Tversky (1979), with their empirically based *prospect theory*, reject probability as a decisive or sole determinant of choice. Instead, they give decisive importance to certain factors, such as risk, that make probability essentially inoperative, and emphasize the weight of potential outcome, including loss. Consequently, a plausible compromising position would seem to be that in some undetermined proportions, both probability and those other factors, risk included, intervene in the computation of prefrontal choice.

To summarize several recent investigations, it is increasingly clear that in the input side, as in the output side of the emotional PA cycle, there are neural structures that attribute value to incoming stimuli as well as to expected outcomes of choices and decisions. The expected value of, and outcome from, a choice or decision results from the neural computation in the prefrontal cortex of certain critical variables that include probability, risk, and amount of reward (Grabenhorst and Rolls, 2011; Knutson *et al.*, 2005; Tobler *et al.*, 2009). Whereas values vary on many scales and by many criteria, it is remarkable that the expected value of practically any sort will reliably activate some areas of the prefrontal cortex.

In addition to the ability to assess a multitude of expected rewards, there is another prospective function of the prefrontal cortex that also benefits and expands freedom. That function consists of the mechanisms to monitor and control the inputs to sensory systems, as these mechanisms are needed for the efficiency of prospective behavior.[12] Indeed, like the cognitive PA cycle, the emotional PA cycle uses functional connections that go from an output, executive, structure, such as the prefrontal cortex, back upon sensory structures to allow forthcoming sensory input into the brain against the background of recent experience and expected action. That is the internal feedback (Chapter 4), which was first postulated by Uexküll (1926) and which is so important for the control of any biological cybernetic cycle. In the nervous system that feedback is the foundation of the control of behavior, of the corollary discharge (Teuber, 1972), of error correction, and of such higher functions as the "cognitive control" (Miller and Cohen, 2001) and working memory (Fuster, 2008). No goal-directed sequence of behavior or language can reach its goal without that internal feedback.

Current evidence indicates that the sources of internal control of emotional inputs are the same prefrontal areas that receive the feed-forward inputs from value selection, notable among them the anterior cingulate cortex, in the medial aspect of the prefrontal cortex. This area is evidently the source of response monitoring and error control signals (Amiez et al., 2005; Bush et al., 2000; Rollnik et al., 2004; Swick and Turken, 2002).

The essential quality of expected reward evaluation and response correction processes – as well as working memory and corollary discharge – is their future perspective. All fall within the prospective capacity of the prefrontal cortex and, therefore, its predictive functions. All weigh heavily on its capacity for prospective memory, decision-making, planning, and creativity that opens the human agenda to freedom, in the short term as well as the long term.

Those prospective prefrontal functions most certainly play a critical role in the postponement of gratification, when and where that is necessary on ethical or economic grounds. In Chapter 4, I referred to a most prevalent phenomenon of expected reward:

---

[12] Feedback servo-mechanisms of sensory control have been successfully computer-modeled by a stellar group of investigators (Friston et al., 1994).

delay discount. Children and emotionally immature or naive adults, like animals, attribute low value to rewards for which they have to wait a long time. They prefer an earlier reward, even if it is smaller than a later reward.

When it is out of control in the adult world, the consequences of this quirk of nature that we call delay discount are enormous. In addition to curtailing everybody's freedom to plan ahead, delay discount can, as we have recently witnessed, bring down well nigh the entire economy of a nation. Ordinarily, a few impatient members of society would not be a problem. A major problem, which can become a disaster, occurs when the financial industry, the advertising industry, and the government all collude to lure a large segment of society to make a large investment, such as the purchase of a home, which it clearly cannot afford with either present or future income.[13] It is nothing short of pathetic to witness the harm that uncontrolled long-delay discount has inflicted on families and family values, on productivity and the work ethic, on the value of saving and on full employment, not to mention pension funds, financial markets, and government obligations.

Above, I have referred to the seemingly general rule that different kinds of rewards share the same brain system (the "reward axis") for processing – not necessarily representing – reward. This appears to be the case even for monetary and social rewards (Lin *et al.*, 2012; Seo *et al.*, 2012). The question is now, where in the brain are the ethical and moral values represented that have such a powerful influence on our behavior, whether we are aware of it or not? Here we must profess ignorance. The only evidence we have on this issue comes either from clinical studies of the effects of brain lesion or from more recent functional – e.g., imaging – studies. Both kinds of evidence, however, are beset with serious problems.[14]

---

[13] Of course, home hyperinflation is itself engendered by the same beast: cheap and reckless credit to a society that cannot and will not wait, and that cannot afford the credit.

[14] A lesion of a given brain structure does not necessarily result in the simple subtraction of the ethical or moral value postulated for that structure. For example, the "moral turpitude" from a lesion of the orbitofrontal cortex (as in the famous case of Phineas Gage [Damasio, 1994]) does not demonstrate that

Nonetheless, the cognit paradigm (Chapter 3) offers a sound rationale for the wide cortical distribution of higher values. Cognits, which are units of knowledge or memory, are hierarchically organized, from the most concrete (sensory or motor), in the lowest associative stages of cortex, to the most complex and abstract concepts in the highest cortices of association (posterior and prefrontal); such is the case for an ethical or moral value.[15]

In the course of life experience, new cognits develop associations with old cognits, which they update and modify. The highest, most complex and abstract cognits are assumed to be the most extensive, made by instantiations of lower, more concrete, and specific cognits. If that assumption is correct, an abstract concept, such as an ethical principle or value, is widely distributed in the cortex, formed by repetition of similar patterns of perceptual or executive experience, which remain nested within the network that forms that abstract concept. Thus that concept is complex in that it grew out of many different patterns. It is abstract in that it unifies the common attributes of all of them. In ethics and morality, that common attribute or set of attributes defines a principle or value – that is, a fundamental belief.[16]

Here the distinction between ethical and moral values is relevant, because they may have different origin and cortical distribution, even though, on psychological and sociological grounds, they are difficult to separate. On neuroscientific

ethical or moral values are localized there, but rather that the orbitofrontal region is the source of powerful inhibitory impulses that modulate social behavior in an adaptive manner. Similarly, the metabolic or neural activation of a cortical region during the exercise of a given ethical or moral behavior does not necessarily mean that the value driving that behavior is localized there. In any case, both lesion and imaging studies are devoid of suitable metrics to measure psychologically a value independent of the brain measure being taken ("inverse inference" problem [Poldrack, 2006]).

[15] Note that the hierarchy is layered transverse to the surface of the cortex, each layer comprising areas of similar phylogenetic or ontogenetic developmental stage (in Figure 3.2, higher stages are symbolized by lighter color, with the highest cognits, concepts, in white areas).

[16] The principle of charity or compassion, for example, may be formed in the higher cortex by many instantiations of direct or indirect experience with good Samaritans. At a deeper level, however, the principle is based on evolution (below).

grounds, the separation is even more difficult.[17] For this reason, here they are together treated simply as *higher values*. They include trust, honesty, compassion, integrity, courage, respect, fairness, and responsibility. The first and the last, trust and responsibility, are the most relevant to freedom, for in fact they are connatural with it. Trust, as we have seen, expands freedom of choice. Responsibility is the accountability to ourselves or to others of every choice we make. We "own" every choice and the responsibility that goes with it, and that ownership is commensurate with the freedom we have to make that choice.

Summarizing the little knowledge we have in this respect, higher values are most probably represented in perceptual and executive cognits of the higher cortex. A good case can be made that those values are solidly based in evolution, and therefore part of natural law (Churchland, 2011; Wilson, 1993). They would be part of our phyletic heritage. Therefore, just as phyletic sensory memory gives rise to perceptual memory, and phyletic motor memory to executive memory, phyletic sentiments and beliefs would give rise to "moral" or "ethical" memory. The latter would consist of a mesh of cortical networks representing higher values of genetic origin, though fine-tuned by social intercourse to serve humankind with a purpose beyond that of the individual.

Animals that are deprived of sensory stimulation right after birth fail to develop a normal sensory cortex, and thus become unable to process sensory information thereafter (Hensch, 2005; Hubel, 1995). The critical period during which sensory input must be present for further maturation varies with the species and sensory system. That period is also called the "vulnerability window," after which the plasticity of the system shuts off or becomes greatly diminished. In the human, the critical period for vision has been demonstrated, though not exactly delimited

---

[17] Ethical values define patterns of behavior, especially with or toward others, which are largely acquired and part of the culture of the individual; they pertain to what is right, good, and just. The fundamental beliefs of morality overlap considerably those of ethics, to which they may give rise or contribute. In general, however, moral values are more associated with a person's character, and more likely to be associated also with that person's relation to higher authority, which may or may not be religious.

(it may be weeks or months), in cases of congenital cataracts corrected by surgery after birth (Gregory and Wallace, 1963). The patients are born blind or with greatly impaired vision. After surgery, they partially recover their vision, but the recovery is slow, halting, and never complete. Most patients show a lingering defect of visual perception, and in some cases outright *agnosia* – that is, difficulty in identifying and naming visual objects. Clearly, the inherited visual system (phyletic memory) must be exercised ("rehearsed") during a critical period after birth so that by natural plasticity it can fully yield perception.

In somewhat similar fashion, children who are deprived of sensory stimulation and maternal care, like Harlow's monkeys[18] fail to develop a normal social life. There are cases in the human literature of extreme parental neglect or isolation of infants (Bowlby, 1951; Rymer, 1994) resulting in severe social as well as cognitive retardation. By the confluence of several factors, the subjects of such cases show also an almost total lack of ethical values; thus they show what we could call "value agnosia."[19] These, however, are extreme cases of generalized disorders of values which do not have a clear-cut critical period. Still, there is evidence that cognitive skills do not develop properly if the child is not exposed to them during certain critical periods. The best example is language.

It is widely known that children are much better at learning languages than are adults, and that generally the ability to learn a new language diminishes with age. What is less known, although some of us have known it since 1967 from the work of Eric Lenneberg (Pinker, 1994), is that there is for the child's

---

[18] Infant monkeys were taken away from their mother right after birth and placed in the company of surrogate "mothers" made of wire and cloth. After a period of exposure to these attendant "mothers," they were returned to the company of their real mothers and other monkeys of various ages. The deprived animals never developed affective or grooming behavior. They were recluses and socially crippled (Harlow, 1993).

[19] The "Klüver–Bucy syndrome" in the monkey (Klüver and Bucy, 1938) is the epitome of object value agnosia. After bilateral lesions of the amygdala, the animals exhibit a pattern of bizarre behavior, characterized by indiscriminate hypersexuality and evident disregard of the biological value of objects, with a marked tendency to explore them with their mouth and to ingest inedible ones, like nails and paper clips.

acquisition of his first language a critical period that extends from age 5 to puberty. After that the adolescent and adult have a much more difficult time acquiring it.[20]

Outside language, we have known since the seminal works of Piaget (1952) and Vygotsky (1978) that in the course of development, cognitive abilities progress though several successive stages marked by certain milestone achievements. This development is not restricted to modern highly technological societies (Greenfield, 2009). With the help of family, peers, and school, the child goes through those achievements, learning to learn and acquiring cognitive as well as emotional knowledge, and thus developing intelligence in both spheres and also acquiring new knowledge in both. There is only scant evidence, however, for a moral-ethical critical period. We know there are periods and stages, but is there a critical period for acquiring the two values, trust and responsibility, that relate most directly to the development of freedom?

Here to help us we have the views of two authorities in child development. Erikson (1993) formulates and explores a critical period for the development of interpersonal trust. According to him, the establishment of basic trust takes place in the open window of the first two years of life. Success of that development within that window of time will mean a happy, secure, and confident child. Failure will mean an anxious, insecure, and mistrustful child.

Vygotsky (1978) integrates the development of social responsibility with the intellectual development of the child and adolescent within a broad period that he identifies as the "zone of proximate development" (ZPD). The ZPD is the difference in time between what the child can do on her own using only her innate intelligence (our hypothetical *phyletic* knowledge) and what she can achieve with the assistance of adult educators. Vigotsky characterizes the process of education as a dialectical one of circular interaction with the social environment (our PA

---

[20] The second, third, and subsequent languages are also known to be progressively more difficult to learn, but there is no clear critical period for any of them.

cycle), in which language would play a critical role. Social responsibility would develop naturally in that process.[21]

If these propositions are shown to be correct, we can confidently assert, taking the argument beyond analogy, that just as perception and action grow on a phyletic base of elementary sensation and movement, ethical values, notably trust and responsibility, grow on a phyletic base of elementary affect and instinct. All takes place in the cerebral cortex with the assistance of limbic structures that constitute the emotional brain. Further, just as the two phyletic "quarries" of sensation and movement (primary sensory and motor cortices) require plastic neural development within a certain critical period, ethical knowledge requires the same through social interaction. If ethical knowledge of trust and responsibility does not develop within that period, the individual remains "value-blind" or "value-crippled" for the rest of his life. His personal liberty will inescapably suffer. As a natural consequence of this individual liability, the liberty of others will suffer too.

PATHOLOGY OF LIBERTY

I am quite certain that, when St. Augustine wrote his famous statement ("love and do what you want"), he was thinking of agape love,[22] not eros love. Agape, according to *Webster's New World Dictionary*, is "spontaneous, altruistic love." Probably Augustine's idea was that agape love will cast out evil, and thus a person would be free, responsible, and able to do good, to adhere to the highest values, and to respect the law and his

---

[21] It is interesting to note that Vygotsky developed his theory in the context of a Marxist collectivist society, in a climate that was essentially inimical to individual liberty, and it is difficult to exclude a degree of indoctrination in the process he describes. This does not invalidate his work, however, which upholds the concept of innate (phyletic) ethical knowledge, and the role of society in expanding it with higher values.

[22] Augustine, *Epist. ad Parthos*, VII, 8 (comment on a letter of John to the Parthians). *Agape*, originally from Greek, means *banquet* (as it does too in Spanish). It refers to the convivial exchange of affect enjoyed by early Christians at a celebratory meal (love feast), where all transgressions were by common understanding precluded from everybody's mind and intent (including presumably gluttony and drunkenness!).

neighbor's values. Under altruism, a person's freedom would be in perfect harmony with his responsibility. It was eminently reasonable advice.

The trouble comes when there is no agape or when there is an imbalance between freedom and responsibility. Or when both are greatly diminished. This section deals with what goes wrong when those things happen because of brain disease. To do that scientifically, however, we would need reliable metrics. But brain science does not give us precise measures of either freedom or responsibility. At best, brain science can give us rough estimates, and thus rough predictions, based on what we know from the phenomenology of brain diseases – that is, from the study of the behavior and mental states of patients suffering from them. Our problem is complicated, however, by the fact that mental and behavioral symptoms are multivariate, the result of interactions of many variables, some of them imponderable or unconscious. In sum, the assessment of the freedom and responsibility of the patient must be couched with circumspection. Here, an analogy with economics seems appropriate.[23]

In Stockholm, in 1974, when Hayek was awarded the first Nobel Prize ever conferred in economics (shared with Myrdal), he gave a famous speech entitled "The Pretence of Knowledge." Talking about inflation and unemployment, wages and prices, he said that the output of an *essentially complex* system like the economy of a nation could not be predicted, let alone planned or manipulated, with any degree of confidence. That output, he said, was the result of many human actions based on incomplete or uncertain knowledge. In comments obviously directed at Keynesians in government and out of it, he counseled humility and caution, for under those conditions people in power, advised by pretentious but ignorant economists ("as a profession we have made a mess of things"), can unleash a massive economic crisis.

---

[23] It is more than an analogy with brain phenomena, and is directly applicable to the phenomena that neuroeconomics and behavioral economics commonly deal with.

Likewise, the human cortex, also an essentially complex system,[24] is subject to so many shifting and imponderable variables that few of its actions can be attributed to any of them. We can only make estimates of relative probability. Every free choice we make is subject to myriad influences that span from genetics to almost every conceivable internal or environmental variable acting on the cortex; perhaps most of them are unconscious. To be sure, in every choice some variables weigh more than others; in this text I have tried to sort them out and to point to the most probable mechanisms by which they intervene in human behavior. Conversely, every failure of free choice can be caused by many factors, some in the individual, some outside. That failure, too, is subject to some factors more than others.

The preceding comments are intended to be a necessary caveat for any scientific treatment of freedom, now especially needed because in this section we are going to deal with a most delicate subject, that of the effects of brain disorder on personal freedom and responsibility. These are questions of interest not only to the brain scientist but also, most definitely, to the judge. We all want to know what occurred in the brain of the individual who so blatantly violated the law, and how personally responsible he was for his transgression. Here is where a Hayekian disclaimer is mandatory, for, sadly, some physicians or psychologists testifying in court as expert witnesses arrogate to themselves a knowledge they do not have.

Nevertheless, there are cases of brain disorder in which a person's ability to stand trial or to take responsibility for a crime (or lack thereof) is beyond dispute. In such cases medical expertise can be confirmatory, some times decisively. There are, however, conditions in which psychiatric or neurological evidence is ambiguous or uncertain. In these cases we must profess ignorance.

Four large categories of brain disorders come frequently before the courts in which liberty and responsibility are more or less compromised: psychosis, depressive/obsessive syndromes,

---

[24] Not coincidentally, Hayek himself, before becoming an economist, had dealt with the complex system of the human cortex in his *Sensory Order*, which was published in 1952, many years after he had done the preliminary writing of it in Vienna (in the 1920s).

drug addiction, and disease or trauma of the frontal lobe. In all of these, there is demonstrable or reasonably inferred brain pathology, easy diagnosis, and clear differentiation from other brain syndromes. In all of them, freedom and responsibility are congruently diminished, though in some individual cases there may be serious questions about civil or criminal responsibility. Other brain disorders, like mental retardation, borderline personality, temporal lobe epilepsy (TLE), hysteria-conversion, etc., also raise questions of freedom and responsibility, though their brain pathology, except for TLE, is obscure.

Psychosis is defined as the mind's breakaway from reality – that is, the "de-realization" of the patient's view of himself and the world around him. The most common and devastating psychosis is schizophrenia, with onset usually in adolescence or early adulthood. Genetics plays an important role in it, although the genes implicated are still uncertain.[25] The most immediate cause of schizophrenia is an imbalance in the connectivity of the cerebral cortex, both old (hippocampus) and new (neocortex). That imbalance affects mainly the dopamine, serotonin, and GABA receptors and transmitters. For this reason, among others, schizophrenia has been deemed to be essentially a disconnection syndrome (Friston and Frith, 1995).

In schizophrenia, cognitive as well as emotional symptoms comingle in a protean syndrome that changes over time and alternates between acute and chronic phases. Among the cognitive symptoms, thought disorders, such as loose associations[26]

---

[25] The reason for that uncertainty may be because there are several forms of schizophrenia, possibly with different genetic makeup, and also because, as in other mental conditions, its phenotype – that is, its overt syndrome – is the result of interactions between several genes, as well as among them and the environment.

[26] Presumably a manifestation of cortical disconnection. As a result of prefrontal disconnection and abnormal dopamine involvement (D-2 receptors), schizophrenia has some characteristics of a prefrontal syndrome (Fuster, 2008; Goldman-Rakic, 1994). This idea is, of course, reinforced by the fundamental difficulties of the schizophrenic patient in working memory and the temporal organization of thoughts and actions. It is incorrect, however, to call schizophrenia a "disease of the frontal lobe." For one thing, no full-fledged schizophrenic syndrome has been observed as a result of prefrontal injury.

and delusions, play a central role, together with auditory hallucinations. Among the emotional symptoms, the patient commonly manifests flat or inappropriate affect and ambivalence. Delusions often take a paranoid form, with a generally mistrustful stance and ideas of thought intrusion and mind control as well as threat and persecution. With regard to the forensic aspects of schizophrenia, Glancy and Regehr (1992), in their excellent review, conclude,

> [there is] an association between schizophrenia and a variety of antisocial behaviors that include violent crime, and even homicide, especially in North America. The literature consistently shows that since the 1950s, schizophrenics have been involved in crime and arrested more frequently than the general population, they are overrepresented in correctional settings, and they represent the majority of those found not guilty by reason of insanity.

The clinical conditions of severe endogenous depression and obsessive-compulsive disorder (OCD) share one characteristic symptom that brings them here under our purview: *the exaggerated sense of guilt*. In the depressed patient, whether suffering from unipolar depression or from the depressive phase of a bipolar disorder, the sad mood is frequently accompanied by deep, completely unjustified feelings of guilt that can be of psychotic proportions and contribute to suicidal ideation. The patient is beset with remorse for imaginary harm that he thinks he has inflicted on his spouse, children, or other persons in his environment. No attempts to convince him to the contrary, even by the supposed victims, can assuage his deep-seated guilt, which in involutional melancholia, a form of age-related endogenous depression, is accompanied by extreme anxiety and can be aptly characterized as "delusional responsibility."[27]

In endogenous depression – that is, in depression brought about by genetic and neurochemical factors – the metabolism and mechanisms of action of the three major monoamines (serotonin,

---

[27] This is one of the few clear indications of electroshock therapy (ECT). Nowadays, however, the procedure is only utilized when pharmacological treatment fails.

neuroepinephrine, and dopamine) are compromised (Malhi *et al.*, 2005). The most common pharmacological agents now in use against depression are serotonergic; they block the breakdown of serotonin in the brain.

Otto Fenichel (1946), a prestigious psychoanalist writer, brought to our attention the close relationship between severe depression and OCD on the issue of guilt. Indeed, psychodynamically, some of the symptoms of OCD (compulsive undoing, checking, repetitive acts, etc.) appear to be symbolic attempts to get rid of guilt or at least to control it. The most telling example in this respect is compulsive hand-washing. The patient is keenly aware of the futility of his compulsions, including hand-washing, yet feels the constant urge to perform them, at least for fleeting relief. Both endogenous depression and OCD epitomize the pathology of responsibility, and consequently of liberty, in psychiatric illness.

Drug addiction is the third robber of liberty that comes to the attention of the psychiatrist (Chapter 4). This one is different from the others in one important respect: in it, the lack, not excess, of responsibility leads to enslavement, a total and sometimes fatal loss of liberty. Sellman, in his authoritative report (2010), claims that 50 percent of drug dependencies are inherited.

Addiction varies somewhat in its effects on the central nervous system depending on the addicting substance. However, all such substances (alcohol, cocaine, amphetamines, etc.) have a common effect on the mesolimbic reward system and related structures (Everitt and Robbins, 2005). In the human and the monkey, that system is overstimulated by drugs of abuse. After extensive abuse in addictive drug-dependency, the system becomes severely depleted of dopamine. Thus the addict desperately and compulsively seeks its replenishment with an ever greater and more frequent intake of the drug (increased "tolerance"). This leads to a life completely absorbed by drug seeking at the expense of any other activity. That frequently leads to crime. Addicts in search of means to maintain their habit commit a very large proportion of violent crime in urban areas.

Comorbidity is extraordinarily common among addicts. That means that such persons are prone to suffer also from other physical or psychiatric disorders, such as AIDS (usually from use of contaminated needles), OCD, and schizophrenia (Dittmann, 1996). Their treatment as well as social rehabilitation needs to take that fact into account. So does the judgment of their responsibility in court.

Finally, patients with frontal lobe disorders commonly raise critical questions about freedom and responsibility. In principle that is to be expected, because the cortex of the frontal lobe is as close as we can get to human agency, where the human brain makes the final assessment of values and prospective choices of organized responsible action before it decides to take it: responsible action, that is, with respect to the agent himself and with respect to his fellow humans. Irresponsible action, ethically or morally, is the frequent result of an infirm frontal lobe. The action may be inconsequential or it may consist of a criminal act.

The prefrontal cortex is the part of frontal cortex most commonly implicated in irresponsible behavior. That behavior will vary depending on the site and extent of the prefrontal lesion or disease process.[28] In general, massive prefrontal lesions do not raise ethical or moral issues. The patient with such a lesion is apathetic, listless, and abulic, deprived of the will to do anything, good or bad, let alone to plan any sequence of goal-directed actions for good or for bad. Not uncommonly, however, depression and anxiety take the place of apathy in the patient with an extensive prefrontal lesion. Lesions of the lateral prefrontal cortex – that is, of the outer convexity of the frontal lobe – lead to what is known as the dysexecutive syndrome, which is characterized by lack of attention and intention, impairment of working memory, and difficulty in the planning or executing of any temporally extended, goal-directed series of actions. Depression is also frequently a part of the clinical picture.

---

[28] The prototypes of frontal-injury cases outlined below are idealized and simplified here for heuristic reasons. In reality, however, frontal lesions are generally mixed and affect several prefrontal areas. Thus, the norm in the single patient is generally the mixture of symptoms from the three categories described. Furthermore, there are some clinical differences between injuries on the right and the left hemisphere.

The lesions or dysfunctions of the ventromedial and orbital prefrontal cortex are those most likely to lead the individual to antisocial behavior and trouble with the law. The typical clinical picture, in the extreme case, is that of an individual emotionally unstable, irritable and jocular, hyperactive and disinhibited, given to temper tantrums and boisterousness, and insensitive to social norms and moral principles. Impulsive, impatient, and risk-loving, he is likely to trample on any law or standard of decency. His disinhibition will frequently result in hypersexuality, excessive eating, and reckless gambling. Most characteristic is the absence of any sense of guilt (unlike OCD or depressed patients). This clinical picture is reminiscent of that of the famous case of Phineas Gage, the New England railroad worker who in the mid nineteenth century, as the result of an explosion, suffered a massive injury of the frontal lobe, which he miraculously survived. The lesion affected primarily his ventromedial prefrontal cortex on one side (Damasio, 1994).

In sum, irresponsible behavior is the hallmark of the individual with pathology of the ventromedial prefrontal cortex. In agreement with this fact is the functional evidence that psychopaths and criminals generally show diminished activation of that cortex as well as of related structures, such as the orbital prefrontal cortex, the amygdala, and parts of the basal ganglia (Blair and Mitchell, 2009; Finger et al., 2011; Raine, 2002). Thus, the aggregate evidence from lesion and neuroimaging studies is that these brain structures are part of an inhibitory impulse-control system whose damage or inactivation, by whatever cause (possibly including genetics), results in irresponsible, antisocial, and sometimes criminal behavior. Such behavior, on the part of the frontal patient in particular, has exacerbated the old debate about the role of nature versus nurture in moral choice, and more broadly about free will (Greene and Cohen, 2004).

In the past two decades, aided in large part by the latest advances in neuroscience, the field of neuroethics has emerged (Churchland, 2011; Farah, 2010; Gazzaniga, 2005; Roskies, 2002). If there is a unifying theme in that field, it is the position that dualism (brain/mind) is indefensible, that all human choice is determined biophysically – that is, by physical events in the human brain – and that moral responsibility is reducible to those events. Consequently, to follow the argument, truly free will does not exist, and culpability is somehow "dissolved," if not "absolved" (my terms), in the physical brain. In support of their position, neuroethicists adduce not only the evidence summarized in the last few paragraphs, but also the latest findings of neuroimaging. Supposedly, this method evinces that not only the moral behavior of mental patients but also that of normal individuals (such as "normal" teenagers) can be predicted by measurable brain variables.[29]

With regard to legal responsibility, neuroscience is yet to make a decisive impact on jurisprudence. However, since the advent of the Enlightenment at the end of the eighteenth century, Western societies have become generally aware of the fact that genetics, brain disease, education, and economics can play a role in the nature of a crime. Philippe Pinel (1745–1826) was the indisputable pioneer in the humane treatment of the mental patient, even if that patient was in trouble with the law. Gradually, the "circumstance" of the perpetrator of a crime has been taken more and more into account. In Western countries, the insanity defense of the mental patient is widely utilized. In large part, this mode of criminal defense is a compromise between society's belief that crime should be punished and the idea that an ill individual should be medically treated.

The result of that compromise is the McNaghten rule, which is the standard of modern courts in dealing with mentally impaired defendants. The rule presumes sanity; in order to acquit the defendant, the judge demands proof from juries and defense counsel that, *at the time of the crime,* the accused was so impaired mentally as not to know the difference between right and wrong *under the law;* or, if he did know it, that he did not know he was doing what was wrong. Successful exoneration on those grounds (by reason of insanity) automatically requires that the defendant

---

[29] In this text, I have said enough about the shortcomings of neuroimaging. Though the method is extremely valuable for exposing the neural correlates of behavior and cognition, I do not think it is reliable enough to produce inculpating or exculpating evidence in court.

be committed to a mental hospital or authorized medical facility for an unspecified period of time and treated for his illness.[30]

In reality, neuroethicists challenge not legal responsibility but moral responsibility. They advocate secular standards of morality in court proceedings and they also appropriately advocate the use of modern neuroscience to refine the medical testimony in those proceedings. Beyond that, however, they have not changed radically the philosophical position of criminal courts. Nor have they changed much the views on liberty or responsibility from the vantage point of neuroscience. Indeed, my views on "free will," responsibility, and the role of the frontal lobe in behavior are fully *compatible* – I use this term advisedly, see Introduction – with theirs. If there are differences, these are of degree, though they may be important. They deserve at least brief restatement.

Against the background of current neuroscience, the treatment of *free will* as a unique indivisible mental faculty or existential entity is in my opinion unreasonable, on the part of defenders as well as detractors. Free will is as free as the laws of thermodynamics allow it to be in the brain. Illness, as we have seen, may disturb those laws to the detriment of freedom. Where there is choice there is freedom, and our freedom is as free as long as we have choices and as these choices have impact on the world, on others, or on ourselves. Thus, we make free moral choices, with limitations.

But a moral choice implies a moral agent. And here we cannot invoke an agent higher than our cortex ("the buck" truly stops there), more precisely our cortex under inputs from itself and from the inner world of emotion, both immersed in the PA cycle. This means also inputs from innumerable cortical

---

[30] The McNaghten rule is named after Daniel McNaghten, who in 1843 was accused of the attempted assassination of the British Prime Minister, Sir Robert Peel. McNaghten, in fact, fired a pistol that fatally wounded the statesman's secretary, Edward Drummond; later he alleged that God had commanded him to kill Peel. After extensive testimony, a panel of judges appointed by the House of Lords acquitted McNaghten on the grounds of insanity, originating the now famous rule that bears his name. The original rule has undergone some modifications by usage in the courts, but in its essence it has continued to be applied in practically all jurisdictions of Western countries dealing with criminal liability in relation to mental cases. It is the foundation for the verdict of "not guilty by reason of insanity" or "guilty but insane."

networks (cognits) that represent ethical and moral patterns of behavior. The fact that many of them are unconscious does not make our cortex less free to weigh, to evaluate, and to choose. No matter that some of those choices are overridden by limbic impulses. Truly free choices are made in the cortex and there is no need for a higher moral authority, or "superego," somewhere in it.[31] Thus, freedom and free will, even for principled action, are graded, determined, or better yet *biased*, by both nature and nurture. Culture is part of both, and is the topic of the next section.

CULTURE

"Culture or civilization, taken in its wide ethnographic sense, is that complex whole which includes knowledge, belief, art, morals, law, custom, and any other capabilities and habits acquired by man as a member of society." This broad definition of culture by Sir Edward Burnett Tylor (1920/1871), the father of social anthropology, is a suitable introduction to the subject of this, the final section of my chapter. As implicit in its last words, the definition contains two fundamental qualifications. One is that, because culture is acquired, it excludes what we have inherited from evolution.[32] The other is the cultural role of symbolic language, a mental faculty that constitutes the most powerful conveyer and depository of culture. Yet another qualification of culture is that it consists of a continuous dynamic process – in other words, that it changes – it "evolves" – in the course of our

[31] There is a dimension of human existence, however, in which the biological grounding of the moral agent in us defies the neuroscientific analysis: human suffering. The capacity to resist, and even to sublimate, physical and moral suffering, overtly challenges a neural explanation of such phenomena. Their reduction to a longing for or pleasure from pain, as a kind of biologically grounded masochism, is woefully simplistic. More plausible would be the rationale that strong belief, cortically grounded, would overcome physical pain, much as the fakir would achieve by training. Most difficult to explain neurologically is the endurance of moral suffering (Frankl, 2000; Fuster, 2005). What is most remarkable in this respect is the sense of inner liberation that some individuals can find in the depths of the most abject oppression. It is the nearest to a metaphysical – indeed spiritual – experience of liberty that neuroscience can encounter and must decline to explain.

[32] Tylor, however, viewed our culture as the result of linear evolution from a "primitive culture."

lives as well as in the course of history. Some of its changes are drastic, sometimes dramatic, as they frequently are for an immigrant, liberated, or subjugated population. In such cases a culture or subculture is called to "acculturate" to a dominant culture, by choice or under duress.

In any case, as far as the individual is concerned, culture has two components, which Tylor does not disambiguate in his definition. The first is culture as the social milieu in which we live. The other is the personal milieu – that is, the internalized culture – which Ortega (1961) called "circumstance." In reality, this is precisely the part of culture that is obliged to acculturate to changes in *external* culture.

Ideally, a democratic culture protects our personal freedoms, while demanding that we fulfill our responsibilities for the protection of everybody else's. The judicial courts at all levels, utilizing civil and criminal laws – made by legislatures in accord with the constitution of the nation – are intended to protect those freedoms. In fact, without adherence to the law on the part of everybody, there is no freedom guaranteed for anybody. This is the way things are supposed to be in a democracy under normal conditions of peace and prosperity. In the course of the past century, however, Western culture has seldom experienced a continuous decade without war or socioeconomic distress. Later, we will consider some of the causes and cultural consequences of current distress in the economies of the West.

Much civil and criminal law is redundant to natural law. We carry in our brain the essence of fundamental virtues or sentiments (trust, affiliation, sympathy, fairness, loyalty, compassion, etc.) that together constitute what has been called the moral sense (Darwin, 1872; Wilson, 1993). The moral sense is essential to social order. That "sense," arguably with a phylogenetic origin,[33] steeped

---

[33] In *The Descent of Man*, Darwin names four factors, growing out of man's social instincts, that lead him to the development of moral sense:

   (1) The social instincts, by their very nature, "lead an animal to take pleasure in the society of its fellows, to feel a certain amount of sympathy with them, and to perform various services for them."
   (2) In man, a superior memory allows him to remember actions that are good for or detrimental to the community.

in emotion and "rehearsed" after birth – first in the family – is most likely the ultimate source of moral judgment, which in concrete situations works on us rapidly by intuition, even before we use our intellect to rationalize that judgment (Haidt, 2001). Going one step further, and based on my view of conscience as epiphenomenal, I would argue that much of what appears to be intuition is already rational, but unconscious. Our cerebral cortex has an enormous database at its command that allows it to compute instantaneously a choice – in this case a judgment – with the speed of a nervous reflex. The fact that unconscious cortical "reasoning," albeit only probabilistic, can be triggered automatically by impulses from the limbic system does not invalidate but strengthens the argument.

The database of natural law probably consists of a vast conglomerate of conceptual cognits – that is, cognitive networks distributed in our cerebral cortex – that embody the aggregate of both our moral experience and our moral agenda. Whether those cognits are innate (phyletic) or not, whether they are made of "honed heredity" or entirely acquired after birth, are matter for serious debate. Nonetheless, my contention has been that moral experience and agenda are always available to the brain and ready to enter the PA cycle at a moment's notice for judgment, choice, or decision. As we have seen in Chapter 4, that cycle has a cognitive circuit and an emotional one, both active in parallel when needed. The need may be immediate or prospective. If it is the latter, the PA cycle involves the prefrontal cortex for the future adaptation of the organism to change, however near or distant that future may be.

There is no reason to believe that man-made law has a cortical distribution different from that of natural law, especially if we accept the possibility that much of the first is subsumed in the second. The structural base for moral judgment, therefore, would be mainly in the posterior cortex, whereas that for moral

(3) With man's mental powers, the power of communication and language also grows stronger, allowing individuals to become aware of the needs of others and to express their own needs to others.

(4) Repeated behavior for the good of the community tends to establish itself as habitual behavior.

These factors work to establish a moral sense of community-friendly behavior.

action would be mainly in the executive cortex. But it is difficult, and probably incorrect, to attempt to separate in the cortex the substrate for the two moral functions at the top of the PA cycle, which is integrative by definition. It would be like trying, for example, to separate a compassionate action from the sympathy for someone's pain.

Man-made law includes a wide gamut of legal codes, ranging from city codes to federal laws, from business regulations to institutional bylaws, from the dress code to the standards of licensed professionals, from copyright law to the ethical standards of writers and scientists. Legal codes have been instituted to protect the rights and freedoms of citizens, trading nations, blue-collar and white-collar workers, business partners, patients, etc. Much of that legislation is relatively stable and immutable once instituted. By and large, that is the part of the law that is most germane to natural law. Another part is more mutable, adaptable to demographic factors, business conditions, environmental factors, societal mores, and so on.

In the past century, major changes in Western culture have forced changes in many legal codes, sometimes preceded or succeeded by societal conflict. The most salient and consequential socioeconomic changes have been: (a) massive migrations from farm to big city, and from underdeveloped to developed countries – and states; (b) gradual transition from a buoyant manufacturing – and agricultural – industry to less productive industries of services and finance; (c) globalization of trade replacing both trade wars and wars for trade; (d) demise of the gold standard or any other stabilizer of the currency; (e) reaffirmation of civil rights; and (f) substantial proliferation of government entitlement programs, some taking the places formerly occupied by private savings, insurance, and personal responsibility.

Conflicts from some of those changes bear witness to the difficulty of a complex system, such as the economy of a nation, to adapt quickly enough, efficiently enough, to any large change. It is as if the collective prefrontal cortex of the nation were unable to predict the consequences of those changes and lacked the necessary information to preadapt to them. We in Western countries are currently experiencing one such situation brought about by economic recession and attendant unemployment. Under present conditions, the self-correction of the system is slow and clumsy, often unable to forestall open social conflict. Of course, nowadays, whatever that conflict, it is magnified by the media and the fact that it affects large populations all at once. In any case, some of the changes enumerated above have taken place to the benefit of our culture, and others not.[34]

I have just made a metaphorical ("as if") reference to the collective prefrontal cortex of a nation. In the present state of our knowledge, a reference of that kind can hardly surpass the level of allegory. Nonetheless, I believe it is more than an idle metaphor to compare the economy of a nation, indeed a complex adaptive system, to that other complex adaptive system that has been the subject of this book: the free and creative human brain. It is obviously more than a metaphor because the two systems are causally interrelated.

In 2004, the psychologist George Ainslie, with J. Monterosso, published a fascinating paper in *Science* entitled, "Behavior. A Marketplace in the Brain?" In it, the authors described their experimental research on delay discount, an important variable in the evaluation of expected reward (Chapter 4). Given that in any real marketplace value (or price) is determined by the actions of many people (Hayek, 1948; Mises, 1998), and given that those actions are ultimately determined by interactions among their brains,[35] I wish to paraphrase Ainslie's question for our final discussion: Is there a marketplace for values in the collective brain of our culture? My answer is "yes," and I shall attempt to

---

[34] One area where there has been cultural change for the better is that of the protection of the environment. In the United States, many individuals and organizations have led the ecological protection initiative over many years. Among the many favorable developments in this respect, two stand out as truly seminal: the creation of the National Park Service (1910s) and California's air pollution regulations (1950s).

[35] Neither of those giants of the Austrian school of economics, Mises or Hayek, indeed both champions of economic freedom, seemed to recognize the importance of biology in the choice of human action. The first referred to "human action as the ultimate given," and the second called it the result of the "pure logic of choice." (To be sure, Hayek in his *Sensory Order* [1952], discussed action at length in the context of perception, anticipating the emergence of the concept of the PA cycle in the cerebral cortex.)

substantiate it in principle, without quantification, leaving the latter to future research.

The first premise for that position is the presence of biological antecedents to the action in the form of a cognitive substrate in the cortex of the agent. The second is that that cognitive substrate is made of networks (cognits) that, when activated, mediate the dynamic relation between the perceptual component of that substrate and its executive component (PA cycle). Those two cognitive components are capable not only of integrating goal-directed action but also of evaluating sensory inputs leading to the action, as well as the expected consequences of it. In previous chapters (especially 3 and 4) I have attempted to substantiate those two premises. As discussed in those chapters, both the evaluation of sensory inputs and the assessed value of expected reward are functions of the prefrontal-limbic compound. Neither of these evaluations is possible without the experience of the agent and his interactions with the internal and external environment in the PA cycle. Nor is any discussion on the neurobiology of value choices possible without taking that interaction into account.

Let us consider a simple example in which the value is monetary, such as a transaction in the stock exchange. Three agents are essentially involved: the buyer, the seller, and the broker. The first seeks a low price ("bid") for a batch of shares, the second and the third seek a high price ("ask" and commission). The transaction basically engages and interlinks two PA cycles, the buyer's and the seller's, with the broker's mediating the two. It is the latter, through telephone or e-mail conversations (i.e., dialectic PA cycles), that reconciles the "bid" and the "ask." The sale brings the three cycles to rest, on the final price.[36]

Changes in cultural values may be caused by monetary factors – such as the prices of commodities, employment, inflation, wages, taxes, interest rates, etc. Or they may be caused by nonmonetary factors, such as developments in government,

---

[36] The transaction has been here greatly simplified without sacrificing the essentials. Even an over-the-counter exchange involves many more people and intraday valuations to determine the final price.

esthetics, immigration, public opinion, and so on. Natural values – that is, those most akin to natural law, such as family values – will be the most resistant to change, and may be amenable only to small modifications or amendments. Others, like esthetic values and fashions, are notoriously subject to media and word-of-mouth.

It is by word-of-mouth, in fact, that changes in most cultural values will take place, through thousands or millions of "dialogues" throughout the world. The fact that media pundits, public-opinion polls, and politicians bias those changes does not completely take away the private nature of free choices of value judgment by the individual or the small community. Nor does the internet alter the dyadic essence of millions of PA cycles in search of a sum total of cultural value. Because each PA cycle goes through one or many pairs of brains, and because each individual brain is free to make choices between opinions that will contribute to that sum total, it is reasonable to conclude that a "collective brain" is deciding on cultural value for all of us. That does not mean we will necessarily agree with it, but then such is the nature of the marketplace of values in a democracy.

In contrast with the benefits from the collective brain of a democracy, I will mention one cultural weakness that is presently quite manifest and deeply disturbing: the societal result of the abuse and manipulation of the people's delay discount by some bankers and politicians.[37] With their actions, the long-term marketplace of our cultural values, especially thrift, is severely distorted. Along with it, our freedom to become financially independent is severely violated. Indeed, a very high delay discount prevents people from saving money for illness and old

---

[37] Delay discount, in financial terms, is the value amount that we discount from an investment if we have to wait to get it back with a profit or benefit of some kind. That value – that is, the discount – increases inversely with the expected return on the investment and the length of time we have to wait to get the invested capital back. A lender – that is, a bank, a private enterprise, or the government – can increase the delay discount by prolonging that time or by decreasing the return. US banks, on behalf of the Federal Reserve, have lately been doing just that by sending to record lows the interest rate on 10-year bonds, for example.

age.[38] Public health and social security are clearly the two major victims of the brutal delay discount that has been forced on our culture. One of the greatest mistakes of this culture has been to transfer to the government the responsibility of people to take care of themselves in the future. It is an insidious transfer that, unfortunately, demagogues know well how to exploit.

Social ills like that can be expected to be temporary, however. In the long run, human society, in the United States in particular, has proven over and over again to be able to rediscover its cultural bearings after they seemed lost forever. We can thus confidently predict that sooner or later traditional values will return, including savings and the joy of working. Immigration is so much a part of our cultural history that we have already made it a habit to live in a multicultural society, where tolerance is natural and discrimination a curse of the past. Unemployment will diminish. Business will prosper again and the promoters of big finance will be muted by much-needed regulation. Freedom, fairness, and democracy will continue to thrive in our cultural brain, and innovation and creativity in its prefrontal cortex.

CONCLUSIONS

Trust in others is an ethical principle of evolutionary origin that develops early in life with the assistance of a trusting and trusted social environment. Trust makes life predictable, as it

---

[38] In former times, public deficits were covered by taxation or inflation, or both. To the dismay of Western governments, however, those tools no longer work to sustain an underfunded welfare state. Taxation can easily reach a point of diminishing returns and inflation seems to be no longer forthcoming or effective, despite record-low interest rates. To overcome recession, in my view, three psychological conditions are necessary that government seems unable to deliver: trust, security, and confidence in the future. The old solutions advocated by economists of the right or the left do not quite work, primarily for lack of those three conditions. Free-market economy, as it was eloquently advocated by Hayek in *The Road to Serfdom* (1944), and vindicated by a powerful post-World War II recovery, hardly works in the massive populations of modern cities, with all their problems of broken families, poor schooling, crime, illegal immigration, and unemployment. The converse economic philosophy of Keynesian economics – that is, the monetizing of the public debt (printing money) and government-promoted employment – hardly ever works reliably for any extended time.

makes predictable the actions of others on our behalf. Immediately after birth, trust is indispensable for life preservation, and later for the acquisition of social skills. In adult life, it becomes essential for the exercise of all freedoms, in family, in society, in business, in the professions, and in public service. Language is both a benefit and a conveyer of trust.

In addition to trust and other moral values, natural goods like food have an evolutionary base of value. Others, like money, have a derivative value. Values are rewarding and, as such, activate the mesolimbic dopaminergic system at the base of the brain – the "reward axis." That system collects inputs from the amygdala and other limbic structures involved in the evaluation of rewards. Those structures, in the aggregate, feed value-coding inputs into large areas of the cerebral cortex. Limbic structures are constituents of the emotional PA cycle, which, in parallel with the cognitive PA cycle, coordinates goal-directed behavior.

The prefrontal cortex is essential for the assessment of expected value, risk, and probability of reward. In addition, it is the source of internal feedback for error correction and monitoring. Prospective prefrontal functions play a critical role in the delay of expected reward for greater gain – that is, in the control of delay discount, which is our natural tendency to depreciate the value of rewards we have to wait for. Failure to control delay discount can be extremely detrimental to private and public economies.

Higher ethical values are presumed to be widely distributed in the perceptual and frontal cortices. Those values are thought to develop within a critical period after birth. Failure of that process can result in a "value-blind" individual. Several brain disorders diminish freedom, and thus moral and legal responsibility. Prominent among them are the psychoses, the OCD/depression syndromes, the addictions, and the disorders of the frontal lobes.

Our internal culture is made, in part, of the moral sense, a wealth of virtues and sentiments, such as trust and affiliation, which are rooted in natural law. Another part of culture is made of learned material, ethical principles, and traditions acquired by experience from family, school, and social life. In a democratic society, laws protect our freedoms; in return, society expects that we act responsibly toward others by respecting theirs. After being established by life experience, the principles of natural as well as man-made law are presumed to be represented by high-level cognits of the cortex, from where they guide cognitive and emotional behaviors through their respective PA cycles.

References

Ainslie, G. (2001). *Breakdown of Will*. Cambridge University Press.

Ainslie, G., and Monterosso, J. (2004). Behavior: a marketplace in the brain? *Science*, **306**, 421–423.

Alexander, G. E., DeLong, M. R., and Crutcher, M. D. (1992). Do cortical and basal ganglia motor areas use 'motor programs' to control movement? *Behavioral and Brain Sciences*, **15**, 656–665.

Amiez, C., Joseph, J. P., and Procyk, E. (2005). Anterior cingulate error-related activity is modulated by predicted reward. *European Journal of Neuroscience*, **21**, 3447–3452.

Amit, D. J. (1989). *Modeling Brain Function: The World of Attractor Neural Networks*. New York: Cambridge University Press.

Ansmann, I. C. (2005). The whistle repertoire and acoustic behaviour of short-beaked common dolphins, *Delphinus delphis*, around the British Isles, with applications for acoustic surveying. MSc thesis, University of Wales, Bangor.

Ardrey, R. (1966). *The Territorial Imperative*. New York: Atheneum.

Ariëns Kappers, C. N., Huber, G., and Crosby, E. C. (1960). *The Comparative Anatomy of the Nervous System of Vertebrates, Including Man*. New York: Hafner.

Aron, A. R., Robbins, T. W., and Poldrack, R. A. (2004). Inhibition and the right inferior frontal cortex. *Trends in Cognitive Sciences*, **8**, 170–177.

Atkinson, A. P., and Adolphs, R. (2011). The neuropsychology of face perception: beyond simple dissociations and functional selectivity. *Philosophical Transactions of the Royal Society of London. Series B, Biological Sciences*, **366**, 1726–1738.

Baddeley, A. (1983). Working memory. *Philosophical Transactions of the Royal Society of London. Series B, Biological Sciences*, **302**, 311–324.

Barkley, R. A. (1997). *ADHD and the Nature of Self-Control*. New York: Guilford Press.

Barsalou, L. W. (1999). Perceptual symbol systems. *Behavioral and Brain Sciences*, **22**, 577–660.

Batthyany, A., and Elitzur, A. (2009). Mental causation and free will after Libet and Soon: reclaiming conscious agency. In: *Irreducibly Conscious:*

Selected Papers on Consciousness. Winter. Heidelberg: Universitäts-Verlag.

Baumgartner, T., Heinrichs, M., Vonlanthen, A., Fischbacher, U., and Fehr, E. (2008). Oxytocin shapes the neural circuitry of trust and trust adaptation in humans. *Neuron*, **58**, 639–650.

Bechara, A. (2005). Decision making, impulse control and loss of willpower to resist drugs: a neurocognitive perspective. *Nature Neuroscience*, **8**, 1458–1463.

Bechara, A., Tranel, D., and Damasio, H. (2000). Characterization of the decision-making deficit of patients with ventromedial prefrontal cortex lesions. *Brain* **123**, 2189–2202.

Bergson, H. (1907). *L'évolution créatrice*. Paris: Presses Universitaires de France.

Bernard, C. (1927/1865). *An Introduction to the Study of Experimental Medicine*. New York: Macmillan.

Berndt, T. J., and Wood, D. J. (1974). The development of time concepts through conflict based on a primitive duration capacity. *Child Development*, **45**, 825–828.

Bernstein, N. (1967). *The Co-ordination and Regulation of Movements*. New York: Pergamon.

Berridge, K. C. (2007). The debate over dopamine's role in reward: the case for incentive salience. *Psychopharmacology (Berl)*, **191**, 391–431.

Bertalanffy, L. von (1950). The theory of open systems in physics and biology. *Science*, **111**, 23–29.

Blair, R. J. R., and Mitchell, D. G. (2009). Psychopathy, attention and emotion. *Psychological Medicine*, **39**, 543–555.

Bodner, M., Shafi, M., Zhou, Y. D., and Fuster, J. M. (2005). Patterned firing of parietal cells in a haptic working memory task. *European Journal of Neuroscience*, **21**, 2538–2546.

Bogousslavsky, J. (2005). Artistic creativity, style and brain disorders. *European Neurology*, **54**, 103–111.

Bolhuis, J. J., and Wynne, D. L. (2009). Can evolution explain how minds work? *Nature*, **458**, 832–833.

Bonin, G. V. (1950). *Essay on the Cerebral Cortex*. Springfield, IL: Charles C. Thomas.

Bookheimer, S. (2002). Functional MRI of language: new approaches to understanding the cortical organization of semantic processing. *Annual Review of Neuroscience*, **25**, 151–188.

Boring, E. G. (1933). *The Physical Dimensions of Consciousness*. New York: Century.

Born, J., Rasch, B., and Gais, S. (2006). Sleep to remember. *Neuroscientist*, **12**, 410–424.

Boroditsky, L. (2003). Linguistic relativity. In: L. Nadel (ed.), *Encyclopedia of Cognitive Science*, pp. 917–922. London: Macmillan.

Bowlby, J. (1951). *Maternal Care and Mental Health*. New York: Schocken.

Broca, P. (1861). Rémarques sur la siège de la faculté du langage articulé, suivi d'une observation d'aphémie. *Bulletin of the Anatomy Society* (Paris), **2**, 330–357.

Brodmann, K. (1909). *Vergleichende Lokalisationslehre der Grosshirnrinde in ihren Prinzipien dargestellt auf Grund des Zellenbaues*. Leipzig: Barth.

(1912). Neue Ergebnisse uber die vergleichende histologische Lokalisation der Grosshirnrinde mit besonderer Berücksichtigung des Stirnhirns. *Anatomischer Anzeiger (Suppl.)*, **41**, 157–216.

Brunia, C. H. M., Haagh, S. A. V. M., and Scheirs, J. G. M. (1985). Waiting to respond: electrophysiological measurements in man during preparation for a voluntary movement. In: H. Heuer, U. Kleinbeck, and K.-H. Schmidt (eds.), *Motor Behavior*, pp. 35–78. New York: Springer.

Buijs, R. M., and Van Eden, C. G. (2000). The integration of stress by the hypothalamus, amygdala and prefrontal cortex: balance between the autonomic nervous system and the neuroendocrine system. *Progress in Brain Research*, **126**, 117–132.

Bullock, M., and Gelman, R. (1979). Preschool children's assumptions about cause and effect: temporal ordering. *Child Development*, **50**, 89–96.

Bush, G., Luu, P., and Posner, M. I. (2000). Cognitive and emotional influences in anterior cingulate cortex. *Trends in Cognitive Sciences*, **4**, 215–222.

Butterworth, B. (2005). The development of arithmetical abilities. *Journal of Child Psychology and Psychiatry*, **46**, 3–18.

Cajal, S. R. (1894). La fine structure des centres nerveux. *Proceedings of the Royal Society of London*, **55**, 444–468.

(1923). *Recuerdos de Mi Vida*. Madrid: Pueyo.

Cannon, W. (1932). *The Wisdom of the Body*. New York: Norton.

Cappelletti, M., Fregni, F., Shapiro, K., Pascual-Leone, A., and Caramazza, A. (2008). Processing nouns and verbs in the left frontal cortex: a transcranial magnetic stimulation study. *Journal of Cognitive Neuroscience*, **20**, 707–720.

Caramazza, A., and Hillis, A. E. (1991). Lexical organization of nouns and verbs in the brain. *Nature*, **349**, 788–790.

Carrington, S. J., and Bailey, A. J. (2009). Are there theory of mind regions in the brain? A review of the neuroimaging literature. *Human Brain Mapping*, **30**, 2313–2335.

Chomsky, N. (1957). *Syntactic Structures*. The Hague/Paris: Mouton.

(1965). *Aspects of the Theory of Syntax*. Cambridge, MA: MIT Press.

(1985). *Knowledge of Language*. New York: Praeger.

(2007). Approaching UG from below. In: U. Sauerland and M. Gärter (eds.), *Interfaces + Recursion = Language?*, pp. 1–29. New York: Mouton de Gruyter.

Christiansen, M. H., and Chater, N. (2008). Language as shaped by the brain. *Behavioral and Brain Sciences*, **31**, 489–558.

Christie, A. (2011). *Murder on the Orient Express*. New York: HarperCollins.

Churchland, P. S. (2011). *Braintrust*. Princeton University Press.

Clark, A. (2008). *Supersizing the Mind: Embodiment, Action, and Cognitive Extension*. Oxford University Press.

Conel, J. L. (1963). *The Postnatal Development of the Human Cerebral Cortex*. Cambridge, MA: Harvard University Press.

Corina, D. P., Loudermilk, B. C., Detwiler, L., Martin, R. F., Brinkley, J. F., and Ojemann, G. (2010). Analysis of naming errors during cortical

stimulation mapping: implications for models of language representation. *Brain and Language*, **115**, 101–112.

Creutzfeldt, O. D. (1993). *Cortex Cerebri*. Berlin: Springer-Verlag.

Damasio, A. R. (1994). *Descartes' Error: Emotion, Reason and the Human Brain*.
New York: Grosset Putnam.

(1996). The somatic marker hypothesis and the possible functions of the
prefrontal cortex. *Philosophical Transactions of the Royal Society of London.
Series B, Biological Sciences*, **351**, 1413–1420.

Darwin, C. (1872). *The Descent of Man and Selection in Relation to Sex*. London:
John Murray.

Davis, J. (1994). *Keynes's Philosophical Development*. New York: Cambridge
University Press.

Dawkins, R. (1986). *The Blind Watchmaker*. New York: Norton.

DeCasper, A., and Spence, M. (1986). Prenatal maternal speech influences
newborns' perception of speech sounds. *Infant Behavior and Development*,
9, 133–150.

Dehaene, S. (1997). *The Number Sense: How the Mind Creates Mathematics*. New
York: Oxford University Press.

De Marneffe, D. (1991). Looking and listening: the construction of clinical
knowledge in Charcot and Freud. *Signs*, **17**, 71–111.

Dennett, D. (2003). *Freedom Evolves*. New York: Viking Books.

Denton, D. A., McKinley, M. J., and Weisinger, R. S. (1996). Hypothalamic
integration of body fluid regulation. *Proceedings of the National Academy
of Sciences of the United States of America*, **93**, 7397–7404.

Dicey, A. V. (1889). *Introduction to the Law of the Constitution*. New York:
Macmillan.

Di Pellegrino, G., Fadiga, L., Fogassi, L., Gallese, V., and Rizzolatti, G. (1992).
Understanding motor events: a neurophysiological study.
Experimental Brain Research, **91**, 176–180.

Dittmann, V. (1996). Substance abuse, mental disorders and crime: comorbidity and multi-axial assessment in forensic psychiatry. *European
Addiction Research*, **2**, 3–10.

Dretske, F. (2000). *Perception, Knowledge and Belief*. Cambridge University Press.

Edelman, G. M. (1987). *Neural Darwinism*. New York: Basic Books.

Edelman, G. M., and Gally, J. A. (2001). Degeneracy and complexity in biological systems. *Proceedings of the National Academy of Sciences of the
United States of America*, **98**, 13763–13768.

Emmerich, W., Goldman, K. S., Kirsh, B., and Sharabany, R. (1977). Evidence
for a transitional phase in the development of gender constancy.
Child Development, **48**, 930–936.

Erikson, E. (1993). *Childhood and Society*. New York: Norton.

Everitt, B. J., and Robbins, T. W. (2005). Neural systems of reinforcement for
drug addiction: from actions to habits to compulsion. *Nature
Neuroscience*, **11**, 1481–1489.

Farah, M. J. (2010). *Neuroethics: An Introduction with Readings*. Cambridge, MA:
MIT Press.

Fellows, L. K, and Farah, M. J. (2005). Dissociable elements of human
foresight: a role for the ventromedial frontal lobes in framing the

future, but not in discounting future rewards. *Neuropsychologia*, **43**, 1214–1221.

Fenichel, O. (1946). *The Psychoanalytic Theory of Neuroses*. London: Kegan Paul, Trench, Trübner and Co.

Finger, E. C., Marsh, A. A., Blair, K. S., Reid, M. E., Sims, C., Ng, P., Pine, D. S., and Blair, R. J. (2011). Disrupted reinforcement signaling in the orbitofrontal cortex and caudate in youths with conduct disorder or oppositional defiant disorder and a high level of psychopathic traits. *American Journal of Psychiatry*, **168**, 152–162.

Flechsig, P. (1901). Developmental (myelogenetic) localisation of the cerebral cortex in the human subject. *Lancet*, **2**, 1027–1029.

Floden, D., Alexander, M. P., Kubu, C. S., Katz, D., and Stuss, D. T. (2008). Impulsivity and risk-taking behavior in focal frontal lobe lesions. *Neuropsychologia*, **46**, 213–223.

Fodor, J. A. (1975). *The Language of Thought*. New York: Thomas Crowell.

Fodor, J. A., and Pylyshyn, Z. W. (1988). Connectionism and cognitive architecture: a critical analysis. In: S. Pinker and J. Mehler (eds.), *Connections and Symbols*, pp. 3–71. Cambridge, MA: MIT Press.

Fox, M. D., and Raichle, M. E. (2007). Spontaneous fluctuations in brain activity observed with functional magnetic resonance imaging. *Nature Reviews Neuroscience*, **8**, 700–711.

Frahm, H. D., Stephan, H., and Stephan, M. (1982). Comparison of brain structure volumes in Insectivora and primates. I. Neocortex. *Journal für Hirnforschung*, **23**, 375–389.

Frankfurt, H. (1971). Freedom of the will and the concept of the person. *Journal of Philosophy*, **68**, 5–20.

Frankl, V. E. (2000). *Man's Search for Ultimate Meaning*. Cambridge, MA: Perseus.

Freud, S. (1891). *Zur Auffassung der Aphasien*. Vienna: Deuticke.

Frisch, W. (2003). *Brahms: The Four Symphonies*. New Haven, CT: Yale University Press.

Friston, K. J., and Frith, C. D. (1995). Schizophrenia: a disconnection syndrome? *Journal of Clinical Neuroscience*, **3**, 89–97.

Friston, K. J., Tononi, G., Reeke, G. N., Jr., Sporns, O., and Edelman, G. M. (1994). Value-dependent selection in the brain: simulation in a synthetic neural model. *Neuroscience*, **59**, 229–243.

Fukuyama, F. (1995). *Trust: The Social Virtues and the Creation of Prosperity*. New York: Free Press.

Fumagalli, M., and Priori, A. (2012). Functional and clinical neuroanatomy of morality. *Brain*, **135**, 2006–2021.

Funnell, E., and Wilding, J. (2011). Development of a vocabulary of object shapes in a child with a very-early-acquired visual agnosia: a unique case. *Quarterly Journal of Experimental Psychology*, 64, 261–262.

Fuster, I. X. (2005). *Sufrimiento Humano: Verdad y Sentido*. Barcelona: Balmes.

Fuster, J. M. (1995). *Memory in the Cerebral Cortex – An Empirical Approach to Neural Networks in the Human and Nonhuman Primate*. Cambridge, MA: MIT Press.

(2001). The prefrontal cortex – an update: time is of the essence. *Neuron*, **30**, 319–333.

(2003). *Cortex and Mind: Unifying Cognition*. New York: Oxford University Press.

(2008). *The Prefrontal Cortex* (4th edn.). London: Academic Press.

(2009) Cortex and memory: emergence of a new paradigm. *Journal of Cognitive Neuroscience*, **21**, 2047–2072.

Fuster, J. M., Bauer, R. H., and Jervey, J. P. (1982). Cellular discharge in the dorsolateral prefrontal cortex of the monkey in cognitive tasks. *Journal of Experimental Neurology*, **77**, 679–694.

Fuster, J. M., and Bressler, S. (2012). Cognit activation: a mechanism enabling temporal integration in working memory. *Trends in Cognitive Sciences*, **16**, 207–218.

Gallagher, S. (2005). *How the Body Shapes the Mind*. New York: Oxford University Press.

Gallistel, C. R. (1980). *The Organization of Action: A New Synthesis*. Hillsdale, NJ: Lawrence Erlbaum.

Gathercole, S. E., Pickering, S. J., Ambridge, B., and Wearing, H. (2004). The structure of working memory from 4 to 15 years of age. *Developmental Psychology*, **40**, 177–190.

Gazzaniga, M. S. (2005). *The Ethical Brain*. New York: Dana Press.

Geschwind, N. (1965a). Disconnexion syndromes in animals and man. I. *Brain*, **88**, 237–294.

(1965b). Disconnexion syndromes in animals and man. II. *Brain*, **88**, 585–644.

Ghashghaei, H. T., and Barbas, H. (2002). Pathways for emotion: interactions of prefrontal and anterior temporal pathways in the amygdala of the rhesus monkey. *Neuroscience*, **115**, 1261–1279.

Gibson, J. (1977). The theory of affordances. In: R. Shaw and J. Bransford (eds.), *Perceiving, Acting, and Knowing: Toward an Ecological Psychology*, pp. 67–82. Hillsdale, NJ: Lawrence Erlbaum.

Gillespie, C. C. (1997). *Pierre-Simon Laplace, 1749–1827: A Life in Exact Science*. Princeton University Press.

Glancy, G. D., and Regehr, C. (1992). The forensic psychiatric aspects of schizophrenia. *Psychiatric Clinics of North America*, **15**, 575–589.

Glimcher, P. (2003). *Decisions, Uncertainty, and the Brain: The Science of Neuroeconomics*. Cambridge, MA: MIT Press.

Goldman-Rakic, P. S. (1994). Working memory dysfunction in schizophrenia. *Journal of Neuropsychiatry and Clinical Neuroscience*, **6**, 348–357.

Goleman, D. (1995). *Emotional Intelligence*. New York: Bantam.

Gothard, K. M., Battaglia, F. P., Erickson, C. A., Spitler, K. M., and Amaral, D. G. (2007). Neural responses to facial expression and face identity in the monkey amygdala. *Journal of Neurophysiology*, **97**, 1671–1683.

Gould, S. J. (1992). Ontogeny and phylogeny – revisited and reunited. *Bioessays*, **14**, 275–279.

Grabenhorst, F., and Rolls, E. T. (2011). Value, pleasure and choice in the ventral prefrontal cortex. *Trends in Cognitive Sciences*, **15**, 56–67.

Grafton, S. T., Woods, R. P., and Mike, T. (1994). Functional imaging of procedural motor learning: relating cerebral blood flow with individual subject performance. *Human Brain Mapping*, **1**, 221–234.

Granger, C. W. J. (1988). Causation in decision, belief change and statistics. In: W. Harper and B. Skyrms (eds.), *Causality Testing in a Decision Science*, pp. 1–20. Alphen, Netherlands: Kluwer.

Greene, J., and Cohen, J. (2004). For the law, neuroscience changes nothing and everything. *Philosophical Transactions of the Royal Society of London. Series B, Biological Sciences*, **359**, 1775–1785.

Greenfield, P. M. (1991). Language, tools and brain: the ontogeny and phylogeny of hierarchically organized sequential behavior. *Behavioral and Brain Sciences*, **14**, 531–595.

(2009). Linking social change and developmental change: shifting pathways of human development. *Developmental Psychology*, **45**, 401–418.

Gregory, R. L. (1970). *The Intelligent Eye*. New York: McGraw-Hill.

Gregory, R. L., and Wallace, J. G. (1963). Recovery from early blindness: a case study. *Quarterly Journal of Psychology, Monograph* **2**.

Griffiths, J. D., Marslen-Wilson, W. D., Stamatakis, E. A., and Tyler, L. K. (2012). Functional organization of the neural language system: dorsal and ventral pathways are critical for syntax. *Cerebral Cortex*, **23**, 139–147.

Guyer, P. (2004). Immanuel Kant. *Routledge Encyclopedia of Philosophy*. London: Routledge.

Habicht, C. (1985). An ancient Baedeker and his critics: Pausanias' 'Guide to Greece'. *Proceedings of the American Philosophical Society*, **129**, 220–224.

Haeckel, E. (1992). *The Riddle of the Universe*. Amherst, NY: Prometheus Books.

Haidt, J. (2001). The emotional dog and its rational tail: a social intuitionist approach to moral judgment. *Psychological Review*, **108**, 814–834.

Harlow, H. F. (1993). *Love in Infant Monkeys*. Scientific American Library: New York: W.H. Freeman.

Harnad, S. (2005). To cognize is to categorize: cognition is categorization. In: C. Lefebvre and H. Cohen (eds.), *Handbook of Categorization in Cognitive Science*, pp. 19–43. New York: Elsevier Press.

Harris, E. E. (1970). *Hypothesis and Perception: The Roots of Scientific Method*. New York: Allen and Unwin.

Hayek, F. A. (1944). *The Road to Serfdom*. University of Chicago Press.

(1948). *Individualism and Economic Order*. University of Chicago Press.

(1952). *The Sensory Order*. University of Chicago Press.

(1960). *The Constitution of Liberty*. University of Chicago Press.

Hebb, D. O. (1949). *The Organization of Behavior*. New York: Wiley.

Hegel, G. W. F. (2002). *Philosophy of Right*. Newburyport, MA: Focus Publishing.

Helmholtz, H. von (1925). *Helmholtz's Treatise on Physiological Optics* (trans. J. P. C. Southall). Menasha, WI: Optical Society of America.

Hensch, T. K. (2004). Critical period regulation. *Annual Review of Neuroscience*, **27**, 549–579.

(2005). Critical period plasticity in local cortical circuits. *Nature Reviews Neuroscience*, **6**, 877–888.

Herrick, C. J. (1956). *The Evolution of Human Nature*. Austin, TX: University of Texas Press.

Hess, W. R. (1943). Teleokinetisches und ereismatisches Kraeftesystem in der Biomotorik. *Helvetica Physiologica Pharmacology Acta*, **1**, c62–c63.

(1954). *Das Zwischenhirn*. Basel: Benno Schwabe.

Hobbes, T. (1968). *The Leviathan*. London: Penguin Books.

Holland, J. H. (1998). *Emergence from Chaos to Order*. Reading, MA: Addison-Wesley.

Huang, P., Qiu, L., Shen, L., Gong, Q., Xie, P., Zhang, Y., Song, Z., and Qi, Z. (2012). Evidence for a left-over-right inhibitory mechanism during figural creative thinking in healthy nonartists. *Human Brain Mapping*, DOI: 10.1002/hbm.22093.

Hubel, D. (1995). *Eye, Brain, and Vision*. Scientific American Library. New York: W.H. Freeman.

Hudson, J. A. (2006). The development of future concepts through mother–child conversation. *Merrill-Palmer Quarterly*, **52**, 70–95.

Ingvar, D. H. (1979). "Hyperfrontal" distribution of the cerebral grey matter flow in resting wakefulness; on the functional anatomy of the conscious state. *Acta Neurologica Scandinavica*, **60**, 12–25.

(1985). "Memory of the future": an essay on the temporal organization of conscious awareness. *Human Neurobiology*, **4**, 127–136.

Jackson, J. H. (1882). On some implications of dissolution of the nervous system. *Medical Press and Circular*, 2, 411–426.

(1915). On affections of speech from disease of the brain. *Brain*, **38**, 107–174.

James, W. (1956/1884). The dilemma of determinism. Repr. in *The Will to Believe*. New York: Dover.

(1890). *Principles of Psychology*. New York: Holt.

Jaynes, E., Bretthorst, G., and Jaffe, A. H. (2003). *Probability Theory: The Logic of Science*. Cambridge University Press.

Jones, E. G., and Leavitt, R. Y. (1974). Retrograde axonal transport and the demonstration of non-specific projections to the cerebral cortex and striatum from thalamic intralaminar nuclei in the rat, cat and monkey. *Journal of Comparative Neurology*, **154**, 349–378.

Juarrero, A. (1999). *Dynamics in Action: Intentional Behavior as a Complex System*. Cambridge, MA: MIT Press.

Kahneman, D. (2011). *Thinking, Fast and Slow*. New York: Farrar, Straus and Giroux.

Kahneman, D., and Tversky, A. (1979). Prospect theory: an analysis of decision under risk. *Econometrica*, **47**, 263–291.

Kandel, E. R. (2000). Cellular mechanisms of learning and the biological basis of individuality. In: E. R. Kandel, J. H. Schwartz, and T. M. Jessell (eds.), *Principles of Neural Science*, pp. 1247–1279. New York: McGraw-Hill.

(2012). *The Age of Insight*. New York: Random House.

Kane, R. (1985). *Free Will and Values*. Albany, NY: SUNY Press.

(2011). Introduction. In: R. Kane (ed.), *The Contours of Contemporary Free-Will Debates*, pp. 3–35. New York: Oxford University Press.

Kant, I. (1993). *Grounding for the Metaphysics of Morals*. Indianapolis, IN: Hackett.

Karmiloff, K., and Karmiloff-Smith, A. (2001). *Pathways to Language: From Fetus to Adolescent*. Cambridge, MA: Harvard University Press.

Karunanayaka, P. R., Holland, S. K., Schmithors, V. J., Solodkin, A., Chen, E. E., and Szaflarski, J. P. (2007). Age-related connectivity changes in fMRI data from children listening to stories. *NeuroImage*, **1**, 349–360.

Keegan, J. (1993). *A History of Warfare*. New York: Knopf.

Keller, H., Lohaus, A., Völker, S., Cappenberg, M., and Chasiotis, A. (1999). Temporal contingency as an independent component of parenting behavior. *Child Development*, **70**, 474–485.

Klüver, H., and Bucy, P. C. (1938). An analysis of certain effects of bilateral temporal lobectomy in the rhesus monkey, with special reference to "psychic blindness". *Journal of Psychology*, **15**, 33–54.

Knutson, B., Taylor, J., Kaufman, M., Peterson, R., and Glover, G. (2005). Distributed neural representation of expected value. *Journal of Neuroscience*, **25**, 4806–4812.

Köhler, W. (1925). *The Mentality of Apes*. New York: Harcourt.

Kowatari, Y., Lee, S. H., Yamamura, H., Nagamori, Y., Levy, P., Yamane, S., and Yamamoto, M. (2009). Neural networks involved in artistic creativity. *Human Brain Mapping*, **30**, 1678–1690.

Kreitzer, A. C., and Malenka, R. C. (2008). Striatal plasticity and basal ganglia circuit function. *Neuron*, **60**, 543–554.

Kroger, J. K., Sabb, F. W., Fales, C. L., Bookheimer, S. Y., Cohen, M. S., and Holyoak, K. J. (2002). Recruitment of anterior dorsolateral prefrontal cortex in human reasoning: a parametric study of relational complexity. *Cerebral Cortex*, **12**, 477–485.

Krubitzer, L. (2009). In search of a unifying theory of complex brain evolution. *Annals of the New York Academy of Sciences*, **1156**, 44–67.

Kuhn, D., and Phelps, H. (1976). The development of children's comprehension of causal direction. *Child Development*, **47**, 248–251.

Lashley, K. S. (1950). In search of the engram. *Symposia of the Society for Experimental Biology*, **4**, 454–482.

  (1951). The problem of serial order in behavior. In: L. A. Jeffress (ed.), *Cerebral Mechanisms in Behavior. The Hixon Symposium*, pp. 112–146. New York: Wiley.

Le Bihan, D., Mangin, J. F., Poupon, C., Clark, C. A., Pappata, S., Molko, N., and Chabriat, H. (2001). Diffusion tensor imaging: concepts and applications. *Journal of Magnetic Resonance Imaging*, **13**, 534–546.

Le Doux, J. E. (1992). Emotion and the amygdala. In: J. P. Aggleton (ed.), *The Amygdala: Neurobiological Aspects of Emotion, Memory, and Mental Dysfunction*, pp. 339–351. New York: Wiley-Liss.

Libet, B. (1985). Unconscious cerebral initiative and the role of conscious will in voluntary action. *Behavioral and Brain Sciences*, **8**, 529–566.

Libet, B., Wright, E. W., and Gleason, C. A. (1983). Preparation- or intention-to-act, in relation to pre-event potentials recorded at the vertex. *Electroencephalography and Clinical Neurophysiology*, **56**, 367–372.

Lin, A., Adolphs, R., and Rangel, A. (2012). Social and monetary reward learning engage overlapping neural substrates. *Social Cognitive and Affective Neuroscience*, **3**, 274–281.

Lorenz, K. (1963). *On Aggression*. New York: Harcourt Brace and Co.

Low, L. K., and Cheng, H. J. (2006). Axon pruning: an essential step underlying the developmental plasticity of neuronal connections.

Philosophical Transactions of the Royal Society of London. Series B, Biological Sciences, **361**, 1531–1544.

Lucas, T. H., McKhann, G. M., and Ojemann, G. A. (2004). Functional separation of languages in the bilingual brain: a comparison of electrical stimulation language mapping in 25 bilingual patients and 117 monolingual control patients. *Journal of Neurosurgery*, **101**, 449–457.

Luria, A. R., and Homskaya, E. D. (1964). Disturbance in the regulative role of speech with frontal lobe lesions. In: J. M. Warren and K. Akert (eds.), *The Frontal Granular Cortex and Behavior*, pp. 353–371. New York: McGraw-Hill.

Malhi, G. S., Parker, G. B., and Greenwood, J. (2005). Structural and functional models of depression: from sub-types to substrates. *Acta Psychiatrica Scandinavica*, **111**, 94–105.

Marcus, G. F. (1998). Can connectionism save constructivism? *Cognition*, **66**, 153–182.

Marías, J. (1970). *José Ortega y Gasset: Circumstance and Vocation*. Norman, OK: University of Oklahoma Press.

Marina, J. (1993). *Teoría de la Inteligencia Creadora*. Barcelona: Anagrama.

Markovits, H., and Barrouillet, P. (2002). The development of conditional reasoning: a mental model account. *Developmental Review*, **22**, 5–36.

Maurois, A. (1986). *The Climates of Love*. London: Peter Owen.

McCarthy, G., Puce, A., Gore, J., and Truett, A. (1997). Face-specific processing in the human fusiform gyrus. *Journal of Cognitive Neuroscience*, **9**, 605–610.

McClelland, H. A., and Rumelhart, D. E. (1986). *Parallel Distributed Processing*. Cambridge, MA: MIT Press.

McClure, S. M., Laibson, D. I., Loewenstein, G., and Cohen, J. D. (2004). Separate neural systems value immediate and delayed monetary rewards. *Science*, **306**, 503–507.

Mehler, J., and Dupoux, E. (1994). *What Infants Know: The New Cognitive Science of Early Development*. Cambridge, MA: Blackwell.

Mele, A. (2006). *Free Will and Luck*. New York: Oxford University Press.

Mill, J. (1829). *Analysis of the Phenomena of the Human Mind*, vol. I. London: Baldwin and Cradock.

Mill, J. S. (1859). *On Liberty*. London: J.W. Parker and Son.

Miller, E. K., and Cohen, J. D. (2001). An integrative theory of prefrontal cortex function. *Annual Review of Neuroscience*, **24**, 167–202.

Mises, L. (1998). *A Treatise on Economics*. Auburn, AL: Ludwig von Mises Institute.

Misztal, B. (1996). *Trust in Modern Societies: The Search for the Bases of Social Order*. Cambridge: Polity Press.

Monod, J. (1971). *Chance and Necessity*. New York: Knopf.

Montague, R. (2007). *Your Brain Is (Almost) Perfect: How We Make Decisions*. New York: Penguin.

Mrzljak, L., Uylings, H. B. M., Van Eden, C. G., and Judás, M. (1990). Neuronal development in human prefrontal cortex in prenatal and postnatal stages. In: H. B. M. Uylings, C. G. Van Eden, J. P. C. De Bruin, M. A. Corner, and M. G. P. Feenstra (eds.), *The Prefrontal Cortex: Its Structure, Function and Pathology*, pp. 185–222. Amsterdam: Elsevier.

Munakata, Y., Herd, S., Chatham, C., Depue, B., Banich, M., and O'Reilly, R. (2011). A unified framework for inhibitory control. *Trends in Cognitive Sciences*, **15**, 453–459.

Murphy, N., and Brown, W. (2007). *Did My Neurons Make Me Do It?* Oxford University Press.

Myers, R. E. (1967). Cerebral connectionism and brain function. In: C. H. Millikan and F. L. Darley (eds.), *Brain Mechanisms Underlying Speech and Language*, pp. 61–72. New York: Grune and Stratton.

Nasar, S. (2011). *Grand Pursuit*. New York: Simon & Schuster.

Noë, A. (2004). *Action in Perception*. Cambridge, MA: MIT Press.

Ojemann, G., Ojemann, J., Lettich, E., and Berger, M. (2008). Cortical language localization in left, dominant hemisphere: an electrical stimulation mapping investigation in 117 patients. *Journal of Neurosurgery*, **108**, 411–421.

Olds, J., and Milner, P. (1954). Positive reinforcement produced by electrical stimulation of the septal area and other regions of the rat brain. *Journal of Comparative & Physiological Psychology*, **47**, 419–427.

Ortega y Gasset, J. (1961). *Meditations on Quixote*. New York: Norton.

Osvath, M., and Osvath, H. (2008). Chimpanzee (*Pan troglodytes*) and orangutan (*Pongo abelii*) forethought: self-control and pre-experience in the face of future tool use. *Animal Cognition*, **11**, 661–674.

Pearl, J., and Verma, T. S. (1991). A theory of inferred causation. In: J. A. Allen, R. Fikes, and E. Sandewall (eds.), *Principles of Knowledge Representation and Reasoning: Proceedings of the Second International Conference*, pp. 441–452. San Mateo, CA: Morgan Kaufmann.

Pessoa, L., and Adolphs, R. (2010). Emotion processing and the amygdala: from a 'low road' to 'many roads' of evaluating biological significance. *Nature Reviews Neuroscience*, **11**, 773–783.

Phelps, E. A. (2004). Human emotion and memory: interactions of the amygdala and hippocampal complex. *Current Opinion in Neurobiology*, **14**, 198–202.

Piaget, J. (1952). *The Origins of Intelligence in Children*. New York: International Universities Press.

Pinker, S. (1994). *The Language Instinct*. New York: Morrow.

Poincaré, H. (1914). *Science and Method*. New York: Nelson and Sons.

Poldrack, R. A. (2006). Can cognitive processes be inferred from neuroimaging data? *Trends in Cognitive Sciences*, **10**, 59–63.

Popper, K. (1980). *The Logic of Scientific Discovery*. London: Hutchinson.

Popper, K., and Eccles, J. C. (1977). *The Self and Its Brain*. London: Springer.

Premack, D. G., and Woodruff, G. (1979). Does the chimpanzee have a theory of mind? *Behavioral and Brain Sciences*, **1**, 515–526.

Preuss, T. M., Caceres, M., Oldham, M. C., and Geschwind, D. H. (2004). Human brain evolution: insights from microarrays. *Nature Reviews Genetics*, **5**, 850–860.

Pribram, K. H. (1973). The primate frontal cortex – executive of the brain. In: K. H. Pribram and A. R. Luria (eds.), *Psychophysiology of the Frontal Lobes*, pp. 293–314. New York: Academic Press.

Price, C. J. (2010). The anatomy of language: a review of 100 fMRI studies published in 2009. *Annals of the New York Academy of Sciences*, **1191**, 62–88.

Prigogine, I. (1997). *The End of Certainty*. New York: Free Press.

Quintana, J., and Fuster, J. M. (1999). From perception to action: temporal integrative functions of prefrontal and parietal neurons. *Cerebral Cortex*, **9**, 213–221.

Rachlin, H., Raineri, A., and Cross, D. (1991). Subjective probability and delay. *Journal of Experimental Analysis of Behavior*, **55**, 233–244.

Raine, A. (2002). Annotation: the role of prefrontal deficits, low autonomic arousal, and early health factors in the development of antisocial and aggressive behavior in children. *Journal of Child Psychology and Psychiatry*, **43**, 417–434.

Ratey, J. J., and Loehr, J. E. (2011). The positive impact of physical activity on cognition during adulthood: a review of underlying mechanisms, evidence and recommendations. *Review of Neuroscience*, **22**, 171–185.

Reiss, S. (2000). *Who Am I? The 16 Basic Desires That Motivate Our Actions and Define Our Personalities*. New York: Putnam.

Rilling, J. (2006). Human and nonhuman primate brains: are they allometrically scaled versions of the same design? *Evolutionary Anthropology*, **15**, 65–77.

Rizzolatti, G., Gentilucci, M., Camarda, R. M., Gallese, V., Luppino, G., Matelli, M., and Fogassi, L. (1990). Neurons related to reaching-grasping arm movements in the rostral part of area 6 (area 6a). *Experimental Brain Research*, **82**, 337–350.

Roberts, A. C., Robbins, T. W., Everitt, B. J., and Muir, J. L. (1992). A specific form of cognitive rigidity following excitotoxic lesions of the basal forebrain in marmosets. *Neuroscience*, **47**, 251–264.

Rollnik, J. D., Schröder, C., Rodriguez-Fornells, A., Kurzbuch, A. R., Dauper, J., Moller, J., and Munte, T. F. (2004). Functional lesions and human action monitoring: combining repetitive transcranial magnetic stimulation and event-related brain potentials. *Clinical Neurophysiology*, **115**, 145–153.

Rolls, E. T., Critchley, H. D., and Treves, A. (1996). Representation of olfactory information in the primate orbitofrontal cortex. *Journal of Neurophysiology*, **5**, 1982–1996.

Roskies, A. (2002). Neuroethics for the new millennium. *Neuron*, **35**, 21–23.

Rowe, J. B., Owen, A. M., Johnsrude, I. S., and Passingham, R. E. (2001). Imaging the mental components of a planning task. *Neuropsychologia*, **39**, 315–327.

Rushworth, M. F., and Behrens, T. E. (2008). Choice, uncertainty and value in prefrontal and cingulate cortex. *Nature Neuroscience*, **11**, 389–397.

Rutishauser, U., Tudusciuc, O., Neumann, D., Mamela, A. N., Heller, A. C., Ross, I. B., Philpott, L., Sutherling, W. W., and Adolphs, R. (2011). Single-unit responses selective for whole faces in the human amygdala. *Current Biology*, **21**, 1654–1660.

Rymer, R. (1994). *Genie: A Scientific Tragedy*. New York: Harper Perennial.

Schoenemann, P. T., Sheehan, M. J., and Glotzer, L. D. (2005). Prefrontal white matter volume is disproportionately larger in humans than in other primates. *Nature Neuroscience*, **8**, 242–252.

Schott, G. D. (2012). Pictures as a neurological tool: lessons from enhanced and emergent artistry in brain disease. *Brain*, **135**, 1947–1963.

Schultz, W. (1998). The phasic reward signal of primate dopamine neurons. *Advances in Pharmacology*, **42**, 686–690.

Scoville, W. B., and Milner, B. (1957). Loss of recent memory after bilateral hippocampal lesions. *Journal of Neurology, Neurosurgery, and Psychiatry*, **20**, 11–21.

Searle, J. (1997). *The Mystery of Consciousness*. New York Review of Books.

Sellman, D. (2010). The 10 most important things known about addiction. *Addiction*, **105**, 6–13.

Selye, H. (1956). *The Stress of Life*. New York: McGraw-Hill.

Semendeferi, K., Damasio, H., Frank, R., and Van Hoesen, G. W. (1997). The evolution of the frontal lobes: a volumetric analysis based on three-dimensional reconstructions of magnetic resonance scans of human and ape brains. *Journal of Human Evolution*, **32**, 375–388.

Seo, M., Lee, E., and Averbeck, B. B. (2012). Action selection and action value in frontal-striatal circuits. *Neuron*, **74**, 947–960.

Shallice, T. (1982). Specific impairments of planning. *Philosophical Transactions of the Royal Society of London. Series B, Biological Sciences*, **298**, 199–209.

Shamay-Tsoory, S. G., Adler, N., Aharon-Peretz, J., Perry, D., and Mayseless, N. (2011). The origins of originality: the neural bases of creative thinking and originality. *Neuropsychologia*, **49**, 178–185.

Shannon, C. E., and Weaver, W. (1949). *The Mathematical Theory of Communication*. Urbana, IL: University of Illinois Press.

Siegel, G. J. (1999). *Basic Neurochemistry*, 6th edn. Philadelphia: Lippincott–Raven.

Siegel, M., Donner, T. H., and Engel, A. K. (2012). Spectral fingerprints of large-scale neuronal interactions. *Nature Reviews Neuroscience*, **13**, 121–134.

Smith, A. (1759). *The Theory of Moral Sentiments*. London: Miller.

Sowell, E. R., Peterson, B. S., Thompson, P. M., Welcome, S. E., Henkenius, A. L., and Toga, A. W. (2003). Mapping cortical change across the human life span. *Nature Neuroscience*, **6**, 309–315.

Spence, S. (2009). *The Actor's Brain: Exploring the Cognitive Neuroscience of Free Will*. New York: Oxford University Press.

Squire, L. R. (1987). *Memory and Brain*. New York: Oxford University Press.
 (1992). Memory and the hippocampus: a synthesis from findings with rats, monkeys, and humans. *Psychological Review*, **99**, 195–231.

Swick, D., and Turken, A. U. (2002). Dissociation between conflict detection and error monitoring in the human anterior cingulate cortex. *Proceedings of the National Academy of Sciences of the United States of America*, **99**, 16354–16359.

Teuber, H.-L. (1972). Unity and diversity of frontal lobe functions. *Acta Neurobiologiae Experimentalis*, **32**, 625–656.

Tobler, P. N., Christopoulos, G. I., O'Doherty, J. P., Dolan, R. J., and Schultz, W. (2009). Risk-dependent reward value signal in human prefrontal cortex. *Proceedings of the National Academy of Sciences of the United States of America*, **106**, 7185–7190.

Tomasello, M. (2000). *The Cultural Origins of Human Cognition*. Cambridge, MA: Harvard University Press.

Trehub, S. E., and Hannon, E. (2006). Infant music perception: domain-general or domain-specific mechanisms? *Cognition*, **100**, 73–99.

Tulving, E., Kapur, S., Craik, F. I. M., Moscovitch, M., and Houle, S. (1994). Hemispheric encoding/retrieval asymmetry in episodic memory: positron emission tomography findings. *Proceedings of the National Academy of Sciences of the United States of America*, **91**, 2016–2020.

Tyler, L. K., Randall, B., and Stamatakis, E. A. (2008). Cortical differentiation for nouns and verbs depends on grammatical markers. *Journal of Cognitive Neuroscience*, **20**, 1381–1389.

Tylor, E. (1920/1871). *Primitive Culture*. New York: J.P. Putnam's Sons.

Uexküll, J. von (1926). *Theoretical Biology*. New York: Harcourt Brace and Co.

Ungerleider, L. G., Doyon, J., and Karni, A. (2002). Imaging brain plasticity during motor skill learning. *Neurobiology of Learning and Memory*, **78**, 553–564.

Vygotsky, L. S. (1978). *Mind in Society: The Development of Higher Psychological Processes*. Cambridge, MA: Harvard University Press.

Walker, A. E. (1940). The medial thalamic nucleus: a comparative anatomical, physiological and clinical study. *Journal of Comparative Neurology*, **73**, 87–115.

Watanabe, M., and Sakagami, M. (2007). Integration of cognitive and motivational context information in the primate prefrontal cortex. *Cerebral Cortex*, **17** (Suppl. 1), i101–i109.

Wernicke, C. (1874). *Der Aphasische Symptomencomplex*. Breslau: Cohn and Weingert.

Wills, G. (1978). *Inventing America: Jefferson's Declaration of Independence*. Boston: Houghton Mifflin.

Wilson, J. Q. (1993). *The Moral Sense*. New York: Simon & Schuster.

Winston, J. S., Gottfried, J. A., Kilner, J. M., and Dolan, R. J. (2005). Integrated neural representations of odor intensity and affective valence in human amygdala. *Journal of Neuroscience*, **25**, 8903–8907.

Wolpert, D. M. (1997). Computational approaches to motor control. *Trends in Cognitive Sciences*, **1**, 209–216.

Woolsey, C. N., Erickson, T. C., and Gilson, W. (1979). Localization in somatic sensory and motor areas of human cerebral cortex as determined by direct recording of evoked potentials and electrical stimulation. *Journal of Neurosurgery*, **51**, 476–506.

Zalta, E. N., Nodelman, U., Allen, C., and Perry, J. (2012). *Emergent properties*. Stanford, CA: Stanford Encyclopedia of Philosophy.

Glossary

Affiliation   Association with, or adoption by, a social group of any kind, such as the family, a sports team, a professional association, a church, a political party, or a business partnership.

Affordance   The quality of an object or environment that allows an agent to perform a certain action or behavior.

Agency   In philosophy and sociology, the capacity of an agent (personal or other) to act on the world. Moral agency refers to the ethical implications of the action.

Amygdala   A conglomerate of nuclei in the depth of the temporal lobe of each side, part of the limbic system. It is involved in emotional life and the evaluation of the motivational or biological significance of external stimuli. Consequently, the amygdala plays a very important role in memory, especially emotional memory, and in emotional behavior.

Antidepressant medication   Currently, the most commonly used antidepressants are tricyclics (e.g., amitriptyline [Elavil]) and SSRIs (e.g., fluoxetine [Prozac]). All potentiate serotonin or block its elimination.

Aphasia

An impairment of language ability. It ranges from having difficulty in remembering words to being completely unable to speak, read, or write.

Association cortex

The part of the cortex that lies outside the primary (specific) sensory and motor areas. It is reciprocally connected with the associative nuclei of the thalamus. It consists of two major components: (a) the posterior association cortex of the parietal, temporal, and occipital lobes (PTO cortex), and (b) the prefrontal cortex. Both association cortices are functionally involved in higher cognitive functions. That is, the first (a) is involved in the sensory-perceptual aspects of cognition – namely, attention, perception, memory, language, and intelligence; the second (b) is involved in the executive aspects of the same higher functions.

Associative thalamic nuclei

Thalamic nuclei that are reciprocally connected with association cortex. This excludes the specific nuclei, which relay sensory information to the cortex, and the nucleus reticularis, which is only connected with itself and with other nuclei, not the cortex. The association nuclei of the thalamus are deemed to be involved in the cognitive functions of the association cortex they are connected with.

Attention deficit hyperactivity disorder (ADHD)	A childhood disorder, sometimes persistent into adolescence and adulthood, characterized by difficulty in concentrating attention and excessive motor activity. Because it commonly affects children in school age, the disorder impairs learning and behavior in the school as well as at home.
Autonomic nervous system	The part of the nervous system that controls visceral functions. It affects heart rate, digestion, respiration, salivation, perspiration, pupil diameter, urination, and sexual arousal.
Basal ganglia	Nuclear masses at the base of the brain (globus pallidus, caudate nucleus, substantia nigra) dedicated to the execution and coordination of movement in muscular-kinetic, cognitive, and emotional processes.
Behavioral economics	Deals with the effects of social, cognitive, and emotional factors on the economic decisions of individuals and institutions and the consequences for market prices, returns, and resource allocation.
Binding	The dynamic linkage of cortical assemblies by re-entry in an activated cognit. It is an inherent characteristic of all recurrent networks.
Biodrive	A biological drive, such as thirst or sex.
Broca's area	An area of the left, inferior, frontal cortex important for the articulation of speech. Broca's aphasia, which results from lesions of that area, is characterized by difficulty in the verbal expression of language.

Cell assembly

Conceptualized by Hebb as a small network of cortical nerve cells participating in the temporal retention of a certain sensory (e.g., visual) feature by some kind of reverberation within it. The concept is thus the precursor of that of the cognit or cognitive network, which is made of interconnected cell assemblies distributed in widespread cortical areas.

Cognit

A memory or item of knowledge in the form of a network of associated cortical neuron assemblies that represent the component elements of that memory or item of knowledge. Thus, cognits are networks that vary greatly in size, that are distributed over greatly variable expanses of association cortex, that share component nodes in common (component features), and that exhibit extensive nesting of small cognits within larger ones.

Cognitive functions

The functions of the mind, based in the cerebral cortex, which mediate the relations of the person with herself and the world around her. The principal cognitive functions are attention, perception, memory, language, and intelligence.

Column

A cortical column is a vertical arrangement of nerve cells, perpendicular to the cortical surface (about 2.5 mm thick in the human), that share certain functional characteristics, whereby they have been identified as "modules" for one neural function or another. The concept has failed, however, on empirical grounds. Instead, cellular aggregates of more or less vertical structure and variable dimensions have been identified in sensory and motor cortices as cell assemblies with common function.

Common law
A legal system developed by judges and juries. It is man-made law in which precedent has decisive importance.

Compatibilism
Philosophical position holding that free will and determinism are compatible, not mutually exclusive.

Computation
Calculation of values in the processing of information. In the brain, as in other physical systems, two forms of computation take place: digital and analog. In the first form, values vary in discontinuous function, all-or-none, such as the action potential of a nerve cell. In the second, values vary in continuous function, such as the frequency of action potentials in an ensemble (cell assembly or network). In the cerebral cortex, even though cells communicate with one another by action potentials, the information (sensory, motor, cognitive, or emotional) transcends the action potential and is processed in analog fashion, by changes in the frequency of such potentials.

Consciousness
Subjective awareness of an external or internal state, object, stimulus, or event.

Content-addressable memory
Memory retrievable by an item of information connatural with its content,

such as a contextual association (for example, the memory of a person by the scent of the perfume she often wears). The cortex and a search engine address memory in this fashion, by associations of content.

Corpus callosum — A wide, flat bundle of nerve fibers, or commissure, that beneath the cortex links the two cortical hemispheres together – mostly symmetrical locations. It serves interhemispheric communication.

Cross-temporal contingency — In a sequence of behavior, language, or reasoning, the logical dependence of an action or event on another having occurred previously.

Cytoarchitecture — Microscopic structure of nerve cells and fibers.

Default network — A network of brain regions that are active when the individual is not focused on the outside world and the brain is at wakeful rest. Also called the "default mode network" or "default state network," its activity is characterized by coherent neuronal oscillations at a rate lower than 0.1 Hz (one every 10 seconds).

Degeneracy — In cognitive neuroscience, it refers to the circumstances under which dissimilar inputs, because of some common characteristic, lead to the same output. Degeneracy is thus a relational property, where similarity leads to constancy. It is the basis of perceptual or executive constancy and the opposite of discrimination.

Delay discount	Depreciation of a benefit, reward, or gain on account of the necessity to wait for it; the longer the wait time, the greater is the depreciation. Delay discount is a major source of consumer credit and a motive for reliance on government at the expense of private savings.
Desert	Ethically justified reward or punishment.
Determinism	The philosophy that states that for everything that happens in the world there is a cause. Events are bound by causality in such a way that any state of physical nature is completely determined by prior or concomitant states.
Drug addiction	Physical – that is, biological – dependence on the continued ingestion or injection of certain toxic agents such as alcohol, cocaine, amphetamines, and opium-derived substances. When severe, it severely curtails personal freedom.
Dualism	In cognitive neuroscience, the position that brain and mind are two different, though interactive, substances.
Economic liberalism	Economic philosophy that advocates the protection of private property, private decisions, and the free market to foster productivity and progress.
Emotional PA cycle	Parallel to, and interactive with, the cognitive PA cycle. It incorporates limbic and autonomic structures of the nervous system in a cybernetic cycle of emotion, where sensing leads to emotional response, which leads to new sensing, and so on.

Episodic memory	Memory of personal experiences.
Epistemology	The nature and scope (limitations) of knowledge in a certain field.
Forensic	Having to do with the law.
Hebbian principles	Laws of synaptic change at the basis of learning and memory, as postulated by Donald Hebb.
Hemicycle of liberty	The aggregate of perceptual and executive cortices involved in the PA cycle, where choices and decisions are made.
Hippocampus	A portion of ancient cortex, part of the limbic system, situated like the amygdala in the depth of the temporal lobe. In the human, it is essential for the consolidation of short-term into long-term memory. It is one of the first brain structures to be affected in Alzheimer's dementia, with its consequent memory problems. In the human and in some lower species, it has also been shown to be involved in spatial navigation.
Homeostasis	Maintenance of equilibrium in the internal milieu of the body.
Hormone	A chemical released by a cell or a gland in one part of the body that sends out messages, through the blood, that affect the functions or metabolism of cells in other parts of the body.
Hypothalamus	Nuclear complex at the top of the brainstem dedicated to visceral functions through autonomic and hormonal outputs. Its key function is the

maintenance of homeostasis. The hypothalamus controls body temperature, sleep, and circadian cycles. It is also involved in instinctual and emotional functions related to feeding, sex, flight, and aggression.

Imagination   The ability to form new images and sensations in one's mind when they are not perceived through sight, hearing, or other senses.

Inhibition   In neurophysiology, the blocking or restraint of neuronal excitation. It acts on synapses, making them less excitable by sources of stimulation. Inhibition may act as a generalized restraint of activity to the benefit of restorative functions like sleep. It is also a fundamental component of attention and selective movement; by reciprocal inhibition of irrelevant material or by relaxation of antagonistic muscles, inhibition enhances focusing and selective contrast, thus increasing the efficiency of sensory and motor functions. In the cerebral cortex, and thus cognitively relevant, the most common inhibitory neurotransmitter is GABA (gamma-aminobutyric acid).

Inhibitory control   An executive function of the prefrontal cortex that, in the processing of attention, planning, decision-making, and working memory, inhibits irrelevant, contradictory, or distracting influences of any source that can in some manner interfere with current action.

Intuition	The ability to acquire knowledge, and to act upon it, without consciousness or the use of reason.
Keynesian economics	Economic philosophy that advocates the intervention of the government by certain measures, such as the monetary policy of the central bank, to stimulate the economy and to minimize the cyclical tendency of private economies.
Limbic system	A set of structures in the middle of the brain, around the major interhemispheric commissures (including the corpus callosum), that support a variety of emotional functions and memory. They include the hippocampus, the amygdala, and the hypothalamus.
Mind	Composite of cognitive faculties that enables consciousness, thinking, reasoning, perception, and judgment.
Monetary policy	The procedure by which the monetary authority of a country (e.g., the US Federal Reserve, the Bank of England, or the European Central Bank) controls the supply of money. Its principal tools are the setting of interest rates and the monetization of public debt (by bond purchases and the like).
Mutation	Accidental change in a gene, a building block of the genome, the molecular carrier of biological inheritance.
Nativism	In psychology, nativism is the theoretical position that holds that certain abilities, such as perception and

language, are hardwired into the brain at birth. This position is in contrast to empiricism. Political nativism is the position that favors the native inhabitants of a country and holds prejudice against immigrants.

Natural law — A system of law determined by nature, and thus universal, supposed to embody a number of inherited binding (ethical) rules of moral behavior.

Natural selection — The process by which in evolution biological traits become part of the organism of an animal species. A trait results from random mutation and becomes established in the population by genetic propagation.

Neuroimaging — Computer-based radiological scanning to visualize the structure and functions of the brain. Structural imaging (for example, magnetic resonance imaging [MRI]) is used to reveal the physical characteristics of brain structures and, for diagnostic purposes, the presence in them of pathological formations, such as tumors and vascular lesions. Functional imaging is used to reveal brain function. It is based on the radiographic exposure of changes in regional blood flow or metabolism assumed to result from, or to accompany, changes in neural activity. The principal functional imaging methods are positron emission tomography (PET) and functional magnetic resonance imaging (fMRI).

Neuron — An electrically excitable cell in the central nervous system that processes and transmits information by electrical and chemical signaling.

Neurotransmitter
An endogenous chemical substance, packed in synaptic vesicles, that transmits information from one neuron to another through their membranes. The most common excitatory neurotransmitters are glutamate, glycine, and the monoamines (dopamine, noradrenaline, and serotonin). The most common inhibitory transmitter is gamma-aminobutyric acid (GABA).

Numerosity
The conceptual and developmental basis of numbers and mathematics.

Ontogeny
Development of an organism or any of its parts.

Orbital prefrontal cortex, or orbitofrontal cortex
Cortex of the inferior part of the prefrontal cortex, immediately above the orbit of the eye.

Oscillatory activity
An electrical manifestation of re-entry in neural networks.

Perception
Organization, classification, identification, and interpretation of sensory information in the making of a mental representation of the external world.

Perception/action (PA) cycle
The circular cybernetic processing of information in the adaptation of the organism to its environment during sequential goal-directed behavior. In it, environmental changes elicit stimuli that are analyzed by sensory structures, which prompt the nervous system to produce reactive responses to those

changes, which produce new outer changes, and so on. The processing flow of that adaptive cycle is reciprocated by counter-cyclical feedback flow from motor to sensory structures, to accelerate the adjustment process and to prepare sensory structures for expected, self-induced change. In the human, the PA cycle involves the perceptual (posterior) and executive (frontal) cortices engaged successively through the environment. A conversational dialogue is a vivid example of two PAs in action, where each interlocutor is the "environment" of the other.

Phenomenology   The philosophical study of subjective experience and consciousness. Initiated by Husserl, this school of thought centers on the appearances (phenomena) of the world in acts of consciousness by the subject. Phenomenology is of extraordinary descriptive value in psychiatry, where it critically assists diagnosis, treatment, and prevention. As applied to neuroscience, phenomenology can be readily differentiated from the Cartesian method, which sees the world as objects, sets of objects, and objects acting and reacting upon one another and upon the brain, independent of phenomenal (conscious) experience.

Phenotype   The sum of the organism's observable characteristics or traits resulting from the interactions of the genome with the environment.

Phrenology	Pseudoscience, based on skull measurements, that maintains that mental faculties are localized in certain areas or "modules" of the brain delimited by external landmarks.
Phyletic memory	The inborn structure of sensory and motor systems in the brain.
Preadaptation	In evolution, the use of a preformed structure for alternate use by descendants. With regard to freedom, creativity, and prefrontal function, to preadapt is to prepare the organism for anticipated changes and to adjust to them ahead of time with the prospective capacity of the PA cycle.
Prefrontal cortex	The cortex covering the anterior poles of the frontal lobes. In the human brain, it constitutes nearly one-third of the totality of the so-called neocortex, the latest cortex to develop in evolution. The prefrontal cortex encodes in its neuronal networks executive knowledge and memory. Cooperating with the posterior association cortex (PTO) in the dynamics of the PA cycle, the lateral prefrontal cortex – external convexity of the frontal lobe – plays a fundamental role in the temporal organization of goal-directed behavior, reasoning, and language. Three executive prefrontal functions serve that basic role: working memory, set, and inhibitory control. The orbital prefrontal cortex, in the inferior surface of the prefrontal cortex, is

essential for the encoding of rewards, the integration of social-emotional behavior, and the control of impulsivity. The medial and anterior cingulate prefrontal region is essential for the monitoring of behavioral performance and error correction.

Priming

Implicit effect of a stimulus on the perception or memory of another, with which it has a tenuous and unconscious relationship.

Procedural memory

Memory of how to do things. It includes skills and habits.

Prospect theory

A behavioral economic theory, associated with Kahneman and Tversky, that describes decisions that involve risk, where the probabilities of outcomes are known. The theory says that people make decisions based on the potential value of losses and gains rather than the final outcome of those decisions.

PTO cortex

The association cortex of the posterior region of both cerebral hemispheres, comprising cortex of the parietal, temporal, and occipital lobes. It encodes in its neuronal networks perceptual knowledge and memory acquired through the senses. The PTO cortex, cooperating with the prefrontal cortex, plays a vital role in the temporal integrative functions of active memory – that is, in working memory, sensory perception, and the acquisition of new memory.

Qualia	In philosophy, individual instances of subjective, conscious experience – ordinarily sensory.
Recursion	In language, recursion has two meanings: (a) the capacity to repeat the essence of a statement or utterance in multiple different ways, and (b) the ability to return to the principal statement or utterance after digression into a secondary or less essential one.
Reductionism	The approach to understanding complex reality by reducing it to the analysis of its parts, often under the assumption that the whole is equivalent to the sum of its parts.
Re-entry	A structural property of neural networks allowing recurrence, whereby one cortical area or group of cortical cells influences another and is in turn influenced by it (positive feedback). It is an essential feature of sustained network activation in working memory, and some say also in consciousness.
Relational code	Definition of an object or item of information by the relations between its elements. Language is the pre-eminent relational code, as all its structures (words, sentences, etc.) are defined by the relationships between letters, phonemes, words, punctuation marks, etc. Geometry is another. In the cerebral cortex, cognits or cognitive networks are most typically relational.
Responsibility	The quality or state of being responsible – that is accountable – for

the effects of one's actions on oneself or on others. The accountability may be mental (psychological), social, moral, or legal. Responsibility is inseparable from freedom, as an agent is responsible not only for his choice but also for the consequences of that choice.

Reward — Positive stimulus, bounty (e.g., money), or pleasure resulting from an action or task, for the performance of which it may have been an incentive.

Reward system — A distributed conglomerate of neural structures at the base of the brain involved in the experience of reward or pleasure, notably including the hypothalamus, the amygdala, the septum, the nucleus accumbens, the orbitofrontal cortex, and the anterior cingulate cortex.

Semantic memory — Memory of facts, meaning, or general knowledge about the world.

Social Darwinism — Application of evolutionary concepts to sociology and politics, with the implicit or explicit assumption that progress results from the outcompetition of inferior groups by superior groups of society.

Superior longitudinal fasciculus — Conglomerate of fiber tracts that connect reciprocally the posterior association cortex (PTO) with the prefrontal cortex. It is critically engaged in all operations of the PA cycle, including language.

Synapse — The point of electrochemical contact between two neurons, through which impulses are transmitted from one to the other. Synapses are at the terminals of fibers (axons) and dendrites that connect one neuron to another. A cognitive network or cognit is made of the neurons, axons, dendrites, and synapses that connect them. The strength of a cognit depends on the synaptic strength of its network. That strength diminishes with aging and lack of cognitive use. In the periphery of a cognit, there are neurons and weak connections that bind the more peripheral elements of a memory or item of knowledge. That weaker penumbra of the cognit is especially liable to forgetting and accounts for phenomena like "priming" and intuition. It may serve the rehabilitation of memory after cortical damage.

Syntax	The rules and principles that govern the structuring of sentences in any individual language.
Teleology	Philosophy holding that nature has final physical causes of prior mechanism, design, or purpose.
Teleonomy	Apparent purposefulness of functions in living organisms that derive from their evolutionary history and are programmed for adaptive and reproductive success.
Temporal binding	Binding of cognitive networks (cognits) across time in the execution of goal-directed behavior.
Thalamus	A conglomerate of nuclei in the center of the brain dedicated to the relay of

sensory inputs to the cortex, the functional connections between cortical areas, and the modulation of subcortical motor systems. It is important in the regulation of sleep and wakefulness.

Universal grammar (UG)
A theory in linguistics, credited to Noam Chomsky, proposing that the ability to learn grammar is inherited and hardwired in the brain. That linguistic ability manifests itself by the ease with which, with minimal learning, children from a very early age can correctly implement grammar and the rules of syntax in their linguistic expressions.

Valence
The intrinsic emotional attractiveness (positive valence) or aversiveness (negative valence) of an event, object, or situation.

Wernicke's area
A portion of PTO – posterior association – cortex important for the understanding of meaning in language. Lesions of this area cause Wernicke's aphasia, characterized by verbose but nonsensical language.

Working memory
Retention of a memory or item of knowledge with an intended purpose in the proximate future, such as the solution of a problem or the attainment of a goal. The content of working memory may consist of an activated old cognit or a recent percept. Working memory can be legitimately considered attention directed to an internal representation.

Index